Red Star over Hollywood

Red Star over Hollywood

The Film Colony's
Long Romance with the Left

Ronald Radosh
Allis Radosh

ENCOUNTER BOOKS
NEW YORK

First paperback edition published in 2006 by Encounter Books, an activity of Encounter for Culture and Education, Inc., a nonprofit, tax exempt corporation.

Encounter Books website address: www.encounterbooks.com

Manufactured in the United States and printed on acid-free paper.

The paper used in this publication meets the minimum requirements of ANSI/NISO Z39.48-1992 (R 1997) (*Permanence of Paper*).

FIRST EDITION

Library of Congress Cataloging-in-Publication Data

Rodosh, Ronald
    Red Star Over Hollywood: The film Colony's Long Romance with the Left / Ronald Rodosh
        p.   cm.
     ISBN -1-59403-146-0
1. Screenwriters—United States—political activity   2. Motion Picture producers and directors—United States—political activity.   3. Motion picture actors and actresses—United States—Political activity.   4. Communism and motion pictures—United States.   5. United States. Congress. House. Committee on Unamerican Activities.   I. Radosh, Allis.   II. Title
PN1998.2.R33 2006
384'.80979494—dc22
                                                    2006012553

10 9 8 7 6 5 4 3 2 1

Contents

Preface

HOLLYWOOD POLITICS HAS BECOME THE SUBJECT OF A NATIONAL COMIC monologue. We are amused by actors who toy with political and social ideas, adopting and discarding them with equal caprice and treating them as the intellectual equivalent of fashion statements. It is now de rigueur to have not only a special "cause" of one's own, but even, *à la* Barbra Streisand, a paid full-time political advisor. The political fads that sweep through Tinsel Town involve career far more than conscience.

Looking back at Hollywood fifty years ago, we see something quite different: a life-and-death political drama that placed the film colony at the center of postwar politics. A script of this drama has been created by a generation's worth of memoirs and histories, as well as films and documentaries. In it, the Communist screenwriters, directors and actors are the heroes—"liberals in a hurry" who knew little about the malignity of Stalinism. The villains in the piece are the House Committee on Un-American Activities (HUAC), which summoned these good people to name the names of their friends and co-workers; the Hollywood moguls who capitulated to the paranoia sweeping through American life and blacklisted honest idealists; the liberals who turned their backs while this outrage took place; and worst of all, the ex-Communist "friendly witnesses" who cooperated with HUAC, testifying about their experiences in the Party and betraying people they had known for half a lifetime.

As a result of this "scoundrel time," so the story goes, Hollywood descended from comity to anger; and from a golden age of socially relevant filmmaking to the escapist and sentimental films of the 1950s and early 1960s. Not only was a great industry wrecked, but even worse, according to this script, the events of that period led America into the "great fear" of McCarthyism and on to Richard Nixon, the Vietnam War and a right-wing takeover by Ronald Reagan (later resurrected by George W. Bush).

This fable of innocence destroyed by malice has acquired an almost irresistible sanctity during half a century of telling and retelling. It has become the consensus view of a troubled time and the story that Hollywood tells itself each night when it goes to sleep.

But is it true?

Our intention is to look once again at what really happened in Hollywood during that fateful episode in our history, and to re-evaluate this legend of good undone by evil. How and why did so many in the film community become enchanted not only with the Left, but with its most totalitarian expression, the American Communist Party? What were their aims and objectives, and how did they set about achieving them? These are questions that have been embargoed for a generation. Until now, the focus of the scores of books, articles, films and plays about the period has been on HUAC and its investigations. We intend to look at the other side of the drama as well, focusing on the specific phe-nomenon—the Hollywood Party—to which HUAC was the equal and opposite reaction. What did the Communists in the film cap-ital actually do? How did they advance their political agenda and how effective were they? These are important questions that have been drowned out by the sound and fury about the "American Inquisition."

Beginning with the aftermath of the Bolshevik Revolution, we will trace Hollywood's fascination with radicalism in the 1930s—when the film industry was growing up and many future Hollywood personalities visited the Soviet Union, saw a future they believed would work everywhere, and returned to make that vision a reality at home. During the Depression and the rise of fascism in Europe, many of those who worked in the film world fell under the influence of such prophets and reacted to the gathering storm by tying their fortunes to those of the political

Left. Hollywood stars, directors and writers came together to create a popular front of liberals and Communists, united by their opposition to the Nazis and their support of the Democrats and Franklin D. Roosevelt. That unity was lost during the years of the Soviet Union's cynical Non-Aggression Pact with Nazi Germany, signed in August 1939. But after Hitler, in June 1941, had invaded the USSR and the Soviets had entered the war, the liberal-Communist alliance was repaired. Once again committed to supporting FDR and defeating the Führer, and promoting themselves as harbingers of history, the Communists achieved even greater influence in the film capital.

After the war had ended and long before HUAC came to town, the growing estrangement between the United States and the Soviet Union terminated the love affair between the Reds and the Hollywood liberals. Some Hollywood personalities, like Olivia de Havilland and Melvyn Douglas, became fed up with the constant intrigues of their old associates and began to see themselves as having been duped by Communists who were always pushing Moscow's interests rather than America's.

By the time HUAC made its first postwar appearance in filmland, not only these liberals (soon to be stigmatized as "Cold War" liberals) but many Communists too had grown disillusioned with the Party and began quietly drifting away. HUAC called for testimony from scores of writers, directors and actors who were widely known in the industry to have been Party members or sympathizers in the 1930s and 1940s. The result of these hearings soon led the studios to dispense with their services and to institute the now-infamous blacklist.

The blacklist has been over for close to fifty years. Yet intellectuals and Hollywood personalities have made sure that it lives on as an object lesson for a new generation. They have refashioned the time of the blacklist into a perverse parody of a golden age. Some contemporary Hollywood personalities try to associate themselves with this dramatic era in an effort to inflate their personae. Actor Sean Penn, for instance, whose father was one of those blacklisted, has tried to argue, when a proposal of his is turned down or a part in a film is given to someone else, that he has been *blacklisted* because of his opposition to the war in Iraq.

And actor/director Tim Robbins, one of the most popular and employable Hollywood stars, complains routinely, when his political opinions are challenged, that he is the victim of a new *blacklist*. It is only a short step from reflexively honoring those actually blacklisted in the past to seeking status as a victim in a fictional blacklist of the present. In both cases, however, there is a denial of reality. That reality is the subject of this book.

1

The Romance Begins

WHAT BETTER PLACE FOR THE RUSSIAN REVOLUTION'S PROMISE OF A utopian classless society to take hold than in Hollywood, the capital of dreams? And who better to promote this dream than the revolutionary entrepreneur and propagandist Willi Münzenberg? Born in Germany in 1889, he dropped out of school at fifteen to become a barber's apprentice and then a laborer in a shoe factory. Handsome, ambitious and dissatisfied, he drifted to Zurich, Switzerland, where at the age of twenty-one he became involved with the Youth Bureau of the Swiss Social Democratic Party. There he crossed paths with a small group of revolutionaries including Lenin, Trotsky and Karl Radek—men who would lead the Bolshevik Revolution.[1]

A born organizer and irresistible public speaker, the charismatic Münzenberg impressed Lenin, who saw a role for him in promoting the new Soviet state. Hardly an intellectual, Münzenberg looked more like the shoemaker he once had been. "One could imagine him," Arthur Koestler wrote, "sitting on a low stool, with a leather apron, driving tacks into an old boot with the energy of a sledge-hammer." A short, squat, heavy-boned man, Münzenberg "gave the impression that bumping against him would be like colliding with a steam-roller."[2]

Believing that it would be difficult to establish Communism in Russia without the support of the European proletariat, Moscow created the Comintern in 1919 to foment world revolution. The Comintern set up Communist parties obedient to Moscow in other countries, trained Communist leaders, and subsidized and coordinated their activities. Lenin requested that Münzenberg become a major player in this effort.

In 1921, when drought inflicted a terrible famine on Russia, Lenin asked Münzenberg to build an international organization to help with relief efforts. Münzenberg created the International Worker Relief and set up offices throughout Europe, where he promoted the politics of the Soviet Union while soliciting aid for its people. Out of these efforts grew a propaganda empire, later referred to as the "Münzenberg Trust," which eventually included firms that published newspapers, books and journals, and produced avant-garde theater and films.

Münzenberg's efforts for famine relief were successful in Europe, but even more so in America, where committees known as Friends of Soviet Russia mushroomed and raised large sums from those sympathetic to the Russian Revolution. Münzenberg saw that when people gave to a cause, they became emotionally invested in it. Reframing charity as solidarity could create a potent political result, a lesson he would later use in recruiting fellow travelers and in establishing front groups for the USSR throughout the Western world.[3]

Like Lenin himself, Münzenberg saw the propaganda potential in the new mass medium of film, which he had exploited in his famine relief effort. In 1924 he helped create a film studio in Moscow called Mezhrabpom, also referred to as M-Russ. He also founded the film production company Prometheus, as well as Weltfilm, to distribute the films internationally. Eventually he planned for "film cells of proletarian art" to be set up throughout the capitalist world.[4] He was given the German distribution rights to Sergei Eisenstein's now-classic film *The Battleship Potemkin* (1925), which depicted the sailors' mutiny during the Russian Revolution of 1905. An example of early agitprop, the film created a sensation in the West and helped establish Münzenberg's credentials.

As the Comintern's chief of political propaganda, Münzenberg was convinced that no medium offered better potential for pro-Soviet publicity than the movies.[5] Only a few short years after the founding of the American Communist Party, Münzenberg was teaching Party cadre about the importance of film. "We must develop the tremendous cultural possibilities of the motion picture in the revolutionary sense," he explained in an article he wrote for the international movement in the *Daily Worker.* "One of the most pressing tasks confronting Communist Parties on the field of agitation and propaganda is the conquest of this supremely important propaganda weapon, until now the monopoly of the ruling class; we must wrest it from them and turn it against them."[6] He quoted Lenin's statement that Communists had to "powerfully develop film production, taking especially the proletarian *kino* [theaters] to the city masses" as well as to the villages. Of all the arts, Lenin admonished, "the motion picture is for us the most important."[7]

Münzenberg was also among the first Communists to insist that, although Marx claimed the working classes would make the Revolution, their goal would never become a reality unless the intellectuals and artists could be won over for the cause. Even if they were gullible romantics, the Party had to gain the service of writers, artists, journalists and other influential "culture workers." While Münzenberg did not invent the political category of "fellow travelers" that would have such a portentous afterlife, especially in Hollywood, his contribution was "to mobilize them and put them in the service of the Communists."[8] These were mainly intellectuals who "without being party members…display active sympathy for Communism and give it moral support." He saw such individuals as being uniquely able to push the Party's secret agenda because they appeared to be motivated only by the fight of good against evil, not by ideology. The Revolution needed these non-Communists who would never have considered joining the Party but would unwittingly do its bidding through their activity in front groups. There were always a few secret Communists (called "submarines") among them pretending to be fellow travelers, because this status would allow them to be more influential and immune to attack.[9]

Münzenberg used the resources of the Münzenberg Trust to create a vast network of what appeared to be independent groups but were actually in service to the Comintern. These fronts, such as the famine relief committees and the antifascist groups of the 1930s, were meant to "ensnare pacifists, moderate socialists, and liberal intellectuals into the Communist camp."[10] Münzenberg, as his lifelong partner Babette Gross wrote, called their members "innocents" and referred to the groups he created as "Innocent Clubs." (Others would later use Lenin's more cynical term, "useful idiots.") According to his friend Arthur Koestler, Münzenberg "produced Committees as a conjurer produces rabbits out of his hat."[11]

Viewed by many as a "Red millionaire," Münzenberg in truth did not even have a bank account, and he held no shares in the many companies he created for the Communist movement. Yet he had a chauffer, wore tailored suits, and enjoyed a seemingly bottomless expense account, courtesy of the Comintern.[12]

Münzenberg was a great success during his first trip to the United States, obtaining an entry visa in 1934 after promising to refrain from any overt political activity. Traveling with the British MP Aneurin Bevan, later to be minister of health in the post–World War II Labour government, he drummed up support for the arrested German Communist leader Ernst Thalmann. "The authorities of this 'country of capitalism,'" Babette Gross noted with astonishment, "put not the slightest obstacle in the way of Münzenberg, the Communist." He spoke at mass rallies in all the major cities, climaxed by a speech to thousands at Madison Square Garden. This resourceful man succeeded in raising thousands of dollars for his various committees while in the United States.[13]

The Romance Begins

Münzenberg and his agents, particularly Otto Katz, who would function as international Communism's ambassador to the film world in the mid-1930s, did not have to start from scratch when they came to Hollywood. The dream of an earthly utopia embodied in the socialist experiment of Russia had already galvanized many who would become leading writers and directors. Among the group of young college students who had visited the revolutionary motherland without any urging from Soviet officials were the future director and writer Joseph Losey; an aspiring documentary filmmaker and writer named Jay Leyda; the future novelist and screenwriter Budd Schulberg, son of a prominent Hollywood producer; Schulberg's childhood friend, the future writer Maurice Rapf, also the son of a prominent producer; and the future screenwriter Ring Lardner Jr., son of the famous short story writer of the same name. They would remain intertwined in the film world and its politics through the 1950s, but their paths first intersected in the Soviet Union when they visited this mythic homeland of the radical imagination where the future was being born every day, and then returned like explorers of an earlier era to tell others of the fabulous revolutionary riches they had seen.

Joseph Losey

Joseph Losey would establish himself as a major director with his first feature, *The Boy with the Green Hair* (1948), an allegory about war and intolerance. Soon afterward he was called before the House Committee on Un-American Activities, where he refused to testify. To avoid the blacklist, he moved to England and continued to work on "message films"—such as *King and Country* (1964), *The Assassination of Trotsky* (1972) and *Monsieur Klein* (1976)—until his death in 1984.

That was the end of a road that began in 1925, when Losey, then sixteen years old, left his home in La Crosse, Wisconsin, entered Dartmouth College, and found his calling when he worked as stage manager and later director for the college's theater group, the Dartmouth Players.[14] After Dartmouth, Losey did a year of graduate study at Harvard, and then decamped to Manhattan with his master's degree and a burning ambition to work in theater. He met a trust-fund baby named John Hammond, who had moved out of his family's East Side mansion and decided to take his name out of the *Social Register*. Hammond, who before long would become America's first impresario of jazz and blues, introduced Losey to various Harlem haunts where they listened to African-American music till early morning. But Hammond's chief contribution, as Losey later acknowledged, was getting him "involved in the earliest stages of my left-wing politics."

In 1931, Hammond made Losey an offer he couldn't refuse:

an all-expenses-paid trip to Europe, starting with a first-class ticket on the ship *Homeric*. For the two idealistic young radicals, it was a glorious and romantic time—"very Scott Fitzgerald," Losey called it. Upon their return, he persuaded Hammond to support him as director of *Little ol' Boy,* a play written for Jed Harris, which New York critics panned as simplistic propaganda. A few years later, Hammond funded Losey's production of *Jaywalker,* a historical drama written by Sinclair Lewis and his brother Lloyd about residents of Kansas who sought to keep slavery out of the state during the Civil War. This play was also trounced by the critics.

Depressed by his theatrical failures and looking for something to hold on to, Losey borrowed five hundred dollars and purchased a third-class steerage ticket to Europe on the *Ile de France*. He felt compelled to visit the Soviet Union, but upon arriving there via Finland, he at first felt "terribly disillusioned." Whereas the famous muckraker Lincoln Steffens had come back from his trip in 1919 and announced, "I have been over to the future and it works," Losey on the other hand said, "I couldn't see evidence of anything much working. I saw extreme poverty, dirt and discomfort, and I didn't see any of the positive things."

Later on, euphoric reports from Russia by journalists like the *New York Times*'s Walter Duranty—who won the Pulitzer Prize for his propagandistic dispatches in 1931 and continued to work as Stalin's favored journalist in Moscow for the rest of his career—led others to believe that things were working gloriously in the USSR and that there was no starvation and no famine. Losey had seen and reported the truth; yet he too became a partisan of the Soviet Union, and even undertook to work as a secret courier for the Communist underground organized by the Comintern.

Why did he distrust his own perception of reality? Because while the Soviet Union may have been a land of poverty and famine, it was also a thrilling new world of artistic experimentation in the Revolution's earliest phases. While Western theater and film depended upon contacts or rich impresarios like John Hammond to fund plays and films, Losey saw the Soviet government sponsoring theater and film, and directors and writers counting among Europe's avant-garde.

Losey met the famous modernist directors Vsevolod Meyerhold and Nikolai Okhlopkov. He attended Meyerhold's drama school and the classes taught by the greatest of Soviet film directors, Sergei Eisenstein. There he met Jay Leyda, a young American filmmaker who had used a grant to travel to the USSR and become Eisenstein's student and protégé. Leyda invited Losey to stay in his apartment on the outskirts of Moscow. On Leyda's recommendation, Losey toured the Ukraine, where in Kharkov and Kiev he spoke to theater collectives under the auspices of the International Revolutionary Theatre, a group that included Erwin Piscator, Bertolt Brecht, Joris Ivens and Hanns Eisler. Losey admitted that going on a speaking tour with these notable figures was in fact "the ultimate presumption," but in exchange for his services he was "fed with Marx and Trotsky and Engels—even Stalin."

Why did he sing the praises of the new Soviet tyranny? "I was fed up with the life that I had led in the USA," he later explained to Michael Ciment, and "wanted to have a goal." Losey even sought out Politburo member Otto Kuusinen and said that he wanted to participate and do something meaningful, like "lumbering in the forests of Karelia." No doubt laughing inwardly, Kuusinen told Losey, "Don't be a fool," and urged him to go back to the United States and work for the Revolution there.

Returning to America, Losey became involved in New York's left-wing theater scene and joined the Theatre Union. He claimed in interviews fifty years later that he had not been affiliated with any Communist groups at that time; yet the composer Virgil Thomson, who knew him then, told Losey's biographer David Caute that he saw Losey as a "sour puss like a great many of those Communist boys," who "spoke the lingo" and who "disapproved of everyone…who were not Communists."

The New Masses, by then the Communist Party's cultural magazine, reported in February 1938 that Losey had participated in a benefit it had sponsored. An unnamed woman interviewed by Caute recalled that in 1936, Losey told her that he was a Party member and tried to recruit her. But most telling was Losey's revelation to his wife that in this period, during his European travels, he was working as a courier for the leader of the American Communist underground, the Hungarian-born Comintern representative known as J. Peters.

Peters, whose real name was Jozsef Peter, was not just another Communist. He had been appointed chief of the New York section of the Party in 1930. Sent to Moscow to be trained by the Comintern, he returned to the United States in 1932 and was assigned, as a Comintern document revealed, "to work in the secret apparatus."[15] The purpose of this underground organization was to ensure the Party's internal security, including countering police surveillance, exposing infiltrators, and protecting Party records. It also prepared Party members for underground work, and carried out surveillance, infiltration and disruption of rival radical groups, especially those of Trotsky's American followers.[16] Most important was Peters' role in putting together espionage networks composed of American government workers who were secretly Party members or willing to engage in espionage for the Soviet government.[17]

Peters not only led the secret apparatus but was in charge of maintaining contact and cooperation with Soviet intelligence. As part of this work, he asked Whittaker Chambers to gather material from secret sources in government, which he would then give to the GRU, the Soviet military intelligence service. Unfortunately, nothing exists to indicate what material Losey carried through Europe on Peters' behalf. But Peters also served as liaison with the European Communist underground, and hence could have used Losey for numerous jobs. As an obscure college graduate, Losey would have been a perfect secret courier.[18] As his biographer writes, his "lifelong loyalty to Stalinism" was based essentially on a "loyalty to his own youthful commitment."

Jay Leyda

Jay Leyda never gained the same notoriety as Joe Losey. To the degree that he is remembered, it is as a man who devoted years to studying the life and work of Herman Melville. The historian Clare Spark has written, "Leyda was such a prodigious Melville researcher that his project to compile a fully revelatory chronology of Melville's life in documents earned the backing of Harry

Levin, F. O. Mattthiessen, and Alfred Kazin," among other leading American scholars.[19]

But in his prior life, in the late 1920s and early 1930s, Leyda
had been active in the world of avant-garde film, theater and
photography, and a member of the American Communist Party.
The FBI had a copy of his Los Angeles membership card for the
cultural section of the Party.[20]

Born in Detroit in 1910, Leyda studied photography in high
school with Jane Reece, a celebrated member of Alfred Stieglitz's
circle. Like others interested in the arts, Leyda moved to New
York City, where in 1933 he informed his friends that he was traveling to Moscow to attend film school there. He explained to one
friend that if at least one member of the Workers Film and Photo
League, a revolutionary Communist-dominated arts group he
had joined, got into the Moscow school, "then we would be a
sharp instrument for revolution here."[21]

Encouraged by his girlfriend, left-wing attorney Carol Weiss
King, Leyda made his journey into the future. In a letter to Lincoln Kirstein shortly after his arrival in the USSR, Leyda urged
his friend to join him in Moscow as quickly as possible. "There's
enough food and excitement…to make up for *any* lack you may
feel," he wrote. Warning him not to engage in "touristy whine"
about unsanitary conditions or a lack of seats on the tram, Leyda
acknowledged that Kirstein would find a "kind of cold" in
Moscow. He was not referring to the famous Russian winter, but
to the "*chistka*," the beginnings of the great Stalinist purges,
which he defined as a "cleaning given by the party members."
The cold wind, Leyda wrote approvingly, blew through "every
unit, trust and union," and every Party member had to rip "open
his past and his mind for inspection by both the cleaning commission and his fellow-workers." Of course, he continued, sitting
"in the slippery comfort of America" one might feel "private
small doubts about the USSR." But upon arriving there, "one
goes in and looks—and knows that it is working and sure of itself.
It's moving toward what it wants—a classless society developing
toward communism."[22] What the Russian Communists were
doing, Leyda wrote in another letter, was "literally making new
people, giving them a solid base and a reason for life."[23]

Leyda left the Soviet Union in 1936, bringing a letter of recommendation from Sergei Eisenstein to Iris Barry, the director of the Museum of Modern Art's film division in New York City. The famed director recommended that Leyda be employed to obtain German and Russian films for MOMA. With such strong support, Leyda was made assistant curator of the museum's film department, where he worked on a history of Soviet cinema. In 1941, Iris Barry asked for his resignation, his history as yet unfinished. Needing funds, Leyda then took a job working for Artkino, the American distributor of Soviet films, which was closely tied to the Soviet government.

While in Russia, Leyda had gravitated toward other young Americans. In addition to providing temporary housing for Joseph Losey, he had also helped arrange and support the trips of other left-wing New Yorkers, especially those involved with the famed Group Theatre. Directed by Harold Clurman, Lee Strasberg and Cheryl Crawford, this radical drama troupe included Stella and Luther Adler, J. Edward Bromberg, Elia Kazan, Sanford Miesner, Clifford Odets and others, many of whom would go to work in Hollywood in the 1940s.

Ring Lardner Jr.

Ring Lardner was one of America's most beloved humorists and writers when he died in 1934 at the age of forty-eight. Until then, all of his three children had always attended only private schools. Now his youngest son, Ring Jr., who was eighteen and had just completed his sophomore year at Princeton, was forced to drop out. To cushion the blow, his mother managed to get five hundred dollars to allow him to travel to Europe before he would have to find a full-time job. He bought steamer passage on the Hamburg-American Line, and arranged with the Soviet tourist bureau, Intourist, to visit the land of revolution for five dollars a day, which covered travel, hotels and meals.

When he arrived in the Soviet Union, Lardner was instantly impressed. Everywhere he saw signs of massive construction, and the people conveyed "hope and optimism." Moreover, he identified the doctrine of Communism with "new, radical trends in social behavior, sexual relations, and art." The teenage Lardner was struck most by the swimming arrangements on the banks of the Moscow River. There were four separate, fenced-off beaches—one of which was for both men and women who chose to bathe nude together.

After U.S. recognition of the Soviet Union in 1933, Moscow University had established an Anglo-American Institute for English-speaking students. Lardner enrolled in a course called "Crime and Punishment in the Soviet Union." At the institute, he met two young men from Dartmouth who would end up in Hollywood with him, the writers Budd Schulberg and Maurice Rapf. The three became fast friends.

Lardner found that the Soviets did not exactly appreciate the Americans' sophomoric college humor. Noticing a wall newspaper on political topics, Lardner and a Canadian friend decided to put up one of their own. It was a formal petition demanding that "double whiskey-and-sodas be served to each student in his bed before breakfast because the menace to student health in having to walk to the dining room on an empty stomach is appalling," and it also demanded "that the Scottsboro Boys be set free immediately."

The Russian professor in charge of the dorm took the petition down immediately and summoned Lardner and his friend to his office. In any Soviet institution, he told them, there could be only one paper, "and that is the one that is sanctioned by the authorities." Moreover, one did not joke about political topics. As for the demand for freeing the Scottsboro Boys—then the major focus of the American Party's propaganda campaign—the professor asked, "How could we free them here in Russia?"

Lardner's friend Maurice Rapf, recalling the same incident, said that in the petition Lardner had "attacked the leadership" of the student group "because we were led by Communists" who had forced them to attend Marxist study groups. Lardner, Rapf said, "was the only one who sounded an opposition voice," and at that point Rapf regarded him "essentially as an anti-Soviet."[24] What prompted Rapf's harsh assessment was that as the dialogue on the wall poster developed, Lardner told the Soviet professor that in the United States there was freedom of the press. The professor replied, "In no country in the world is there more free-dom of the press than…in Russia," where the "press belongs to the people." When Lardner explained that their paper was meant as humor and parody, he was told that in the Soviet Union, "humor for the sake of humor" did not exist.

Aside from what in retrospect was a rather mild rebuke by his Soviet overseer, Lardner had a great time consuming caviar and vodka and flirting with girls from Sarah Lawrence College. He also was taken on tours of courtrooms and prisons as part of his sociology course. Here, Lardner learned that "all punish-ments were designed for re-education and rehabilitation, and in keeping with this principle of Soviet jurisprudence, the maxi-mum prison sentence was ten years, even for murder." As for the death penalty, this was reserved for serious "crimes against the state." Thievery and prostitution still existed as "hangovers" from the old society, he was told, but were on their way out. Most impressive, Lardner heard that unlike the United States, the USSR had no political prisoners. Such "facts" deeply influenced him. Lardner thought that Russia was "already practicing what only the most advanced criminologists in the West were propos-ing": curing criminality rather than merely punishing it.

Lardner sought to confirm his own impressions by checking with others——older people whom he expected to be wiser and politically more sophisticated. Unfortunately, the man to whom he turned was the *New York Times*'s man in Moscow, Walter Duranty, whom the British writer Malcolm Muggeridge called "the greatest liar of any journalist I have ever met." He was refer-ring to Duranty's now well-known coverup of the Ukrainian famine, in which an estimated six million people died as a result of Stalin's forced collectivization.[25]

After spending an evening with the "charming and erudite" fellow-traveling journalist, Lardner adopted Duranty's view that anything negative said about the Soviet Union was "not to be trusted."

By the time he returned home, Lardner had become radi-calized. Through Stanley Walker, the city editor of the *New York Herald-Tribune* and a great admirer of his father, he landed a job as a reporter at another New York newspaper, the *Daily Mirror*.

As the youngest reporter on the staff, he covered suicides, murders, robberies and strikes. This last assignment moved him further to the left, since it brought him into contact with pivotal figures in the newly aroused working class, like the firebrand John L. Lewis and other leaders of the breakaway industrial union, the Congress of Industrial Organizations (CIO).

In the summer of 1935, Herbert Bayard Swope Sr., the father of Lardner's roommate at Princeton, introduced him to producer David O. Selznick at a party that Swope Sr. was giving at his home in Sands Point on Long Island. A few months later Selznick offered Lardner a job, and the twenty-two-year-old jumped at the chance to go to Hollywood, following "some of the most important writers in the New York newspaper world [who] had already made the leap."[26] Lardner was assigned to the publicity department and soon began to work with Budd Schulberg on doctoring already developed scripts.[27] While they were working on *A Star Is Born*, Budd, who had joined the recently organized Hollywood branch of the Communist Party, recruited his friend. According to Lardner, it took Budd just five minutes to accomplish his goal.[28]

Maurice Rapf and Budd Schulberg

Unlike Losey and Lardner, Maurice Rapf and Budd Schulberg were born into Hollywood's royalty. Rapf was the son of the prominent MGM producer Harry Rapf. When the new film company MGM was created in 1924, it was Louis B. Mayer, Harry Rapf and the young Irving Thalberg who built it and also created the Loews Theater chain.[29] Budd Schulberg, who grew up one block away from Rapf, was the son of B. P. Schulberg, the head of production at Paramount Pictures. They first met at age eleven and started to do everything together. While other kids their age were playing sandlot baseball, Rapf and Schulberg spent their free weekends on the MGM back lot playing with costumes and props gathered from the prop department. If *Ben-Hur* was being filmed, they used Roman helmets and breastplates; when it was *The Big Parade*, a war film, they borrowed soldiers' bayonets. They would spend their entire day playing on the film sets.

The Malibu Beach film colony in which they lived was a small, privileged world. Schulberg captured the atmosphere in this vivid description: "With a tennis court adjoining our house and with the Pacific for a swimming pool, with track meets, ball games and boxing matches, Grauman's openings, Trocadero floor shows, dances at the Grove, symphonies under the stars, and barbecue beach parties under the moon, with the children of famous stars, directors and producers for playmates, ours was not exactly a proletarian or Marxist background."

Returning from Dartmouth during his 1933 summer vacation, however, Schulberg noted how world events such as the waterfront strike, bank failures, breadlines, apple vendors, the National Recovery Administration and the Reichstag fire had intruded even into this charmed world. He and his friends talked incessantly about Hitler, anti-Semitism and the threat of war. "We were afraid of Adolf and the munitions makers," he recalled.[30]

Like most college students at the time, Schulberg and Rapf, who was at Dartmouth with him, were anxious for peace and initially found themselves attracted to isolationists and even the America First movement. But Rapf happened to study the Soviet Union in some courses where the Soviet "experiment" was generally treated favorably. Dropping by the student activities building one day during his junior year, he saw a notice announcing a three-month trip to the USSR during the 1934 summer break. It was organized by the National Student League, a group he described as an official "communist youth organization," and the cost was $325. The two young men decided to enroll. Rapf's parents initially objected, but Maurice's arguments about the chance to see the Moscow Art Theatre, then considered one of the most exciting in the world, swayed them.

The trip was perhaps the first educational exchange program in which American undergraduates studied in Russia. Rapf, however, understood its purpose: "converting U.S. youth to a pro-Communist point of view."[31] He and Schulberg joined the forty-five other American, Canadian and Chinese students at the Anglo-American Institute in Moscow, where they lived in a palace formerly occupied by Russian royalty. Rapf, conscious of his Jewish heritage, was responsive to the myth that the Soviets had outlawed anti-Semitism and were inherently antifascist. What "probably made me a Communist," he later said, "was that anti-Semitism was illegal in the Soviet Union, and that the Soviets were very anti-Fascist, which the United States was not." When he had to pass through Germany on the way back to the States, the contrast was chilling. "I saw the Brownshirts marching down Unter den Linden," he still remembered decades later. "Anti-Semitism was really flagrant, but nobody in the United States was paying much attention."

Schulberg's impression of life in Russia was not so rosy. He was not prepared for "the frightful housing, the near-starvation of many workers, their lack of shoes, the homeless children begging on the streets." But like Joe Losey, who had witnessed the same disillusioning scenes, he got "caught up in the most exciting theatrical activity" he had ever experienced. He saw a production of Alexander Ostrovsky's *The Forest* at the Meyerhold Theatre that he never forgot. Vsevolod Meyerhold was a genius who was "creating new, anti-traditionalist forms for traditional plays," using a bare-stage "constructivist" setting similar to that of American plays like Thornton Wilder's *Our Town* and *The Skin of Our Teeth.*

Rapf too found the living conditions of average people "appalling," but he identified with the "writers and artists [who] were, at this time, given special rewards in terms of living quarters and an occasional car."[32] Communism might be tough on the proletariat, but for someone whose concern was theater and cinema, the freedom given to pro-regime artists was more important.

Unlike many other young revolutionary pilgrims, Schulberg already had some familiarity with Soviet cinema, having met Sergei Eisenstein when he came to Hollywood in 1930 under contract to Paramount Pictures. Eisenstein proposed films such as one he called *The Glass House,* a drama set in a modernist apartment with transparent walls. His radical proposals, however, did not go down well with Paramount executives—including Budd's father, B. P. Schulberg. Eisenstein then proposed *Sutter's Gold,* a film in which, he later wrote, "I wanted to express the disastrous role of the gold strike on Sutter's California lands, the destruction and ruin of his fertile estates," including a depiction of "those mountains of waste being disgorged."[33] This proposal too was rejected. Finally, the Soviet director tried to sell David O. Selznick a film based on Dreiser's *An American Tragedy*. When Selznick refused, Eisenstein turned to the best-selling writer Upton Sinclair, then running for governor of California, who raised money for Eisenstein to make a film to be shot in Mexico, part of which was released under the title *Thunder over Mexico*. When the film failed, Eisenstein went back to Russia.

Parlaying their brief acquaintance, Schulberg spoke to the director several times on the phone after the latter's arrival in Moscow. Eisenstein seemed uneasy. Only later did Schulberg learn that he had not made a film since his return, and that some of his proposals had been rejected by the Soviet authorities for being too mystical and even religious. Still, when they finally got together, the director took him to a Moscow film studio, where he informed Schulberg that only in the Soviet Union were pictures produced on the basis of true democracy. Scripts, he told the impressionable youngster, were "not chosen and approved exclusively by the 'bosses' as in Hollywood. Everyone in the studio, from the star and director to the lowliest stage-hand and office-boy, has an equal voice in the production." Filmmaking had become the egalitarian dream come true. The world's most famous director, Schulberg said, served "happily as a servant of the great revolutionary proletariat."[34]

The precocious Schulberg came to Moscow with a contract to write a book on Soviet youth. His contract and Hollywood background allowed him to meet leading figures in the world of drama, film and literature. The great Meyerhold, he said, "showed me through his theater and made an effort to describe some of his theories of constructivism." And Schulberg was invited to the apartment of the young playwright Afinogenov, whose play *Fear* was one of the hits of the season. Afinogenov reminded him of "a prosperous Hollywood writer," with royalties pouring in from all over Russia and with a new car, awarded by the Soviet government, which he planned to use for driving to his summer home.

The highlight of Schulberg's trip was the First Congress of

Soviet Writers. This event was important in the history of the growing Party control over literature because it was here that the doctrine of "socialist realism" was introduced. For the young Schulberg, however, being in the presence of his Russian literary heroes blocked out the ominous implications of this development. Schulberg saw the congress as a move away from the "tight strait-jacket" that the proletarian literature movement had been forcing writers to wear. He was not alone; the entire group of well-meaning but naïve Western visitors were virtually incapable of seeing how the congress was in fact initiating a new age of repression.[35]

Schulberg's memory of the details of the writers' congress became hazy over the years; yet he easily recalled "the general impression of enthusiasm, optimism and universality." André Gide expressed his faith in the Soviet Union as "the champion and defender of world culture." André Malraux shared the platform with Gorky while "the grand old man of Soviet literature" expounded on socialist realism. As Schulberg saw it, the new doctrine, rather than demand the celebration of the state, would permit Soviet literature to draw upon the bourgeois realism of nineteenth-century writers such as Balzac, Tolstoy and Stendhal. He heard the brief introductory speech by Andrey Zhdanov, Stalin's literary henchman, who "reminded writers that artistic truth must never be separated from 'the task of ideological remolding and re-education of the toiling masses.'" Schulberg, however, saw it as merely an example of a "Soviet orthodoxy" that did not stand in the way of "tolerance and comparative artistic freedom." He did not comment on the speech by Karl Radek, in which Stalin's foremost propagandist and Willi Münzenberg's mentor condemned Western writers such as James Joyce and John Dos Passos.

Schulberg also failed to mention a leaflet addressed to Western guests that was distributed at the conference, perhaps because copies were confiscated by OGPU-NKVD agents. The leaflet was the work of dissidents who wanted the political pilgrims to learn the truth about the writers' lives: Soviet freedom was "a gargantuan lie presented to you as truth." For seventeen years, "any possibility of free speech" in Russia had been "completely out of the question." The writers were compelled to be like prostitutes, selling not their bodies but their souls. Were they to disobey, they and their families would suffer "death by starvation." When they spoke of the Revolution's "brilliant achievements," it was by necessity and was intended for "consumption in the West."[36]

By the time Rapf and Schulberg returned to the United States, they were converts whose paths had been set. They had seen Moscow and the Soviet Revolution, and they wanted to help create humanity's future in their own homeland. Rapf was particularly ecstatic. "I think Communism is the coming thing for the world," he wrote home to his parents. He urged them to understand that there was nothing "horrible or violent about Communism." Contrary to the propaganda of the American press, "a Communist state would mean more good for a greater number," whereas American workers, the majority of the country, now received "the fewest benefits from society."[37]

The two young men were unprepared for the dismay that their opinions caused their parents and the Hollywood community. Budd Schulberg's parents were slightly more understanding and sympathetic, being more liberal than the other studio moguls. B. P. Schulberg had supported Upton Sinclair for governor and considered himself to be an Al Smith Democrat, eventually backing Franklin Roosevelt. His mother was something of a leftist, a friend of both Sinclair and Lincoln Steffens, who often visited at their home. She had made the journey to the Soviet Union herself in 1931 and regarded Russia as "an interesting social experiment."[38]

Maurice's father, Harry Rapf, on the other hand, was alarmed and very critical of the direction that Maurice and his friend were headed in. His concern was aroused when the "very strongly pro-Communist" letters began to arrive from Moscow. But there was more: Rapf was so taken with the Soviet Union that he had shaved his head and grown a Lenin-style goatee. Schulberg followed suit, admitting that the two of them looked "absolutely ridiculous." Meeting Will Rogers on the ship back from Europe, Rapf took the actor's advice and had his goatee removed in the SS *Majestic*'s barber shop.[39]

When Rapf arrived, his parents met him at the dock, having come to New York from Los Angeles to try to talk sense into him. "I could never have a career in movies if I was going to be a Red," Harry Rapf told Maurice. Reluctant to confront his son directly, Harry sent him to friends who proceeded to lambaste him for his "pro-Soviet leanings." Young Rapf was made to visit, among others, Harry Warner, who said he would end up destroying the movie industry and would "bring anti-Semitism down on the heads of all the movie people." Harry's brother Jack added, "you're a god-damned little fool, and you will cause a lot of trouble for all of us." Rapf got the same treatment from Louis B. Mayer, Irving Thalberg and David O. Selznick. Mayer's point was similar to Warner's: "[W]hat I was doing was bad for the Jews…[and] would strengthen the view that Jews and Communists were synonymous."[40] Furthermore, "It's people like you who cause anti-Semitism in the world."[41]

Schulberg likewise remembered that when they returned from Moscow, "there was a great complaint about it at the studio and so we went to see Thalberg. 'Send them to Thalberg' was the cry. It was like 'Go see the Wizard.' Thalberg was sort of the high priest of Hollywood and the producers, especially Mayer, felt he could straighten us out." Described by Neal Gabler as "young, ethereally handsome, boyishly charming, confident, intelligent, and, above all, possessed of a natural refinement," Irving Thalberg, who was MGM's legendary top producer and was like a surrogate son to Louis B. Mayer, talked to Schulberg and Rapf as if one day they would "take over the reins of these studios," except that their "extremely immature" politics would interfere with this destiny.[42] His warning was not farfetched. "We were," Schulberg says of himself and Rapf, "in the line of absolute succession."[43]

Inviting them to his bungalow for lunch, Thalberg told them that in his Brooklyn high school days, he had been a member of the Young People's Socialist League and "had made ardent street-corner speeches."[44] He then deputized his assistant Albert Lewin, a former New York critic who had done graduate work at Harvard and Columbia and who claimed to be an expert on Marxism, to talk further to the fledgling radicals. "He was quoting stuff I didn't know anything about," Maurice admitted later on. This made him realize that he didn't "know a goddam thing about Marxism." But instead of prompting him to reconsider his commitment, the humiliation in front of Thalberg made Rapf decide to study so he could better defend his left-wing convictions.[45]

After graduating from Dartmouth, Rapf moved to New York City, where he sought to work with left-wing filmmakers affiliated with the Film and Photo League. But the league could not offer him paying work, so his father got him a job in Hollywood as a junior writer on a film called *We Went to College*. When he met playwright Lillian Hellman through his father's contacts, she asked him to join the newly formed Screen Writers Guild, a writers' union being organized by Hollywood Communists. There he found himself meeting with people such as Dorothy Parker, Dashiell Hammett and Samson Raphaelson, all idols of his. Guild membership soon led him to a weekly Marxist study group, the first step before joining the Party. Its members, he was amazed to find, all worked for his father at MGM. Within four months, Rapf joined the Young Communist League.

When Budd Schulberg graduated, he too returned to Hollywood. The path he followed was almost the same as that taken by Rapf. Joining a Marxist study group, Schulberg found that it "gradually and unceremoniously evolved into a Communist youth group."

Writing to his parents when he was still in Moscow, young Rapf had said, "I can't go into the picture business and work into the big money and at the same time fight for Communism and be convinced that Communism is the right system for the world." To do this would mean "living like a capitalist by day and like a Communist at night." Now that he had joined the Party, this was a fairly good description of how he and Schulberg and other Hollywood Communists would live.[46]

2

The Hollywood Party

DESPITE WILLI MÜNZENBERG'S EXHORTATIONS TO USE FILM AS A PROP-
aganda medium, Los Angeles Communist Party chairman Sam
Darcy made a speech to Party cadre in 1933 where (according to
a FBI report) he "severely criticized one of the comrades for
mentioning the possibility of penetrating the motion picture
industry." Communists, Darcy said, "had no business wasting
their efforts in 'swanky Hollywood'" Communist work should be
confined to "the industrial districts, the shipyards and the harbor" where the "real work was to be done."[1]

In his critique, Darcy was just following the current ultra-
left Party line, which from 1929 to 1934 held that revolution was
imminent in the capitalist West and that Communists must
organize for revolution, avoiding coalitions with liberals and
social democrats. While Party organizers were willing to tap Hollywood wealth for their causes and send young Party recruits to
organize tenant farmers, Darcy and the other bosses were slow
to grasp the opportunities for organizing right in the film capital itself, and for that matter to understand the growing
importance of movies in American life after the advent of the
"talkies."

When Warner Brothers introduced sound in *The Jazz Singer*
in 1927, this crucial innovation created vast new markets for Hollywood's products and launched a rapid industry expansion.
Over the next three years, the industry's total assets tripled to $1
billion.[2] The studios rushed to sign up writers who could come
up with fresh script ideas and snappy dialogue. Among the

screenwriter recruits were dramatists coming out of the radical New York theater, young college graduates looking to enter the industry, and established novelists—many of whom were later accused of having sold out—included William Faulkner, Robert Sherwood, Elmer Rice, Clifford Odets, Bertolt Brecht and Aldous Huxley. For some, it became a gold mine. Huxley, for instance, received $15,000 from MGM for eight weeks of work, at a time when the average weekly wage for a writer was only $120.

But even booming Hollywood was not Depression-proof. Before the crash of 1929, more than eighty million Americans were going to the movie theaters each week, spending roughly $720 million each year. By the early 1930s, twenty million fewer Americans attended the movies and box office receipts fell by one-third. Out of sixteen thousand theaters nationwide, only eleven thousand survived.[3] Paramount and RKO declared bankruptcy; Twentieth Century Fox, Warner Brothers, Universal Studios and Columbia Pictures were on the verge of doing likewise. Only MGM remained in sound shape. The studio heads responded to the crisis by asking their workers to accept a pay cut of up to 50 percent, depending on their weekly salary.

The industry issues were made even more explosive in 1934, when socialist author Upton Sinclair ran for governor on an EPIC—"End Poverty in California"—ticket. One of his campaign promises was to raise funds for the state and for the poor by imposing a higher tax on the movie business. Hollywood responded by producing phony "newsreels" showing hordes of the unemployed and hobos descending upon the state, with the implication that they were flooding into California because they would be able to live on the dole once Sinclair became governor. The studio bosses also asked that their highest-paid employees, including writers and actors, contribute one day's pay to the campaign of Sinclair's opponent, Frank Merriam. The producers went so far as to write checks in their employees' names and press them to sign.[4]

The prospective pay cuts, combined with confiscation of a part of their salaries for the anti-Sinclair campaign, helped fuel the union movement in the studios. The Screen Actors Guild and the Screen Writers Guild were organized, both being craft unions that aimed to limit the power of the studios to dictate pay and working conditions. The Writers Guild was largely the creation of Communists and fellow travelers. Some writers complained about misuse of their creativity, others about working conditions. Americans who felt themselves fortunate if they had any job at all were not particularly sympathetic.

Yet there *was* something bizarre about the studios' attempts to run what amounted to a scriptwriting assembly line. Milton Sperling recalled that he was required to punch a time clock: "They would walk around and see if everybody was typing. There'd be a lookout in the writers' building. When Warner or Cohn would be seen coming toward the building, somebody would say, 'He's coming!' And all the typewriters would start."[5]

Michael Blankfort remembered that the main topic of conversation at the studio commissaries was how "stupid the producers and directors were.... The resentment was the resentment of the coal miner who resents the boss because [while] he's digging coal, he's getting all dirty [and] the boss is nice and clean and sitting in an air-conditioned office."[6] Moreover, most of the studio chiefs regarded writers as "separate but unequal, necessary but troublesome, independent and often irreverent," a group whose ideas were often seen as radical and hence as "a potential threat to any corporate structure." While producers and directors ate in the executive dining room, writers could gain access only if they had won an Academy Award. This so-called "class system" fueled demands for "studio democracy."[7]

Although regarded by the public as birds fluttering about in Hollywood's gilded cage, actors had their grievances too, albeit somewhat more subjective. As one officer of the Screen Actors Guild put it, actors feared being passed over for a role, or experiencing only a brief run of good luck, or being typecast in an ever-dwindling pool of roles. And when they were able to work, they found conditions far different from those that prevailed in the theater. An average workday might last from twelve to fourteen hours. Robert Montgomery, a major star of the 1930s and 1940s, recalled one film in which "we were actually on the set and working for over thirty-five hours without a break."[8]

The uncertainty of their profession, as much as the working

conditions, gave actors a strong incentive to organize. Since 1919 they had been represented by Actors' Equity in the New York theater. Hollywood offered quite different prospects for stage actors trying to make the transition to film. Although reaching a greater audience, they had little bargaining power with employers. In other industries, Communists moved to the forefront of the labor movement. The volatile boss of the Coal Miners' Union, John L. Lewis, hired Communists as organizers to recruit workers into the new federation of unions, the Congress of Industrial Organizations (CIO). And the Communist Party, now recognizing its earlier error in writing off Hollywood, reacted to the situation with equal fervor. Already having a base among those who had migrated from New York City's radical theater milieu, Communists became the leading figures in organizing Hollywood talent.

The comrades' presence in Hollywood was duly noted. "Communism is getting a toehold in the picture industry," *Variety* reported, with "red movie recruits" obtaining studio jobs as writers, scenarists, authors and adapters of material. These people's goal was nothing less than "a fantastic sovietizing of the lots," as the Hollywood Reds planned at weekly meetings to get the studios "writer-controlled" rather than run by producers. Most of the leaders, according to the story, were "easterners who have hit Hollywood during the past two years."[9]

This breathless account was rather exaggerated; the Party had little success in organizing sound stage and back lot workers. But it did play a significant role in organizing the two major guilds, especially the Screen Writers Guild. When the Motion Picture Academy approved the producers' newly announced wage cuts, Lester Cole, later one of the Hollywood Ten, met with other writers in the back room of Rose's Bookshop, one of their Hollywood hangouts, where they drew up an organization statement that they later circulated through the studios. They demanded such things as a standard writer's contract, in which writers would receive a percentage of gross receipts against royalties, as well as the right to gain screen credit for their work. More to the point, they rejected the producers' "recommendation" to cut salaries in half.[10]

A more formal meeting took place on February 3, 1933, at the Knickerbocker Hotel, when John Howard Lawson, who became the most influential figure in the Screen Writers Guild, convened several writers to discuss what could be done to improve their position. Cole attended, as did Samson Raphaelson, a Chicago advertising executive turned playwright, whose Broadway play *The Jazz Singer* had been turned into the first talkie. John Bright was also present. Best known for writing the gangster picture *The Public Enemy*, starring James Cagney, Bright was described by writer Nancy Lynn Schwartz as a "flamboyant character, with a penchant for booze, big shiny cars, and hanging out in the black section of town."[11] The guild grew quickly and had 750 members by October 1934.[12]

John Howard Lawson

Lawson was easily elected the first president of the new Screen Writers Guild. With a loud booming voice, which would later become famous throughout the country via newsreels of his 1947 HUAC testimony, Lawson seemed a born agitator. In his capacity as head of the Screen Writers Guild, he sought in 1934 and 1935 to establish Hollywood writers not simply as artists, but as members of the American working class.

A generation older than Budd Schulberg and Maurice Rapf and other young people who had become Communist converts as a result of trips to the USSR, Lawson came to Hollywood with an established reputation in the New York left-wing theater. His immigrant father, Simeon Levy, who Americanized his name to Lawson, had assimilated against great odds and in the face of prejudice.[13] An itinerant journalist traveling through the American West in the late 1800s, he later started an English-language paper in Mexico City, and then became chief of the East Coast division of Reuters news service. Although he converted from Judaism to Christian Science, he nevertheless endured anti-Semitism. Booking reservations at upper-class WASP resorts in New York's Catskills and arriving by coach with footman and staff, the Lawsons would still be turned away when hotel managers heard his thick Yiddish accent.

John Howard Lawson, however, was educated at Christian schools and accepted at Williams College in Massachusetts. Precociously talented, he had a play produced on Broadway by George M. Cohan and Sam Harris while he was still in college. In 1924, when his most famous play, *Processional,* debuted on Broadway, one critic commented that it was a "dazzling recreation of Aristophanic comedy" in which "a West Virginia strike is treated like a running gag in a vaudeville show" and the main characters were "slow-witted blacks, whining Jews, and comic-strip Communists."[14]

Lawson's son Jeff later described the play as showing a "Victorian, overbearing, over controlling, angry, capitalist father." Not surprisingly, Jeff saw *his* father in the same way, as an "aloof, very, very angry, and driven man who seldom spoke to me, who was not affectionate, and toward whom I felt fascination and awe but also fear." It was John Howard Lawson's own "angry Victorian controlling father," he thought, who had made him "an angry and driven radical man."[15]

By 1926, Lawson was working in New York at the New Playwrights' Theatre, along with young Harold Clurman. Lawson's first brush with Hollywood came soon after, when MGM asked him to create dialogue for a new film starring Greta Garbo. Desperately needing money, Lawson then accepted Cecil B. De Mille's proposal that he write the screenplay for the filmmaker's first sound film, *Dynamite.* Lawson got his money, but was burned when he found out that he had not received screen credit for his script. This embittering experience prompted him to quickly pack his bags and return to New York, where he became part of Clurman's newly formed left-wing dramatic ensemble, the Group Theatre. "We were determined," he told interviewers, that "we would not return to Hollywood."[16]

The Group Theatre, founded by Harold Clurman, Lee Strasberg and Cheryl Crawford, was the foremost theater group in the 1930s. Lawson's work was considered so good that one of the first plays they produced was his *Success Story.* The play focused on the rise of Sol Ginsberg, a Jew working in a New York ad agency, who leaves his youthful radicalism behind and seeks to replace the company's owner. It was, Lawson said, "an indictment of the whole system of values which capitalism imposed upon us."[17] But Clurman, who regarded Lawson as a man who "by his love of discussion, even of dispute," was irreplaceable, later wrote that at this time he also "vented opinions that led us to believe that he was violently opposed to official Communist doctrine" and was even considering writing a play to be called *Red Square* that would deal with the contradictions of the worldwide revolutionary movements.[18]

At the same time as he was working with the Group, Lawson continued to moonlight for Hollywood. After signing a contract with RKO, he wrote three original screenplays while in New York. In 1931, as Hollywood was trying to weather the Depression, Lawson and his family decided to relocate in the film capital, because "we didn't have enough money to sustain a permanent program of living in the East."[19]

The dean of the proletarian New York authors, the Communist Mike Gold, whose book *Jews Without Money* became the only best-selling novel written by a Communist in the 1930s, mercilessly attacked Lawson for the decision. Calling the playwright a "bourgeois Hamlet" in the Party cultural journal *New Masses,* Gold blasted Lawson for "political indecisiveness" and accused him of "squandering his talent on inferior plays and scripts." Lawson's characters, Gold argued, were lost—constantly repeating "the same monotonous question: 'Where do I belong in the warring world of the two classes?'"[20] Gold's diatribe hit hard; Lawson responded in a penitent fashion, agreeing with Gold's criticisms but insisting that his work showed "an orderly development" away from "bourgeois romanticism" and the doctrine of "art for art's sake" toward "art as a weapon."[21]

Harold Clurman later witnessed Lawson's appearance before what he called "a radical literary club," probably the New York City chapter of the Party's John Reed Club. Lawson was greeted by a "host of indictments," echoes of Gold's attack that harped on how "confused" Lawson was. Clurman was shocked to find that when Lawson finally had his turn, "he talked like a man with a troubled conscience, a man confessing his sin, and in some way seeking absolution."[22]

Lawson tried to honor the demand that he make closer

contact with the working class. He took a break from writing and became a full-time activist. Working as a journalist, Lawson went south and wrote up the case of the Scottsboro Boys, a group of black Alabama youths who had been framed and sentenced to death for rape. The lesson he learned from the case and from being arrested for opposing white vigilantism was simple: "My brief adventures in the south deepened my conviction that commitment is essential to the artist's creative growth."[23]

When Lawson presented his next theatrical work, *Marching Song*, a play about a striker, Clurman was disappointed, finding it "cold, artificial, a creature of the author's will—lacking in spontaneity." Clurman committed the unpardonable sin of telling Lawson that he was far better when writing about the middle class, to which he actually belonged. "Don't you think proletarian plays should be written at this time?" Lawson responded. Clurman thought this "should be written" implied a "very dangerous position for an artist to take." He told Lawson: Maybe so, "but not by you."[24] Years later, Clurman concluded that, although Lawson had perhaps become a "more useful citizen" as a result of his Communism, he was "no longer working as an artist."[25]

After this, Lawson gave up his bicoastal artistic identity and focused on Hollywood. Over the next few years, he became the Party's enforcer in the industry; ironically, in this capacity he subjected others to the same treatment that he, as a young playwright, had been given by Mike Gold. Later, Party members such as Paul Jarrico regarded Lawson as someone who had committed "intellectual crimes" against his comrades. To Jarrico, a self-proclaimed Party "revisionist" (who thought some might even call him a "right-wing opportunist"), Lawson was "an infantile leftist, a sectarian sonofabitch." Similarly, the Party's future West Coast chairman Dorothy Healey saw him as a "tragic figure," a man of talent who was "struggling so hard to prove he was not a petty-bourgeois intellectual" that he could not write a word without submitting it to the appropriate Party body for approval.[26]

Lester Cole

Lawson's comrade-in-arms in organizing the Screen Writers

Guild was Lester Cole, who until his death in 1985 also remained a hardcore Communist, as the title of his autobiographical memoir, *Hollywood Red,* suggests. Cole had his first exposure to radical politics when he heard his father, an immigrant from Poland, speak from soapboxes as he campaigned for New York City's Socialist Party mayoral candidate Morris Hillquit. Although his father was a committed socialist, Cole's mother was an equally committed entrepreneur. She established an astounding array of small businesses—thus epitomizing petit-bourgeois ambition to her Marxist husband. His refusal to borrow money to set up a business of his own eventually led to their divorce.

While his father's "way of thinking of…working people and a socialist world made sense" to him, Cole explained in his memoir, his mother's "driving ambition for wealth did not." After dropping out of high school, he promised his mother that he would eventually become "a lawyer, doctor, or dentist."[27] But in 1926, like other radicals of his age, he was deeply affected by the trial and execution of the anarchists Sacco and Vanzetti (who were convicted of a payroll robbery in Braintree, Massachusetts). Viewing the affair as a "scandalous, inhuman frame-up," Cole attended protest meetings where he heard John Howard Lawson speak.

Finding a job as a stage manager in a touring theater company, the twenty-two-year-old Cole was fortunate enough to be seen by Cecil B. De Mille while directing a rehearsal of *The Miracle* in Los Angeles. The legendary director offered him a job in Hollywood; but when Cole arrived there, De Mille was nowhere to be found and Cole was forced to take a job digging ditches on the back lot of the Warner Brothers studio. While doing manual labor, Cole read Maxim Gorky's famous novel *Mother,* whose namesake character witnesses her revolutionary son being killed while leading a strike. As Cole was to put it, "I desperately wanted to be that young striker, and that mother to be my mother." The novel led him to Communism.

Determined to get a job in the industry, he approached Sid Grauman, the owner of Grauman's Chinese Theatre on Hollywood Boulevard. Amazingly, Grauman told the young man that he too had been at the rehearsal of *The Miracle* on the same day as De Mille. The impresario offered Cole a job as assistant director at the new Chinese Theatre. While employed there, Cole wrote and sold a play, and this led to a writing job at MGM, where he had the desk next to Lillian Hellman. Cole came to be known as a trustworthy journeyman screenwriter, someone with "a sense of plot, a social conscience, a talent for creating a reasonably authentic urban milieu peopled by the proletariat, politicos, prostitutes and criminals."[28]

With Lawson and others, Cole became one of the principal organizers of the Screen Writers Guild, a role that brought him notoriety and a reputation for militancy. As a result, he was invited to join a "Marxist study group," the path through which all future Hollywood Communists began their apprenticeship in the CP. In this milieu they were expected to learn the basic tenets of Marxism-Leninism and prove that they would be solid comrades worthy of Party membership.

Within a month, Cole was visited by a man—most likely Stanley Lawrence—who introduced himself as organizer of the Party's Hollywood section. This group, he was told, was not a club but a "revolutionary party," to which writers had "perhaps the greatest obligation to give as much of their time and ability as humanly possible."[29]

Organizing the Hollywood Party

By 1935, the CPUSA leadership, seeing that Communism was a growth industry in Hollywood, decided to create a Hollywood branch and put the New York headquarters in charge of it. Until then, Party members in the film capital had been loosely controlled by the southern California branch. Within a year, the Hollywood branch had over one hundred members; after three years, there were three hundred.

The new arrangement brought Hollywood Party members under the control of the Central Committee's "cultural commissar," V. J. Jerome, who came to personify the Party's secret and harshest face. A full-time apparatchik working in the Party's national office in New York City, Jerome was a third-rate writer whose real job was seeing to it that Party doctrine was always enforced, particularly when new and important chapters were created. Born Isaac Romain in Poland in 1896, and naturalized in 1928, he was a former bookkeeper and high school teacher who had once intended to become a rabbi. Short, chubby and bald, and wearing horn-rimmed eyeglasses, Jerome looked like a benign professor. But his features turned steely—indeed, frightening—when he confronted even well-known writers and forced them to grovel before the correct Party line.

As his envoy to Hollywood, Jerome chose Stanley Lawrence, described by Neal Gabler as a "shaggy dog [who] had been a Los Angeles cab driver who had gone overseas to help organize workers." Seymour Stanley Robbins, Lawrence's real name, was actually a skilled operative of the Comintern who had been active in the international Communist movement in Europe.[30] After attending Cornell University from 1925 to 1929, Robbins was accepted at medical school in Vienna, where he joined the Communist Party of Austria on the eve of fascism's triumph. Upon graduating in 1935, Robbins transferred his membership to the American CP. Jerome gave him the nom de guerre "Lawrence" and assigned him to the Los Angeles section in May of that year. His principal role as financial secretary was to recruit and organize in the motion picture industry.[31] The writer Samson Raphaelson described Lawrence as "my first true international communist" and regarded him as "absolutely brilliant," someone who could explain Marx's theory of surplus value without a hitch.[32]

Maurice Rapf remembered Lawrence as an organizer who regularly came to his parents' home, where he would help himself to breakfast and drop off Marxist literature that Rapf was to distribute at unit meetings in the evenings. Producer Harry Rapf was not happy about his son's regular guest and made it clear that the weekly visits had to stop. One afternoon when Harry Rapf found Lawrence sprawled out on a damask loveseat in the elegant, white-carpeted living room, he "blew his stack." The powerful producer ordered him out: "If you have any consideration for my son, you will stay away from him."[33]

Budd Schulberg recalled that Lawrence came out of nowhere, suddenly appearing in the middle of their lives. After establishing a Marxist study group for Rapf and Schulberg to attend, he gave the two young would-be moguls their first assignment: to organize tenant farmers in the fruit fields of California's Central Valley. "We would go to Grange meetings and try to organize," Schulberg said. "Farmers would ask us: 'Who the hell are you two? Why are you here? Who needs you?'"

The Party leadership chastised Lawrence for giving these well-connected young men such an assignment. According to Schulberg, V. J. Jerome "came down hard on Lawrence" and told him that "the focus of the Party ought to be in the Hollywood film community, and in getting Leftists to join the Party and hand over ten per cent of their salary as dues." According to Schulberg, the Party punished Lawrence by falsely accusing him of siphoning off money from the Party treasury for his own use and of mismanaging its funds. ("He never had a cent. We used to have to give him car fare and lunch money.")[34] Then it sent him off to fight in Spain. Eventually it was announced in the Party's paper, the *Worker*, that Lawrence had been shot as a traitor. "I didn't understand it," Schulberg said. "Orwell did."[35]

James Cagney and the Uses of Celebrity

Young enthusiasts like Rapf and Schulberg were important, but the Party needed celebrities, especially those with access to big salaries. As an FBI informant told the bureau, "from among the fabulous-salaried executives, directors, actors, scenario writers…of the motion picture industry, have come the Communist Party's most liberal financial supporters." Each month a reliable Party member visited key contributors and collected money, much as ministers do in their congregations. They did their best to keep the names secret, allowing only a "trusted few" to know who the contributors were.

This was especially true in the handling of the actor James Cagney, who became closely acquainted with a number of Communists and was a major contributor to the causes they supported. Cagney (an FBI informant noted) was "among those at the head of the list of heavy contributors, who could be counted upon to make additional contributions…as well as to maintain his monthly payments." From their experience with Cagney, Party leaders learned that they had to move to protect such high-profile supporters from unwanted public scrutiny.[36]

Born in New York City's Lower East Side on July 17, 1899, to a poor family headed by an alcoholic father, Cagney had a background that made him a logical target of the Party. Irish on his father's side and Irish-Norwegian on his mother's, Cagney escaped from life on the street by entering the drama program of the Lenox Hill Settlement House on East 69th Street, which was headed by two socialists, Florence and Burton James. He performed in their plays, and before long he was touring in vaudeville and appearing in Broadway reviews, where he was discovered by producer Jack Warner and signed to a contract.[37]

Once Cagney was established, the Communist screenwriters John Bright and Sam Ornitz took him under their wings, introducing him to the Party's most important causes, including the Scottsboro Boys and Tom Mooney cases, and taking him to meetings of new fronts, such as the Film and Photo League.

When Cagney expressed interest in meeting Theodore Dreiser and Lincoln Steffens, Bright took him to San Francisco, where he joined the distinguished authors for dinner at John's Rendezvous restaurant before attending a ten-thousand-strong workers' rally at the Longshoremen's Amphitheater. The organizers saw to it that the visitors were seated on the platform next to the secretary of the California Communist Party, William Schneiderman. When Jack Warner saw the story in the Hearst press, he called Bright and Cagney into his office and raised hell with them for being "Communist dupes."[38]

But Cagney ignored him. For a while, he even rented a house in Carmel near the home of Party sympathizer Steffens and his wife, Ella Winter (whom Comintern agent and "Münzenberg man" Louis Gibarti called "one of the most trusted party agents for the West Coast").[39] Privately, by the 1930s Steffens had actually adopted Communism. "My chief argument for communism in the U.S.," he wrote to Los Angeles district Party organizer Sam Darcy, "is that it so exactly solves our problem."[40]

Steffens seemed to realize that his effectiveness would be increased if he remained formally outside the Party's ranks. Thus he told Darcy, "I am not to be trusted in the Party or in the front rank of the struggle that is on."[41] Darcy, writing to Party chairman Earl Browder, assured him that Steffens was "one of the few famous intellectuals who is sincere and acts to aid our movement" and that in the next presidential election Steffens would "speak in support of the Party as often as his strength allows."[42]

According to John Bright, Steffens and Winter "sort of adopted Cagney," much to the dismay of the movie star's rather traditional and conservative wife. The actor Lionel Stander, another Hollywood Red, recalled meeting Cagney at the home of Winter and Steffens, when he and John Steinbeck came to a fundraiser for a lettuce workers' strike. Cagney responded emotionally to the conditions in which downtrodden workers lived. When Ella Winter wrote a series of articles about cotton workers on strike in the San Joaquin Valley, he immediately sent her a check for the strikers.[43]

This spontaneous generosity caused problems for Cagney. The Sacramento district attorney, Neil McAllister, was grandstanding by opposing the Communists and currying favor with the growers by opposing the CP-led strikes. As part of this effort, he mobilized his private Red squad on the watch, and at times managed to screen private mail sent by Communist Party members. He saw the letter in which Winter told Caroline Decker, secretary of the Communist-led Cannery and Agricultural Workers Union: "I have Cagney's money again," with the added comment that the actor "is going to bring up other stars to talk to Stef about communism." Soon there appeared a banner headline in the *New York Times,* courtesy of McAllister: "FILM ACTOR NAMED IN COAST RED PLOT."[44]

When Martin Dies, chairman of what eventually became the House Committee on Un-American Activities, first came to investigate Hollywood Communism in 1940, Cagney was one of those he called to testify. On the day of Cagney's appearance, and before he testified, a former Hollywood Red named John L. Leech testified that Cagney belonged to the CP, had given the Party large sums of money, and had sent letters of endorsement to the cotton strike leadership in 1934.[45] When Cagney's turn came, he denied Leech's allegations. Admitting only to giving money to the San Joaquin Valley strikers—because the evidence had already been made public—he vigorously denied being a Party member.

His donation, said Cagney, had been in response to "a direct request to the Screen Actors' Guild as a fellow union…to help out." He also acknowledged giving money to the Scottsboro and Tom Mooney defense committees because, he said, his friend Lincoln Steffens had asked him to. These groups, of course, were all Communist fronts and major Communist Party causes, as was the Committee to Aid Republican Spain, to which Cagney later donated money to buy ambulances for the Loyalists.

"Under the circumstances under which I was raised," Cagney told the committee, "I saw poverty on all sides for a long time. Such a thing leaves its impression; you can't go through life and build a wall around yourself and say 'Everything is fine for me and to hell with the other fellow.'" He had also joined the Hollywood Anti-Nazi League after receiving an "emotional appeal" from a friend. Cagney claimed to have asked its sponsors whether they were left-wing or Communist-led, never receiving an answer. The dreaded Martin Dies was charmed and satisfied. Unlike his HUAC counterparts in the late 1940s and early 1950s, he told Cagney that they were bringing no charges against him. Nor was Cagney asked to name his associates. "We are just as anxious as you," Dies stated, "to defend innocent people and their names as we are to expose those who are guilty." He advised Cagney to go to "dependable" agencies that "aid those who are in distress." Cagney replied that he would not give money in the future to those who worked against the American system and sought to do it harm. From then on he distanced himself from his friends on the Communist Left.[46]

Cagney later claimed that he was just someone who grew up poor, believed in fighting for the underdog, and was completely ignorant of the political associations of friends such as Ella Winter. "What the hell did I know about the ebb and flow of political movements," he asked, "or even what they meant?…[I]t all seemed so sensible: take from the overrich, give to the poor. Distribute the wealth. How does one do that?…In any case, at the time, left seemed right."[47]

3

The Popular Front: 1935–1939

IN AUGUST 1935, COMMUNISTS THROUGHOUT THE WORLD WERE informed that the "left turn" had been declared over. No longer were Franklin Delano Roosevelt and the New Deal to be portrayed as an American variant of fascism. The Seventh Comintern Congress, chaired by the Bulgarian Georgi Dimitrov, announced that henceforth Communists would unite with liberal democrats throughout the West in a Popular Front.

Following the Münzenberg blueprint, the American Communist Party went into overdrive in the effort to create new front organizations. Through these groups, as Walter Krivitsky, one of the NKVD's first defectors, put it, "Moscow now entered the citadels of capitalism as the champion of peace, democracy and anti-Hitlerism." The Party sought to convince "New Deal officials, respectable business executives, trade-union leaders and journalists that Soviet Russia was the forefront of the forces of 'peace and democracy.'"[1]

The new policy helped the American CP grow in influence and in numbers. Party chief Earl Browder proclaimed the new slogan, "Communism is twentieth-century Americanism," and the Communists began to cite Lincoln, Washington and Jefferson as much as they did Marx, Lenin and Stalin. Now it was FDR's enemies, not the president himself—whom they had previously called a fascist—who were to be opposed. The CP now attacked only the Republicans and urged their electoral defeat in 1936. While Browder himself ran on a Communist presidential ticket, he made it clear that his membership should vote for

Roosevelt on the Democratic line. Within a few years, the Party moved into the Democratic Party itself, seeking influence within its ranks; and after October 1937, when FDR called for "quarantining the aggressors" of Germany and Japan, the Party moved to embrace Roosevelt completely, hailing him as the leader of the Popular Front in America.[2]

The national Party focused on its Hollywood chapter, seeing the Popular Front as a way of dramatically increasing its power there. Its specific goals were later summarized by a Communist screenwriter named Max Silver when he testified before the House Committee on Un-American Activities in a secret executive session in 1951. First, Silver explained, the CP stipulated that Hollywood "influences the country not only culturally but politically." Second, in terms of film content, the Popular Front emphasis was to subtly insert ideology "in an ordinary John and Mary movie where millions go…[rather] than to put in a whole thesis." Third, the film capital was a major trade union center. Because of CP influence in some Hollywood unions, it could "reflect that influence in the [Los Angeles] Central Labor Council." Finally, Silver explained that Hollywood was "a source of finances for broad campaigns" such as the antifascist movement or the Scottsboro Boys.[3]

Recruitment and Financing the Party

During the years of the Popular Front, because many liberals did not see any difference between their own goals and those of the Communists, the Party's strategy for consolidating its beachhead in Hollywood worked. The actor Lionel Stander recalled that the Communist Party always "took the frontal position" in expressing "all the things that everybody wanted to hear."[4] Thus it became comfortable, even fashionable, to be thought of as a Red. "The Marxist explanation for what was happening in society was most convincing," said Budd Schulberg. "Once we were told that we could be Communists and still support the New Deal and Roosevelt, and that the CP was simply a more advanced group going in the same general direction, it was pretty heady…stuff to us."[5]

Screenwriter Richard Collins, who became one of the most

hard-line Reds, was similarly attracted to the Party because it "enunciated a program against prejudice, for trade unions, for higher wages, social justice and civil liberties," and because it presented "the Soviet Union as the great enemy of Nazism and the friend of the democracies." It did not talk of revolution, but of day-to-day tactics. Many who joined during the Popular Front, Collins explained, "had no idea that we were embracing, in whole or in part, another tyranny."[6]

Martin Berkeley, who in the 1950s named more names of Communists before HUAC than any other screenwriter, testified that he would never have joined the Party in 1936 had he known that he was joining a revolutionary movement. "I joined," he told HUAC, "because I was anti-Fascist, because I believed in social reform, because I felt the Party was the only vocal, active enemy of Hitlerism."

Hollywood director Frank Tuttle felt that not enough attention was being given to Hitler's rise to power, and when he met Stanley Lawrence, the CP's chief Hollywood organizer, the latter emphasized how the Communists had been instrumental in forming antifascist organizations. Tuttle became impressed with "the idea that the Communists were responsible for this work, which I considered good." Two years after meeting Lawrence, Tuttle joined the Party in 1937.[7]

Meta Reis Rosenberg, a script reader for Warner Brothers, met Party member Madeleine Ruthven at a meeting of the Hollywood Anti-Nazi League. Ruthven stressed how the CP was the main force backing the Loyalists in Spain and how it also was "very active in support of Roosevelt," as well as being "the most militant organization in the United States in terms of their opposition to Hitler." Since Rosenberg already believed in these goals, it was a natural step for her to join "the most effective organization" working for them. She became a Communist in 1938.[8]

Hollywood could be a very lonely place where newcomers were largely ignored; there was cut-throat competition for jobs and assignments, and social relations were typically strained and hierarchical. The Party reached out to young people who were trying to make it in the film world, offering them an instant community, membership in an organization with worthy goals, and access to successful and influential Hollywood insiders. When Frank Tarloff came to Hollywood as a screenwriter for MGM during the war, Lester Cole and his wife spoke to him about joining the Party. Tarloff enthusiastically signed on and was thrilled with the results. "I found myself collecting Party dues from Dalton Trumbo and other famous writers," he recalled. "They were wonderful, and the only way that I could have gotten to know them was through the Party. Dalton was making five thousand dollars a week, but we were comrades.... I was welcome at the 'red table' at MGM where all the left-wing writers ate."[9]

In effect, the Communist Party became the place to be for many of the most socially conscious people in Hollywood. For years, according to screenwriter Abraham Polonsky, it was "the best social club in Hollywood. You'd meet a lot of interesting people, there were parties, and it created a nice social atmosphere."[10] For many, social life was a CP meeting or a Party recruitment session. "Some of the more prominent [actors and writers] even joined the Party itself, standing by their swimming pools with clenched fists," Budd Schulberg remembered, "looking towards that 'better world in birth' where beckoned that benign social engineer 'Uncle Joe' Stalin."[11]

After Stanley Lawrence was disciplined for putting Schulberg and Rapf to work organizing farm workers, the Party assigned them their proper role: recruiting new members. Schulberg was especially successful at this. Although in 1936 he was only twenty-two years old, Budd had already published well-received short stories. Moreover, his wife, Virginia Ray—known as "Jigee"—was an attraction herself. Jigee and her sister, Anne, despite having grown up with an anti-Semitic father, "found a new world of talk and ideas and humor" with the largely Jewish group of Communist writers.[12] Budd and Jigee married on New Year's Eve, 1936, and the couple quickly became "the prince and princess of Hollywood."[13] Looking at her, Ring Lardner Jr. proposed a slogan: "The Most Beautiful Girls in Hollywood Belong to the Communist Party." He saw Budd and Jigee as "the ideal representatives of our generation."[14]

Milton Sperling recalled, "We used to have Marxist study groups in B. P. Schulberg's house in Benedict Canyon. B. P. never suspected, of course. Jigee was the hostess, and I think we couldn't deny the appeal of meeting in a fine Beverly Hills house to talk of revolution with such a glamorous young hostess. These study groups usually numbered eight to twelve people and most of them were men—young writers—and everyone was a little in love with her."[15]

Often the study groups were prime recruitment opportunities, where seasoned Communist cadre led newcomers into the world of Marxism, carefully identifying novices who might be good candidates for Party membership. Maurice Rapf, for instance, quickly graduated from the study group to the Young Communist League, where he was told to "recruit friends in Hollywood who might be ripe for joining...but not quite ready for the CP itself."

Maurice Rapf was a great catch for the Party, not only because of his industry connections but also because his family had a beach house in Malibu, where he held very popular soirées for prospective CP members. In his memoir, Rapf describes a "Malibu Beach CP Recruiting Party." Writers Paul Jarrico, Sandy Kibbee, Ring Lardner Jr., Perl Slutzky and Richard Collins were there, along with Rapf's wife, Louise, and Jigee Schulberg—all sitting near the surf, drinks in hand. For the most part, the attendees sunned themselves and went swimming, played volleyball and just got "to know beautiful people." There was also time for indoctrination, but it was not exactly, Rapf slyly comments, what Lenin meant when he talked of the life of a professional revolutionary.[16]

Future screenwriter Robert Lees found employment in the film capital through his family's connection to Harry Rapf's brother Joe. Lees had grown up in San Francisco; he described his family as "liberal Reform Jewish" and Republican until FDR was elected, when most of them became Democrats. When his father's business faced retrenchment during the Depression, Robert dropped out of UCLA and took a job as a shipping clerk. His father, thinking he would do better in Hollywood, called upon the Rapfs for help. Joe Rapf, who once worked for Lees's father, was now working at the costume department at MGM. As a result, in 1931 Robert got work as an extra, a bit player and a

chorus boy.[17] Eventually, Lees ended up in the MGM junior writers' department, working on scripts alongside other young
people fresh from college. There he would become a partner of
Fred Rinaldo, one of Rapf's and Schulberg's classmates at Dartmouth. Years later, they would make their mark as the writing
team for Bud Abbott and Lou Costello. Working at the studio
when Hitler was rising to power in Germany, Lees saw the Communists as "the leadership" in the resistance to fascism.

In 1939, shortly before the announcement of the Nazi-
Soviet Pact, Lees was hosting a party at his house after some
left-wing affair. Fellow screenwriter Paul Jarrico approached him
and asked, "Have you ever thought of joining the Communist
Party?" Lees hesitated. "What's bothering you so much?" Jarrico
asked. "Half the people outside in your living room are members
of the Party." Lees and his wife had only two questions: Should
they join, and "What was wrong with us that they took this long to
even ask?"[18]

The Party not only offered members a community, it also
supplied them with a "correct line" on matters large and small.
Richard Collins joined the Party in 1937 and moved swiftly up
through the ranks over the next ten years, becoming the head
of his cell and a board member of the Screen Writers Guild. The
son of a successful dressmaker whose shop was on the fashionable corner of New York City's 57th Street and Park Avenue,
Collins had attended the Browning School, where he was one of
three Jewish students. The family relocated to California, where
Collins' father got a job at Twentieth Century Fox as the head
designer in the costume department. While attending Beverly
Hills High School, Collins soon became friends with Budd
Schulberg and Maurice Rapf, visiting them at the Rapfs' beach
house and hearing about their experiences in the Soviet Union.

After graduating, Collins went off to Stanford, where his
freshman English professor introduced him to socialism. The
abstract ideas became concrete when Collins was forced to drop
out of school after his first year because his family had lost their
money during the Depression. Collins observed that the only
Stanford engineering students getting jobs were those who had
moved to Soviet Russia.[19]

Collins left Palo Alto for New York in 1935, where he joined the New Theatre League, from whose ranks he was recruited into the Young Communist League. "When I joined the Party," Collins later wrote, "I was handed ready-made friends, a cause, a faith and a viewpoint on all phenomena. I also went through ten years of constant reinforcement and re-commitment and education. I learned the party view on psychoanalysis, on existentialism and Sartre, on almost every writer living and dead, on folk music, on religion, on everything under the sun."[20]

An airtight, readymade worldview came along with a Party card. Philip Dunne, a liberal activist who joined many Popular Front groups, later recalled being approached by two "earnest young gentleman" during the mid-1930s. "Their Party, they said, offered guidance, discipline, and above all, peace of mind. Under its benevolent control, I would be able to concentrate my energies in the areas I know best and where I could best perform. Moreover, they said, I would be spared the agony of thinking my way through difficult issues: all the thinking would be done for me by an elite corps of trained cerebrators...."[21]

After recruitment, in trying to find uses for its new cadre the Party was obviously interested in money. Most high-salaried Hollywood CP members gave 4 percent of their income after payment of their 10 percent agents' fee. During his years of membership, Frank Tuttle, for instance, paid between $9,000 and $10,000 in annual dues to the Party; these were cash contributions with no formal accounting for income tax records.[22]

The Party also realized the importance of being associated with what was later called the celebrity culture. "There was a real feeling," Collins put it, "that the concentration of creative people would be useful in the sense of prestige."[23] Learning from the Cagney fiasco, however, the Party worked to protect its most illustrious stars and intellectuals from being identified. They were recruited and handled by members whom Ring Lardner Jr. called "our most steadfast section leaders." Dorothy Parker, Alan Campbell and Lillian Hellman were such members. To protect their identities and to keep their CP membership secret, they met with Party representatives individually or in very small groups. Schulberg, who recruited Campbell and Parker, met regularly with Parker to fill her in on Party news and especially to collect her dues.[24]

The Guilds

Party members were also given the task of reconstituting the Screen Writers Guild in 1937, after it was decimated by the desertion of its members to the Screen Playwrights, a company union. Richard Collins recalled that the Party was in fact the main organizer of the revived guild. V. J. Jerome, the Party's New York–based cultural commissar, and later John Howard Lawson held meetings to explain to the writers how they should work to organize a union. They called a series of eight or nine meetings on the same night at different homes. To each of these meetings, twenty or thirty writers were invited. At least one person at each meeting had previously met with V. J. Jerome and hence "knew what the demands were." Then, the "Screen Writers Guild was organized," said Collins, "...with about 200 people" all put together by the Party apparatus.[25]

Guild rules required only 10 percent of the membership to be present in order to obtain a quorum. The Party could be depended upon to make sure that all of its members attended critical meetings. They would be in control when the non-Communists tired and left in the wee hours of the morning; or alternatively, if they saw a vote going against them, the members would withdraw from the meeting so that a quorum could not be obtained.

Such tactics had worked elsewhere. In the early 1930s, a small Communist cell had attempted to gain control over the Group Theatre, a left-wing troupe. Some Party members, such as Elia Kazan, became disturbed about what he would later call a "game of conspiracy." The methods employed at the Group Theatre and Actors' Equity meetings in New York were similar to those that later became commonplace in Hollywood: "The secret caucuses before, the clever tactics during, the calculated positioning of our 'comrades' in the meeting hall to create the effect of a majority when the fact was that we were a small minority."[26]

The Party had other ways of exerting influence in front

organizations and the guilds, with the result that its importance exceeded its actual numbers. All Party members were assigned to broad mass movements. In Budd Schulberg's case, this meant supporting the Spanish Loyalists and forming a Young Democrats chapter in Hollywood. But Schulberg's special responsibility involved the Screen Writers Guild. Party members contrived to elect him to its board of directors. Those in the left-wing caucus of the guild, he recalled, were instructed to create an illusion of independence by not sitting together at meetings. They were instructed instead to befriend and sit with non-Communist liberals in the guild. He selected as his target Jesse Lasky Jr., the son of Paramount's California studio chief, with whom he had grown up.

"I would have dinner with Jesse before a meeting," Budd recalled, "and talk to him about the issues and what I thought had to be done. Jesse would get interested and supportive, and I worked on him to assure backing for resolutions and actions desired by the Party. Then I would say, look, I'm shy of getting up and making a resolution myself, especially since sometimes I stammer. You get up and make the resolution and I'll second it."

Such tactics turned many liberals off. Morrie Ryskind, who had belonged to the Dramatists Guild in New York, was made a member of the Screen Writers Guild board of directors when he got to Hollywood. He soon observed that seven of the fifteen board members always voted the same way, no matter what the issue; so even though they were a minority, they usually managed to win every point. For the 1937 board election, Ryskind helped put together and campaign for a non-Communist slate of candidates. Going into the meeting, he calculated that his slate had a three-to-one majority of those members present and also had about five hundred proxies. But he suspected the Communists would have "some kind of trick," and he was not disappointed. During the meeting, after guild president Charles Brackett had declared it a healthy sign that the guild had two tickets to choose from, Lester Cole got up and said, "Let's not split among ourselves. We have only one enemy—producers. Any fight among ourselves will be welcomed by the producers.... Let's reelect the old board who served us so well in this first year of our trouble by unanimous acclamation." Then all the Communists, who had spread themselves around the room, jumped up and started cheering and applauding. The board was returned for another year.[27] Experiences like this led Ryskind several years later to help found a new anti-Communist group, the Motion Picture Alliance for the Preservation of American Ideals.

Although he was a novice, the Party elevated Maurice Rapf, along with Schulberg, into a leadership position in the Screen Writers Guild. He was put on the guild's board and then made secretary. He was assigned to guild committees charged with negotiating with the studio producers. The Party knew that Rapf would be negotiating with his father's friends and associates.[28]

Rapf remained a Communist in his mind and in his principles, but soon found that the political activities the Party demanded of him interfered with his ambition to be a productive screenwriter. Producer David Selznick had given him good—but unheeded—advice when Rapf returned from his 1934 trip to the Soviet Union and was praising Communism. "You have to choose," Selznick said, "between politics and making movies." Having to attend two or three meetings a week, being forced to read verbose and useless articles, Party propaganda and reports, as well constantly trying to recruit new members, left him no time for creative work. The Party had also ordered him to run for office in the Democratic County Committee, which entailed yet more political commitments. For a good Communist, the worst offense was to regard a political event as "another evening down the drain every week," which was precisely Rapf's point of view.[29] Eventually, to escape the demands on active Party members, he left Hollywood altogether.

Budd Schulberg faced the same problem. Party members, on the model of the European underground, were organized in cells of eight or nine people each. "We'd meet each week with a definite agenda. Everybody had an assignment." Most important was that each member "had to work in a front organization. Somebody would work on the Young Democrats, the Screenwriters Guild, someone in the group against war and fascism." They all worked diligently, Schulberg recalled, and "it took a lot of time and study and energy."[31]

Richard Collins proved to be an exemplary member, attending an average of five or six meetings a week. The groups that Collins had joined included the Anti-Nazi League, the Committee to Aid Agricultural Workers, the Screen Writers Guild, the Motion Picture Buyers Group, the Hollywood Writers Mobilization, the Hollywood Democratic Committee, the League of American Writers, the American Peace Mobilization, and other fronts as well.[30]

Otto Katz and the Hollywood Anti-Nazi League

The major front group established by the Party in the period of the first Popular Front was the Hollywood Anti-Nazi League. Behind the work was Comintern agent Otto Katz, Willi Münzenberg's right-hand man, dedicated to building the Soviet-run antifascist campaign of the 1930s.[32] According to the influential British Communist journalist Claud Cockburn, Katz "was the most successful man of his period in the mobilization of non-Communist and even Conservative opinion on a broad anti-Nazi basis," even though in Europe he always openly identified himself as a Communist.

Katz had contacts everywhere. Thin, of medium height, dark and handsome, Katz had, according to Cockburn, "large melancholy eyes, a smile of singular sweetness and an air of mystery—a mystery into which he was prepared to induct you, you alone, because he loved and esteemed you so highly." And indeed, "he was at the heart of a lot of important and secret affairs."[33] Katz had the mannerisms of a spy, which added to his mystique. Arthur Koestler, who worked with him and Münzenberg in Paris, described him "as the type of person who, when lighting a cigarette, always [closed] one eye, and his habit became so fixed with him that he often closed his left eye while thinking out a problem even when he was not smoking."[34]

Many people found Katz likeable and charming. He was also quite a ladies' man. Cockburn remarked that Katz "made love to every good-looking woman he met." Katz told people that he was Marlene Dietrich's first husband and that they had worked together at a theater in Teplitz where he held his first job, as a cashier. Babette Gross claimed that Katz "had an extraordinary fascination for women, a quality which greatly helped him in organizing committees and campaigns."[35] Koestler noted that he was particularly attractive "to the middle-aged, well-intentioned, politically active types, and used them to smooth his path."[36] He fit into Hollywood perfectly as a speaker and dinner guest—a star in the antifascist struggle.

In September 1935, Katz and his wife, Ilse, entered the United States. When Katz needed an extension beyond his initial three-month stay, he told authorities it was to research and write a book on American expeditions to the Arctic that he was doing for Editions du Carrefour of Paris, a publishing firm that Münzenberg had acquired as part of his far-flung empire of front organizations.[37]

Katz assumed a fictive persona when he got to Hollywood. He was now Rudolph Breda, a refugee from Nazism who had put together the famous Communist "Brown Book" detailing Nazi atrocities. At other times he was "André Simone," or "O. K. Simon." But Katz was actually a Sudeten German from a Czech upper-class Jewish family, born and raised in Prague. He had made a mark in the avant-garde Berlin theater scene of the 1920s and had worked for the famous radical director Erwin Piscator as his administrative director.[38] Now Piscator was the head of the Drama School of the New School for Social Research in New York City, was involved with the Group Theatre, knew many actors and producers, and could provide introductions for Katz in Hollywood.[39]

Katz reveled in the fact that Münzenberg had assigned him to the world's film capital. "Columbus discovered America," he boasted, "and I discovered Hollywood."[40] By the time Katz arrived in southern California, Hitler's anti-Semitism was beginning to frighten the Jewish community in particular. There was also a functioning Party network for him to draw upon in setting up the Anti-Nazi League in Hollywood. Katz had help when Münzenberg sent Prince Hubertus zu Lowenstein, the former leader of the Catholic Center Party in Germany, to Hollywood. The prince, an opponent of Hitler, had aligned himself with the German Communists in support of the new Popular Front policy. Escaping from the Nazis just in time, Lowenstein had traveled to Paris, where he met with Münzenberg and agreed with him that motion pictures were the key to developing a broad antifascist front.[41]

When Lowenstein went to Los Angeles for a lecture tour, Erwin Piscator helped organize small meetings for him at the houses of film stars, where he spoke about the menace of fascism. The prince and Katz soon teamed up to raise money for the anti-Nazi campaign. Donald Ogden Stewart, a fellow traveler and soon-to-be Party member, was recruited to host a dinner party to introduce them to more of Hollywood's most important glit-terati. Stewart did not disappoint them. The guest list included Irving Thalberg, Mary Pickford, Norma Shearer, David and Irene Selznick, Sam and Frances Goldwyn, and Walter Wanger. According to Stewart, "The Prince and Herr Breda [a.k.a. Katz] quickly won sympathy for their cause (the prince was an extremely impressive nobleman, Breda was irresistibly intelligent and sincere, and the champagne was very good, too)." Plans were made to have a large, elegant, $100-a-plate black-tie dinner where Stewart would serve as toastmaster.[42]

Katz had chosen wisely when he decided to work through Stewart. A graduate of the elite Exeter prep school and Yale University, Stewart was a true Republican blueblood and the epitome of the 1920s playboy, throwing wild parties and becoming known for living life in the fast lane. After graduation and a period of service in the Navy, he moved to the rarified literary world of *Vanity Fair*, where he was a regular at the famous Algonquin Round Table.

By the early 1930s, Stewart was working in Hollywood. One of his efforts, *Philadelphia Story*, became one of the most highly regarded films of the day. He lived in a Bel-Air mansion and threw the most lavish parties in town. While most Americans suffered through 1934, for Stewart, as he noted in his 1975 memoir, it was a year filled with weeks at Palm Beach, "including warm sandy beaches and all gin fizzes, daily golf and nightly visits to the gambling tables at Bradley's, and a large party at a night club" that he gave for a famous investment tycoon. As he left in a chauffeured car, he threw money to a "small crowd of Negroes" who had surrounded the vehicles of the wealthy, asking for hand-outs.[43]

When screenwriters staged a picket line to boycott the annual Academy Awards banquet that year, Stewart was inside at producer Irving Thalberg's table. He was shocked later on when writers he knew and liked came to his office and called him a "fink." Traveling to Europe on the maiden voyage of the luxury liner *Normandie,* Stewart began his own voyage "into the strange new world of left-wing politics." As he searched for a theme for a new play, he wrote, "deep within me had been growing the dis-quieting realization that my childhood gods had played me false, that my quest for security through social and financial success had let me up the garden path," which "seemed to have come to a dead end.... It suddenly came over me that I was on the wrong side. If there was this 'class war' as they claimed, I had somehow got into the enemy's army."[44] Soon Stewart began to think "romantically" of himself as a Communist. His next step was to join the Party.

In April 1936, Stewart hosted a dinner at the Victor Hugo Restaurant. It was a tremendous success—every table was "crowded with top-bracket Hollywood names." When Katz/Breda gave his speech describing the Nazi terror, "the details of which he had been able to collect only through repeatedly risking his own life," Stewart was "proud to be sitting beside him, proud to be on his side in the fight." Katz, however, had not been in Ger-many at the time and had not risked his life. Stewart, like others in attendance, accepted Katz's false claim, which had been devel-oped by the Münzenberg apparatus to enhance his credentials. One guest who was not enamored was the archbishop of Los Angeles, John Cantwell, who left in a huff before Katz's speech, having been informed that the charismatic speaker was actually a European Communist.[45]

Soon after, the Hollywood Anti-Nazi League was formed. Stewart was its president, and on its executive board were figures such as actor Fredric March and writer Dorothy Parker, a secret Party member. That the league was a Communist operation did not at first raise opposition from the studio heads; in fact, they welcomed its creation and helped rent its offices. Eventually, however, many of the producers became suspicious and withdrew their support. An exception was the Warner brothers, who gave the group use of their radio station for weekly programs. Jack Warner told Stewart that "Hitler was the enemy" and he was "willing to use any help, even from Reds, to fight him."[46]

The Anti-Nazi League continued to grow, drawing members from across the political spectrum, and eventually had a membership of around five thousand.[47] According to Neal Gabler, between 1936 and 1939 the league became the "primary vehicle for most of the community's left-wing activism.... [They] picketed for everything from condemnation of the Germans and, after their invasion of China, the Japanese to support for Roosevelt's beleaguered Federal Theater Project." They also sponsored two weekly radio programs, put out the newspaper *Hollywood Now,* and created numerous subcommittees to reach out to various constituencies.[48]

The stars on the league's masthead were really just glamorous window dressing. Aside from the use of his name and an occasional speech, Donald Ogden Stewart's contribution to running the league was negligible. Looking back, he had to admit that "All the daily grind of collecting dues, planning meetings and radio programs, and getting out the newspaper was done by four or five devoted members who were, I had been told, members of the Communist Party. In this, as in other organizations of which I belonged [*sic*], it was largely the Communists who did the work."[49]

Until August 1939, when Stalin made his pact with Hitler, the German and Central European émigré community in southern California were among the most ardent supporters of the Anti-Nazi League. In the late 1930s, their numbers began to swell as Jewish intellectuals and artists fled their homeland. The studio heads had helped some by offering "lifesaver contracts," which allowed them to receive a U.S. visa and an income for one year. By the 1940s, many observers were calling Hollywood "Weimar on the Pacific"—home to leading literary figures such as Thomas and Heinrich Mann, Franz Werfel, and Lion Feuchtwanger.[50] Such people were joined by those more directly concerned with theater and film: actor Peter Lorre, composer Hanns Eisler, producer/director Otto Preminger, director Fritz Lang and play-wright Bertolt Brecht.

At the center of this community were Salka and Berthold Viertel. The Viertels' house on Mabery Road in Santa Monica became a popular gathering place on Sunday afternoons. Salka welcomed the creation of the Anti-Nazi League, although she was well aware that "Rudolph Breda" was actually Otto Katz, whom she knew to be a Communist because in 1932 he had offered her and Berthold jobs at the Mezhrabpom Studio in Moscow. At the time, she had told her husband that Katz's offer was "insane": "I would like to see you in Russia, watching every word you say, con-trolling your temper!"[51] While she may not have wanted to live in Stalin's Russia, Viertel apparently deemed the Hollywood Communists harmless. When director Ernst Lubitsch told her that he was quitting the Anti-Nazi League because it was domi-nated by Communists, she replied that the only way to combat fascism was through a front. Anyway, she told Lubitsch, "all these people do is sit around their swimming pools, drinking highballs and talking about movies, while the wives complain about their Filipino butlers."[52] Salka's main concern was getting Jews out of Europe and helping them get on their feet once they arrived in the United States.[53]

One of the émigrés closest to Katz was Fritz Lang, arguably Germany's most important film director. Born in Austria in 1890, Lang became a pioneer in the silent film industry in Berlin in the 1920s. Famous for using film to express his fascination with cru-elty, fear, horror and death, he created *Der Spieler* (1922), about a master criminal; *Metropolis* (1926), an expressionist drama about a futuristic slave society; and most famously *M* (1931), star-ring the young Peter Lorre as a serial killer of children.

In what may be an apocryphal story, Lang was said to have fled to Paris in 1933 after the culture chief Joseph Goebbels asked him to take charge of Nazi film production. He moved to the United States in 1934, eventually becoming a naturalized citizen. In America he made films such as *Fury* (1936), about mob violence; Westerns such as *Western Union* (1941); and the anti-Nazi film *Hangmen Also Die* (1943), which he wrote in col-laboration with Bertolt Brecht, a Communist.

Some claimed that Lang was a CP member. Testifying before the Dies Committee in 1940, John L. Leech, a former California CP organizer who had turned against the Party after the Nazi-Soviet Pact, said he had once attended a criticism session at Lang's home about the very successful film *Fury*. Although this film, starring Spencer Tracy and Silvia Sidney, was a major commercial success, Communists were upset by it. "His direction of the moving picture *Fury*," Leech said, "was antiworking class from the Party's point of view." He claimed that Lang acknowledged his "mistakes" as a result of the meeting and promised "that he would attempt to devote the major part of his motion picture direction to pictures which would have the approval of both the Communist Party in Los Angeles and the group of Hollywood people with whom he was associated."

Lang was particularly close to Otto Katz and dedicated to the antifascist cause. As Katz wrote to Lang, "it means a great deal to us to find people and artists like you who believe in our cause."[54] Lang said that Katz's mere presence had given him "the feeling that I could at last do something, no longer just sitting around waiting...that I could be active...for a cause which is close to one's heart."[55]

Despite serious illness, weeks of recuperation, and fights with the producers, Lang sought to combine his work with his politics. While directing *You Only Live Once* (1937), produced by Walter Wanger and starring Silvia Sydney, Lang even succeeded in making the relatively conservative Walter Wanger a member of the Anti-Nazi League.[56] Although Lang got Wanger to join the front group, he was not as lucky in gaining the producer's cooperation when he tried to inject left-wing content into the film. During the filming, Wanger put him "under stiff control," he complained to Katz, "and crossed out every political or social allusion in the manuscript."[57]

Still attempting to infuse propaganda into his films, Lang told Katz that he was on to something big: "an absolutely new form of film with music and songs about [a] social theme which is very important for America, but written in a jolly, light and humorous way." It might, he thought, be "possible to say much more in this way." The music in the film, to be titled *You and Me*, was to be written by his fellow German exile Kurt Weill, longtime collaborator with the playwright Bertolt Brecht.[58] Katz liked the idea. "It seems to be a great experiment," his wife, Ilse, wrote on her husband's behalf. "We will press our thumbs [keep our fingers crossed] that it will be as successful as a film as has been 'The Three Cash [Three Penny] Opera' in the theater." Nothing came of Lang's suggested new form of agitprop.[59]

With antifascism as their new calling card and Otto Katz as their suave salesman, the league's Communists saw their influence grow rapidly. They had a simple and popular new message, one that avoided the issue of their other, more problematic allegiances and one that met with wide approval. Throughout California they created new leagues, fronts and associations—all for the purpose of exercising maximum influence without having to dilute their propaganda, which consisted almost exclusively of pro-Sovietism. The ostensible goal was no longer proletarian revolution or a Soviet America, as it had been in the 1920s, but the defense of democracy all over the world. Stalin and FDR were depicted as allies in this effort. And the new policy would be most evident in the one cause that galvanized the entire liberal community: the Spanish Civil War.

The Spanish Civil War

On July 17, 1936, General Francisco Franco led a rebellion of military officers against the legally elected left-wing Popular Front government in Spain. The fight to save the regime—a fight supported by the Left throughout the world—was played out against the backdrop of the epic struggle between fascism and Communism, with Germany and Italy backing Franco and the Soviet Union supporting the Republic, while England, France and the United States remained neutral.

To the European and American Left, defense of the Republic became a symbol for all that was good and decent, as the "progressive" world organized against the tide of reaction. The fact that Stalin sought to make Spain a puppet of Moscow was lost in the urgency of the drama.[60]

Hollywood did not perceive the gray tones of the conflict.

The cause of Spain was immediately made the most urgent of the fights waged by the Popular Front groups, with new ones created especially to raise funds for the Republic. These included the American League Against War and Fascism (which changed, in a sign of the times, into the American League for Peace and Democracy during the years of the Nazi-Soviet Pact). Numerous other front groups, often interacting with each other and containing virtually the same membership, included the North American Committee to Aid Spanish Democracy, the Medical Bureau to Aid Spanish Democracy, the Spanish Refugee Relief Campaign, Friends of the Abraham Lincoln Brigade, the United American Spanish Aid Committee, the Hollywood Committee for Writers in Exile, and the Motion Picture Artists' Committee to Aid Republican Spain.[61]

The urgency of the Spanish cause was such that Otto Katz left Hollywood in mid-1936 to go to Barcelona, where, he wrote Fritz Lang, he "experienced the entire fight and victory of the people's front over the uprising military-fascistic reaction." He saw "poorly equipped workers" destroy seven cavalry, infantry and artillery regiments "with courage and enthusiasm that is beyond comparison." Katz told Lang to show his letters to other left-wingers in Hollywood, particularly the Communist writers Sidney Buchman and Frank Tuttle.[62] And, he added emphatically in a telegram that was obviously more than an afterthought, the film community must "do everything" possible to raise large sums of money for medical aid to the Loyalist troops.[63]

There was also the new problem of the anti-Hitler German Communist volunteers in Spain; unable to return to Germany, and forced out of Spain, they were literally starving. Admonishing Lang that "it is a duty of honor to help these people who have made the greatest sacrifice against Hitler," he asked the director to help raise at least $5,000, which could feed and clothe the German volunteers for six weeks.[64]

At the commencement of the Spanish Civil War, Münzenberg and the pro-Communist Spanish foreign minister Alvarez del Vayo set up the Agence Espagne news agency in Paris to provide the French press with news from the Republican government.[65] Katz, now using the name André Simone, was put in charge of the campaign in Western Europe, an operation that developed branches in England, Scandinavia, Belgium, Holland, Czechoslovakia and Switzerland. According to the FBI, Katz also acted as a courier and a liaison for the French and Spanish Communist parties during the war.[66] Using funds from the Spaniards as well as the Comintern, Katz subsidized papers, made bribes and "in his smooth way in social circles brought influence to bear with the right people." He also used the money to build Popular Front groups with the German émigrés in Paris.[67] Babette Gross said that Katz paid hefty sums to get French journalists to print pro-Soviet and pro-Communist articles, for which he came to be regarded by many who knew him as a "tool of the Russians."[68]

When Lillian Hellman had dinner with Katz in Paris in the fall of 1937, she described him as a "weary-looking, interesting man who had moved in many circles" and was "brave and kind."[69] At some point Katz and Hellman had an affair.[70] Katz had convinced her to visit Spain to write about the war, but when he caught up with her there in late October, he was dismayed to find that she planned to go to the front. "Have courage enough not to go," he told her. "It is a foolish, dangerous waste." As they walked around Madrid, Katz admitted that although he was still in his forties, he felt like an old man. He had been a Communist since he was "a young boy, almost a child," Katz sadly recalled, and it was even more difficult to be one in Spain. Pressing Hellman's arm, he said, "Don't misunderstand. I owe it more than it owes me. It has given me what happiness I have had. Whatever happens, I am grateful for that."[71]

Perhaps the most notable activity of Hollywood in defense of Spain was the nationwide presentation of the film *The Spanish Earth*, made by the Dutch Communist director Joris Ivens. He had worked for Münzenberg's Mezhrabpom Studio in Moscow and was reporting to them on his activities while in the United States. The project was put together by a group calling itself "Contemporary Historians," made up of Lillian Hellman, Archibald MacLeish, John Dos Passos and Ernest Hemingway. Arguably America's most popular writer, Hemingway wrote part of the script and narrated the movie, giving the film a wide appeal. Ivens consciously sought to make the film appear to be above ideology. Communists who appeared favorably in the movie were not identified as such; ideological lectures were studiously avoided. In one sequence, Ivens showed speakers presiding over abolition of the Party militias and their integration into the official government army. Among those on the screen were Enrique Lister, identified as a stonemason; José Diaz, identified as a printer who had become a member of parliament; and Gustav Regler, who was said to have gone to Spain to fight for his ideals. Omitted from these identifications was the fact that Diaz was general secretary of the Spanish Communist Party; that Lister had trained in the USSR and was a member of the Party's Central Committee; and that Regler came from Moscow, where he had been appointed political commissar.

It was a classic Münzenberg operation. He had put together the committee that created the film in Paris in 1936, and Ivens' new film group worked "in close consultation with party and Comintern functionaries."[72] In Spain, Ivens had prepared for his film by meeting with the Italian Communist Vittorio Vidali, political commissar of the Fifth Regiment, who was known in Spain as Comandante Carlos or Carlos Contreras. One of the most brutal of Stalin's thugs, Vidali was notorious for his habit of killing those he claimed were fifth columnists by shooting them in the back of the head.

Ivens' main goal had been winning Ernest Hemingway over to the Communist side. He suggested that "Comrade" Hemingway write an article about "the great and human function of the political commissar at the front," challenging those who opposed the Comintern's control over the Spanish army. He also made sure that the novelist had full access to the Soviets who stayed at the Gaylord Hotel—part of his "plan for Hemingway."[73]

The film premiered at the White House in an exclusive showing for FDR and thirty guests. The president was receptive, despite Ivens' opposition to the administration's nonintervention policy. Ivens touted the film as a simple plea for taking the stolen land away from the large landlords and giving it back to the Spanish people. According to Ivens, President Roosevelt appreciated the film's "values" and its "fine continuity."

In Hollywood, the first screenings of *The Spanish Earth* netted $20,000 for the Committee to Aid Republican Spain, which announced it would use the money to purchase ambulances for the war zone. On July 11, 1937, Ivens presided over the public premiere, where, according to news reports, the film colony's "great names" shelled out five dollars apiece. At the second night's screening, the glitterati gathered at actor Fredric March's home, where Robert Montgomery, Luise Rainer, Silvia Sidney, Dorothy Parker, Lewis Milestone, Fritz Lang, Lillian Hellman, Dashiell Hammett, Errol Flynn, Joan Bennett, Donald Ogden Stewart and Lionel Stander all gave the film their approval, promising to pass the word that seeing it was "a must." Writing to Otto Katz about the affair, Fritz Lang reported that they had raised a lot of money from all the showings. Only one thing annoyed Ivens: Errol Flynn, invited even though he was not a left-winger, fled the event through March's bathroom window just before Donald Ogden Stewart made the fundraising pitch.[74]

Ivens and his company sought a distributor so that the film could be shown in major theaters. Here they did not have as great a success; the major film distributors did not believe *The Spanish Earth* would attract a large general audience. It fell to a left-wing group to release it at smaller venues. The film opened at the Fifty-fifth Street Playhouse in New York, and then was screened in over three hundred theaters and at various labor union halls and movement fundraising events. The triumph was complete when a major film critics' group declared it one of the three most important films of the year.[75]

The Spanish Civil War was not only a financial windfall for the Hollywood Party but also a recruitment opportunity. Budd Schulberg brought his friend, the author William Saroyan, to attend a welcoming rally in Los Angeles for the French writer André Malraux, future minister of culture for the postwar De Gaulle government. Schulberg thought that Saroyan was living in a vacuum, and hoped that hearing Malraux would move him toward commitment. Malraux, he recalled, was "his lean, intense, effective apocalyptic self and the antifascist multitude responded with emotional if vicarious '*No pasaráns!*'" Salka Viertel was amazed to see that when Malraux finished his speech and thanked the cheering crowd, he then raised his fist in the Communist salute. In response, she wrote, "ladies in mink [were] raising and clenching their bejeweled hands."[76]

Schulberg was so ecstatic that he was convinced he was winning Saroyan over to the cause. Afterward, however, he found that Saroyan "was still his own sweet apolitical self," explaining that although he was for the people defending themselves against Franco, he also was for "the poor peons trying to keep themselves alive in Franco's army." Saroyan persisted in arguing that there were always two sides and each had its claims.[77]

Others were more impressed. Sometimes appearing on the same platform with Hemingway, the romantic Malraux, Schulberg wrote, "outglamour-boyed Robert Taylor, Gary Cooper and Cary Grant."[78] The Malraux event was screenwriter Paul Jarrico's first step toward joining the Communist Party. He ran into an old friend who was a CP organizer, who asked him, "Are you in touch with people in the Party?" He said that he was not, but would like to be. Soon afterward he received an invitation to a luncheon at the Hillcrest Country Club, where several young Communists looked him over. Jarrico recalled feeling strange, "sitting in this den of wealthy iniquity with two sons of film executives"—most likely Rapf and Schulberg—who were asking him to join the Communist Party.[79]

Spain also afforded the wives of actors, directors and writers a new role to play. Elizabeth Faragoh (wife of screenwriter Francis Faragoh,) told Nancy Lynn Schwartz, "I remember that in 1936 we were playing poker for Spain," and she found that "William Faulkner was the most marvelous poker player."[80] Dorshka Raphaelson's datebook for 1936 showed that on Saturday nights in April and May, she and her husband, Samson, attended a banquet for the Anti-Nazi League, a dinner for Prince Hubertus zu Lowenstein, a Scottsboro Boys fundraising party and a dinner at the home of Dorothy Parker.[81]

With the defeat of the Spanish Republicans and the growing threat of a new world war, it became increasingly difficult for Katz to raise money for his fronts. In late 1938, Fritz Lang wrote to him that the situation in Hollywood had changed in the one year he had been there.[82] The film colony, with its appetite for novelty, was tiring of the old causes. More catastrophically for the

Communists, the Nazi-Soviet Pact of 1939 was about to bring their close collaboration with liberals to an end.

4

The Nazi-Soviet Pact and Its Aftermath

OVER THE YEARS, ACTOR MELVYN DOUGLAS CAME TO REPRESENT THE quintessential Hollywood liberal: opposed to fascism, supportive of the Roosevelt New Deal, but suspicious of the Communists. From his first years in Hollywood—a time when he was playing opposite the most important actresses of the day, including the legendary Greta Garbo, in roles that often mirrored his own qualities of dependability and principle—Douglas was as interested in politics as he was in acting and in films. Along with his wife, the actress and future member of Congress (and early victim of Richard Nixon) Helen Gahagan Douglas, he had joined the Anti-Nazi League, despite his awareness that it had been formed by Hollywood Reds. The reason was clear. It was, Helen Douglas explained, "the only organization in California that was speaking out against Hitler."[1]

Douglas's involvement in California politics began in earnest in 1938, when liberal Democrats supported Culbert Olson for governor against the Republican incumbent, Frank Merriam, who had defeated Upton Sinclair—with the help of the studios—four years earlier. Like Sinclair, Olson supported public ownership of private utilities, restructuring of the tax code, an end to infringements on civil liberties, and better conditions for the state's migratory laborers. To help Olson in his campaign, Douglas and other liberals in the film capital created a new group, the Motion Picture Democratic Committee (MPDC), which sent groups of actors barnstorming throughout California on behalf of Olson. The group included Communists who appeared to be fighting only for liberal ideals—a tactical alliance on Douglas's part.

The legendary Hollywood figure Philip Dunne was also responsible for creating the MDPC, perhaps even more than Douglas. Dunne's films over a forty-year career as screenwriter, director and producer included *How Green Was My Valley, Pinky, Ten North Frederick, The Late George Appleby* and *The Ghost and Mrs. Muir.* Dunne believed that the best way to achieve their antifascist goals was to elect government officials who understood the international situation; he realized that this meant it would sometimes be necessary to work alongside the Communists.

In Dunne's eyes, the Communists were fellow travelers of the liberals, rather than vice versa, since during the Popular Front era they downplayed revolution and created reformist groups. Dunne seemed to be unaware that the Communists dominated organizations in which liberals worked; he correctly perceived, however, that the Reds were adroit at "hitchhiking on the liberal line."[2]

Some former Communists—John Bright, for example—would later claim that Melvyn Douglas "very reluctantly accepted support of the Communist Party in the MPDC" and that liberals as a group were "very reluctant to work with the Party."[3] Douglas may well have been reluctant, but journalist Ronald Brownstein points out that the Communists "were so entrenched that it was not possible to develop independent, non-Communist liberal institutions in the film industry."[4]

With Communist Party member Dashiell Hammett as president and John Ford, Miriam Hopkins and Philip Dunne as vice-presidents, the Motion Picture Democratic Committee became the foremost political action group in the film capital. When Hammett became ill, Dunne assumed the presidency, but Melvyn and Helen Gahagan Douglas were, as Dunne later wrote, the two major "powers in the MPDC."[5]

Working closely with the AFL-CIO and its California political action committee, chaired by Harry Bridges, the Communist chief of the longshoremen's union, the MDPC began to move "some political mountains in California." Culbert Olson won the gubernatorial race, which was a political triumph for the Left.

Their second victory in the state was the election of Fletcher Bowron, also a well-known liberal, as mayor of Los Angeles. The MPDC contributed to the transformation of a traditional and conservative Democratic machine into a fundamentally left-liberal operation.[6]

As a result of its participation, the group was able to call in some bills due from the candidates it supported. Perhaps the most famous campaign of the Communist Party in the 1930s, nationwide as well as in southern California, was to free Tom Mooney, a labor leader who had been sentenced to life in prison for allegedly bombing a Preparedness Day parade held in 1916.[7] Although overwhelming evidence proved that Mooney had not planted the bomb, years of appeals were to no avail. "Free Tom Mooney!" became the rallying cry of the entire political Left.

By the early 1930s, the official solidarity committee working for Mooney's freedom had been taken over by an ex-inmate named Arthur Scott, who had befriended Mooney in San Quentin and subsequently joined the CP. Mooney's mother toured the country in 1932 as part of a Communist front group's new campaign, and in that year the Communist Party began to run the Mooney defense, although Mooney himself was not a Communist.

Culbert Olson had vowed to free Mooney if elected governor. In office, he began to back away from his pledge. To pressure him, a delegation traveled to the state house to discuss the issue. Led by Melvyn Douglas and Philip Dunne, who were joined by Harry Bridges and AFL executive Jack Shelley, the group told the new governor that if he did not pardon Mooney he would lose the labor and liberal support that had won him the election. On January 7, 1939, Olson signed the pardon.[8]

Mooney's release was a major victory for the California and Hollywood Communist Party. But it turned out to be one of the last triumphs of the Popular Front in Hollywood. A few months later, on August 23, 1939, the liberal-Communist honeymoon ended when Nazi Germany and the Soviet Union signed their Non-Aggression Pact.

The USSR's announcement of its new relationship with Hitler sent shock waves through all the Communist parties of the

West. For years the Party had proclaimed that it was the one force dedicated to stopping fascism; now Stalin, the leader of the world's Communists, had declared a new alliance and his foreign minister had stated publicly, "Fascism is a matter of taste."

When they heard the news, Philip Dunne bet Melvyn Douglas, in Dunne's words, that "the next morning there wouldn't be more than a dozen Communists left in all Hollywood." Douglas responded, "Write out your check now, so I don't have to remind you tomorrow." Douglas was right. Recounting the story years later, Dunne acknowledged that his friend "knew a religious fanatic when he saw one." No mass defections from the Party took place, and Dunne concluded that "a good wheel-horse Communist has a digestive system like a goat's and apparently can swallow anything."[9]

Yet the pact was a severe shock to Communist intellectuals and to all fellow travelers. Charles Glenn, who covered Hollywood for the *People's Daily World,* reported that among his comrades "nobody knew what to think." Paul Cline, the local Party chairman, suddenly went on vacation. Party chief Earl Browder skipped town. The switchboard at the *People's Daily World* was flooded.[10]

The Party leadership knew it had to stop the defections. On August 24, the *New York Times* reported that Browder had cut his vacation short and had come to New York to "set the public straight." Far from a betrayal, Browder said, the pact was a "wonderful contribution to peace and a victory for the enemies of fascism." It was actually "part of the long-declared and established policy of the Soviet Union" that would "weaken Hitler at home," and was a "marvelous example of how to show Hitler the way to peace."[11] Browder's language had been dictated by the Comintern. Identical statements appeared in *L'Humanité* in Paris and in the *Daily Worker* in London, thereby assuring what Walter Krivitsky called "unity of opinion throughout the Communist Parties of Europe and America…a well-organized echo to everything which [Stalin] declares in Moscow."[12]

Screenwriter Herbert Biberman's reaction was typical of the robotic about-face made by the faithful. Douglas recalled that the night before the pact was announced, Biberman chaired an antifascist rally sponsored by the Anti-Nazi League. At the meeting, rumors were afloat that an agreement between Hitler and Stalin was imminent. According to Douglas, Biberman had pounded on the table and called the rumors "fascist propaganda." The next day, after the pact was announced, "we did not see much of Biberman and his political friends."[13] A few weeks later, Dunne asked Biberman what had become of collective security, their old rallying cry. He responded opaquely: "Collective security for peace." Decades later, Dunne was "still trying to figure out what he meant."[14]

How did the majority of Hollywood Reds rationalize the Non-Aggression Pact and remain active Communists? Ring Lardner Jr. explained that "to remain a Communist you had to believe the following":

1. That in the Munich Pact of 1938, the ruling forces of Britain and France had sold out Czechoslovakia and abandoned the policy of collective security with the purpose of turning Hitler against their real enemy, the Soviet Union.
2. That to forestall this plot, the Soviets had no choice but to make a purely tactical deal with Germany, enabling them to strengthen their borders and build up military power.
3. That [the Soviet Union's] occupation of eastern Poland and southeastern Finland were not aggrandizing acts but necessary defensive moves against Germany.
4. That the best interests of the United States lay in neutrality.[15]

Whether or not they had private doubts, most Party members parroted these explanations, proving to their former liberal allies that for them the interests of the Soviet Union came first.[16]

The result was a stunned sense of betrayal among those liberals who had accepted the Popular Front as a necessity, and among a few Communists who had jointed the Party because they saw it as the best vehicle for fighting against fascism. Screenwriter Donald Ogden Stewart was still a relatively new Party member at this point and president of two of the anti-Nazi front groups. His first reaction was complete shock: "How can that guy Stalin *do* this to us?" he wondered. However, considering himself only an "amateur" Marxist in comparison with the great Soviet leader, he accepted on faith that Stalin had good reasons for the pact. Marxism had come to him as a "cry for help from a man who was drowning in a world which didn't make sense." He could not relinquish his new faith: "I didn't think I could abandon Stalin without surrendering my life raft."[17]

Stewart hit the "lowest depths" when he confronted his old friend, humorist Robert Benchley. At dinner Benchley began lecturing him about his "hypocrisy as an anti-Nazi in not attacking Stalin's pact with Hitler." All Stewart could do was respond that "Stalin must have good reasons." Benchley shouted back, "What reasons?" At this moment Stewart saw in Bentley such a violent contempt that he could not answer. Feeling "sick and betrayed," Stewart went outside and hailed a cab. The driver, noting his depressed mood but mistaking its cause, said to him, "If you ask me, Mac, I think that guy Stalin ought to be hung."[18]

With the posturing of the Popular Front a thing of the past, it was obvious that liberals and Communists did not share the same goals; it was now impossible for liberals who were patriotic Americans to work with the Reds in the old groups. But when liberals attempted to take control of these organizations, they discovered that the Party's control over them was stronger than they had thought. The Hollywood Anti-Nazi League, which had almost five thousand members in its heyday, became a ghost organization. The Jewish members of the league were especially outraged over the pact. "The known Reds were in hiding," Charles Glenn put it, "afraid to stick their heads out of doors because the Old Country Jews, the ones who had fled Hitler, would have torn them apart."[19]

When the league finally held a meeting, MGM story editor Sam Marx told the group that he now thought "communism was the same as fascism." Marx may have believed such an observation to be obvious, but he was drowned out by a cascading echo of boos and hisses.[20] Attempts of liberals like Marx to rescue the league from Communists were doomed to failure. Instead, the Party, which controlled the organization more firmly than ever once many liberals had dropped out, changed the group's name to the Hollywood League for Democratic Action, which quickly folded into another pro-peace Party front, the American Peace Mobilization. This group united with isolationists in the America First Committee and was dedicated to keeping America neutral and out of any potential European war.

Just as the Party could no longer countenance an organization that was devoted to fighting fascism, it could no longer support the Motion Picture Democratic Committee's connection to the Democratic Party, FDR and the New Deal. Douglas and Dunne introduced a resolution reaffirming the support of Roosevelt's anti-Nazi foreign policy and denouncing the Non-Aggression Pact. To their surprise, the organization's executive committee passed the resolution without one negative vote. They discovered that this had happened because the vote was taken on the very night of the pact's announcement, and before the members had been given the new Party line. At the next board meeting a few weeks later, a new motion to rescind the resolution passed by a vote of ten to seven, which Dunne realized was "an indication of the extent to which the party had succeeded in infiltrating our executive board."[21]

Douglas, Dunne and their liberal allies knew they would have to fight hard to save the MPDC. Traveling to Washington, D.C., Douglas met with a group of key New Dealers, including Tommy Corcoran, FDR's close advisor who was known as the "assistant president," and another FDR aide, Harold Ickes. Douglas told them that the MPDC "was willing to do what it could for the New Deal," but the problem was "two or three Communists, rather prominent in the organization, who will have to be sidetracked since they continue to be apologists for Stalin."[22]

After the meeting in Washington, Douglas returned to Hollywood and wrote a report to the executive board of the MPDC that made the case for supporting Roosevelt's foreign policy. The issue of the Nazi-Soviet Pact and the Russian invasion of Finland, Douglas wrote in a bold understatement, "had caused a very sharp difference of opinion in many liberal organizations." Some had turned on FDR and the administration with "drawn swords." Douglas became specific: "The fountain head of these attacks has been the Communist Party." It was not surprising, he went on, "that the Communist Party…suddenly turned against an administration foreign policy which they had so recently supported." That earlier support, he now thought, was "not because of any real conviction but for opportunistic reasons." Douglas therefore wanted the MPDC, his own group, to come out against the CP. Finally, Douglas warned those "who have taken the pro-Soviet position in the events of the past few months" that they had become "a drag around the neck of any liberal organization which does not hold the same position."[23]

The report was met with a barrage from Hollywood Reds attacking Douglas's anti-Communism. It was a preview of the ploy that would be repeated *ad infinitum* into the Cold War years. Anyone critical of the Communist Party was a Red-baiter whose tirades served only the right wing. The Communists did not see the irony in the fact that, by their sudden isolationism, they were themselves now aligned with the far Right.

The discussion of Douglas's report took place before a board dominated by Communists and fellow travelers. They argued that the resolution violated "the principle of free democratic discussion," that it amounted to "reactionary phrasing," that it would create a split in the MPDC and was a "form of political purging." The resolution was called to a vote and defeated by an overwhelming majority.[24]

Douglas and Dunne were not yet ready to give up the fight. Convening an emergency board meeting in Dunne's home a few days later, they fought to introduce a rewritten resolution rejecting any alliance with groups that did not support FDR's foreign policy. Dunne was candid, affirming that his resolution was "frankly intended to define our split of purpose and opinion with the Communist Party—since we can get no place until we do state this split…. This resolution is a repudiation of the Communist Party."[25]

The resolution was voted down, although the board agreed to submit the issue to a full membership meeting. The meeting took place on January 30, 1940, at the Hollywood Women's Club offices. Dunne offered a new amendment to the Statement of Policy condemning all aggression, "including Soviet aggression," and specifically the American Communist Party's "support of that aggression."[26]

Fellow-traveling members immediately rose to condemn him. Joan Storm replied that "we are not here to discuss the rights and wrongs of the Communists. We are concerned with progressive action." Harold Buchman followed, saying that Dunne's position was intended "to lay the basis for outright suppression of the Communists," a position that was "making a dangerous contribution to the general hysteria." It was nothing but "the reactionary tactic of red-baiting." To follow Dunne would be to "fall victim now to a witch-hunt, no matter how the...resolution is disguised with liberal phrases."

With his resolution's defeat, Dunne joined Melvyn and Helen Douglas in resigning from the MPDC, "as well as from the other popular front organizations which were destroyed in similar fashion by the same wrecking crew, as all over town the industrious Communist tail wagged the lazy liberal dog."[27]

The MPDC had now become just another totally controlled Communist group. A May newsletter proclaimed that America was now on the road to fascism as the administration "exploited" the actions of Hitler and Mussolini "to force a peaceful people into slaughter."[28]

☆

The political spectacle in Hollywood was studied carefully by Congressman Martin Dies, whose House Committee on Un-American Activities was planning a visit to Hollywood. One of the areas that Dies looked into was the role and influence of Hollywood's Popular Front groups, which, as Ronald Brownstein writes, served "a chilling warning that the price of alliance with Communists was rapidly rising."[29]

Compared with HUAC hearings of the 1950s, however, the Dies Committee proved to be somewhat tame. Despite the *New York Times* scare headline on the first day of the hearings—"Hollywood Stars Accused as Reds before Grand Jury"—the report focused on the testimony of John L. Leech, who had joined the Party in 1931, became executive secretary of the Los Angeles section, and was expelled from the Party in 1937.[30] Leech had named as possible Communists some of Hollywood's most prominent figures, including Melvyn Douglas, Humphrey Bogart, James Cagney, Fredric March and Franchot Tone. Obviously, by including someone like Douglas on his list, Leech was

implicating anyone who had joined a Popular Front group, even
if they were opponents of the Reds. As for Bogart, Leech said
that he had "sat in organized study groups, organized by the
Communist Party, and [I] have known Mr. Bogart to contribute
money to the Communist Party." Leech then acknowledged that
he personally had not seen Bogart give the Party any money. "I
have never desired to injure any of these people," he added, and
had nothing "but the kindest feeling toward them" and did not
wish to "slander or in any way injure them."[31]

Bogart, appearing before the Dies Committee, strenuously
denied all of Leech's charges. He was not a Communist and had
never given the Party any money. He did not know of any Communist activity in Hollywood, and when he saw people involved
in politics, "I don't know whether they're communistic activities,
or liberal activities, or activities of misguided people." He had
"suspicions" about who might actually be a Communist, Bogart
added, and he thought "Hollywood people are dupes in the most
part" who didn't know "what they were getting into when they
started out." Congressman Dies, unlike his counterparts on
HUAC a decade later, did not press Bogart, but dismissed the
star, telling him that "this committee has absolutely no evidence
in its possession that involves you in any un-American activity."[32]

Similarly, Dies let off actor Franchot Tone, a former member of the Group Theatre who had gone to Hollywood. Tone
denied knowing either Leech or Stanley Lawrence, the other
Party organizer, and said he had given money only to labor
organizations in the "interest of human betterment." As an advocate of what he called "social theater," he saw the Communist
Party as "just another political party." When shown proof that he
had given money to the Scottsboro Defense Committee and the
Tom Mooney Defense, Tone claimed to have had suspicions
about the groups and gave Dies a simple explanation: "You see
when you have so much money thrown into your lap your conscience is aroused, especially when some people get so much for
so little effort." Dies was visibly moved by this "worthy feeling in
any man's heart."[33]

Dies called actor Lionel Stander, one of the most involved
of Hollywood Communists, who also denied Party membership.

Stander told Dies, "I believe the Moscow [purge] trials were conducted fairly." Even though he claimed that he knew no
Communists and believed only in democracy, a blatant lie to
those who knew of his CP involvement, Dies exonerated him
also, saying, "Your heart has changed evidently since the Stalin-
Hitler Pact."[34]

When Philip Dunne heard that he too was on Dies' list, he
called his contacts in Washington and was told to see Dies and
put all his "cards on the table." Dunne tracked the congressman
down in San Francisco, where he received a hearing at the Fair-
mont Hotel, "complete with steno typists and newsreel cameras."
Telling Dies there was no truth in rumors that he was a Red,
Dunne "entered into the record photostatic copies" of articles he
had published criticizing "Communism and Communists, as well
as newspaper and trade-paper reports of the battles I had fought
with various popular front organizations."[35]

Melvyn Douglas was also easily able to clear himself. A simple telegram to Dies—along with a telephone call to Dies from
actor Robert Montgomery—removed him from investigation.

One reporter wrote that Hollywood had "spiked Mr. Dies's
guns."[36] But despite his clearance of Dunne, Cagney, Bogart,
March and others, Dies correctly observed that there were
"numerous actors and screen people, out of humane motives,
who have made contributions to, and let their names be used by,
certain organizations which the Dies committee has unanimously
found to be organized under communist leadership."[37]

Leaving the Party

As one of the Hollywood Party's most notable members and
enthusiastic recruiters, Budd Schulberg was concerned that Dies
would target him. Later he recalled that Dies' arrival was accom-
panied by an announcement in the newspaper that there were
six leading Communists in Hollywood and that he was one of
them. Dies then invited anyone who felt he was being treated
unfairly to contact him. Schulberg went to the Biltmore Hotel,
where hearings were in progress, and told a committee investigator that he had seen the notice and didn't think it was right to

make such allegations about people "before they have had a chance to come down and at least talk with you." Schulberg said, "I can't prove it, but I just have a strong hunch that that list is a faulty list." He was told to wait, but was never interviewed.[38]

A far larger crisis for Schulberg was that his commitment to the Party was waning. He was affected by the furor over the Nazi-Soviet Pact, but his problems with the Party centered on the question of his freedom to write fiction. Schulberg's parents held literature in high esteem; love was expressed through "educational and artistic prodding." By the time he was twelve, Schulberg was writing short stories and on his way to forming an identity as a writer.[39]

Around 1937, when Schulberg joined his first Marxist study group and then the Young Communist League, his short stories were already being published in magazines. Much to his surprise, his Communist Party cell told him that the stories "were not exactly what would be expected of someone writing as a Communist"; they were found "too depressing, decadent, ...etc." His response was to continue to write as he pleased, while supporting the Party on political issues.

This compromise didn't work, even though he tried to make sure that his fiction had "the Popular Front phrases of the day." The problem was that he couldn't make the stories conform to the Party line. One of them, for instance, about the individual struggle of a Polish Jew to escape pogroms and find a homeland, was criticized by his Party group for failing to show faith in the masses. Schulberg was told that he had not cured himself of "'individualism' and other reactionary habits of thought." He found himself in a strange in-between land, still a "member in good standing of my generation's left-wing," but at the same time one who was branded by his comrades a "literary 'deviationist.'"

The conflict came to a head when Schulberg decided that he wanted to turn a short story he had published in *Liberty* magazine called "What Makes Sammy Run?" into a novel. His comrades told him that it was a "destructive" idea that "didn't begin to show what were called the progressive forces in Hollywood." The fight over "Sammy" took him by surprise. When Schulberg requested a leave of absence from his Party work to write the novel, John Howard Lawson told him that he would have to submit an outline of the book first.[40]

The pressure on Schulberg not to develop "Sammy" was intense. "They talked about it every goddamned week," he recalled years later, "hoping that I would give in." Seeking support from a senior Communist, he went to see a man he thought to be the best of the Party writers, Albert Maltz. Later to be a screenwriter, Maltz had written stage plays and a prize-winning short story, "The Happiest Man on Earth," and had taught playwriting at New York University. Maltz expressed sympathy but, still under the sway of the Party, he would not back Schulberg against the Party leadership. "I know how you feel and I sympathize with you," he said, "but you had better go see Lawson." When he finally met with Lawson, the Party chief told him that his bourgeois background was keeping him from understanding "how a writer must function in the Communist Party."

Growing up in Hollywood, Schulberg had already objected to the way writers were treated as word slaves by studio chiefs like Louis B. Mayer, and now he was getting "the same feeling from the other side." He was also tired of his self-censorship and the schizoid internal dialogs it produced: "I think Faulkner is a very, very good writer. But Faulkner cannot be a good writer, Faulkner is a reactionary." Most of the so-called "proletarian" literature offended him as "self-conscious, bloodless, and written from the outside." Schulberg much preferred F. Scott Fitzgerald and John O'Hara to writers like John Steinbeck and James T. Farrell, then "literary gods of the Popular Front."

With difficulty, he came to the conclusion that if he was ever going to become a writer, he had to "pay no more dues, listen to no more advice, indulge in no more political literary discussions, and go away from the Party." Conferring with his wife, Jigee, he expressed worry that if he stayed in California he would never be able to write his book. Random House had given him an advance of $250, and he desperately wanted to take a year off to do nothing but write *What Makes Sammy Run?* Jigee reluctantly agreed to support him. Without informing or resigning from the Party, the couple fled Hollywood. It was, he put it years later, "a major act," since he had not asked permission from the Party.

Arriving in Vermont, as far away as he could get, in May 1939, Schulberg felt as if he had "escaped from prison."

He returned briefly to Hollywood in March 1940, after he had completed *What Makes Sammy Run?* but before it was published. Since he had not actually resigned from the Party, his status was ambiguous. Richard Collins caught up with him in Los Angeles and chastised him for leaving without transferring to another Party group on the East Coast. Collins told him he should come back to the group and discuss the issues that concerned him. But after his vacation from Party discipline, Schulberg was more disillusioned than ever. Not only had the Nazi-Soviet Pact caused further doubts, he was disturbed about the growing repression he was hearing about in the Soviet Union.

In one last effort to open a dialogue, he went to a Party meeting, taking with him a short essay he wrote attacking the pact, and offered fifteen reasons why he thought Stalin was wrong. "I thought we were going to argue those things out and discuss them," he told an interviewer. "...I thought I might even change minds." His old comrades weren't interested. He had learned the hard lesson: in its "democratic centralism" the Party was "far more centralized than it was democratic."[41]

In an attempt to rehabilitate Schulberg, a pair called "the great explainers," future Hollywood Ten screenwriters Herbert Biberman and Sam Ornitz, told him that because of his bourgeois origins, his understanding of the working class was confused. In a last-ditch effort to redeem Schulberg, the Party's cultural commissar, V. J. Jerome, came to Hollywood representing the Central Committee. In this crisis, Schulberg reluctantly agreed to see Jerome at a comrade's apartment on Hollywood Boulevard. Jerome harangued him and told him that his "entire attitude" was wrong: "I was wrong about writing; wrong about this book; wrong about the Party; wrong about the so-called peace movement." When it was over, Schulberg thought to himself that he had seen "the real face of the Party." He realized that there was no turning back.

Later Schulberg summed up the process of quitting the Party. "Before the step is taken," he explained, "you don't know quite how to make it. You sit there for a long time wanting to get out, and you can't find the words to say it. You go on maybe for a year in which you think about how to get out and not really agreeing with it, but [you are] still in it. One day you say 'What am I doing here? I am not a Communist', and finally you go."

Schulberg had dealt with his withdrawal by burying himself in *What Makes Sammy Run?* The novel's key figure, Sammy Glick, is a grasping, ambitious young Jew on the make. Raised in poverty on New York's Lower East Side, Sammy dedicates himself to reaching the top rungs of Hollywood by any means necessary. He achieves his goal by stepping over everyone in his way. Working at a newspaper in New York, he steals a writer's idea and sells it to a Hollywood tycoon, who pays him $10,000 and brings him out to the film capital. From then on, the once-poor Jewish boy ascends to the top without ever doing anything on his own to attain his position. Sammy does get his comeuppance in the end by marrying a woman even more callous than he. The book was at once a critique of the studio system and a blast at the producers and their exploitation of writers.

Schulberg asked his father to read the manuscript in advance of publication. Noting the obvious similarities between the Glick character and many of the producers he knew, B. P. Schulberg praised his son's book but asked him not to publish it. "He said I would be ostracized and not allowed back in town again," Budd said, and he asked "how would I live, how would I survive?"[42] The one disturbing criticism his father made echoed the sentiments of some of his Party comrades who had seen the manuscript. The novel, B. P. thought, might be construed as anti-Semitic. Schulberg gave the book to three people he trusted most, Maurice Rapf, Ring Lardner Jr. and F. Scott Fitzgerald.[43] None of them thought it was anti-Semitic, particularly since some of Sammy's victims, as well as some positive characters, were also Jewish.

After correcting the galleys in New York, Budd returned to Hollywood shortly before the novel was officially published. Much to his consternation, he found that some of his old Party comrades had obtained advance copies and were angry. They felt, he later told HUAC, "that all the storm warnings that had been raised against me had been disregarded, and that the work that was about to come out was even worse than anyone could imagine."[44] *Sammy* caused many bitter fights within Party circles after it was published.

What prompted the Party's suspicion and fear of the book? Nancy Lynn Schwartz surmises that "coming as it did in the middle of the Stalin-Hitler Pact," it "aroused the defensiveness of the Party, out to prove that it was not anti-Semitic, though it was linked with Hitler in a nonaggression alliance."[45] Schulberg himself saw another possible explanation. While he took the side of the fictional screenwriters he had portrayed in their union struggle against the producers, ardent Marxist-Leninists like Lawson still objected that "the novel was elitist and dealt only with the screenwriters, not with the workers in the backlot," the real Hollywood proletariat.[46] As Schulberg saw it half a century later, the problem was that the book "failed to meet the Hollywood Communists' high standards for social realism à la Stalin," a criticism he thought ridiculous, since *Sammy* was the first novel "to side with the Writers Guild in its bitter struggle against Mayer, Thalberg & co."[47]

Finally, several writers were invited to Herbert Biberman's house to listen to Budd's feelings about his book. Ring Lardner Jr. knew that "heavy-handed criticism of this sort was fairly common in the Party, and some people ignored it without suffering any harm. For Budd, however, the experience was apparently an epiphany, inspiring feelings of kinship with the Russian artists and writers persecuted under Stalin and leading him away from the movement into which he had recruited me just a few years earlier."[48]

The Party's view of *Sammy* became public in reviews in the *Daily Worker* and the *People's Daily World,* the Party's West Coast paper. Charles Glenn, the Party's Hollywood correspondent and an admirer of Schulberg's, had bumped into him at a Los Angeles bookstore and asked if he could get an advance look at the galleys. Glenn hailed *Sammy* as "the best work done on Hollywood" and praised Schulberg as a major novelist of the future. "For slightly fewer years than they have awaited the great American novel," Glenn wrote, "...American bibliophiles and critics have been awaiting the Hollywood novel…. I've a feeling that all critics, no matter their carping standards, will have to admit they've found *the* Hollywood novel in Budd Schulberg's *What Makes Sammy Run?*"[49]

Schulberg was relieved. Despite all the alarm, the Party's official voice had come to his defense. His relief was transitory. Soon, Schulberg heard that all hell had broken loose in Party headquarters as a result of the review. Lawson demanded an audience with Glenn, who experienced what he called "the most tortured hour and a half I'd ever spent." Lawson told him that he "had to retract." Glenn proposed that Lawson write a letter to the editor and that he would publish it as an article, and that they could then have a discussion in the pages of the Party newspapers. "No discussion," said Lawson. "Just write the review."[50]

A good comrade, Glenn followed his orders. On April 23, the *Daily Worker* in New York ran a second review of *Sammy*. This time, Glenn told his readers that "On the basis of quite lengthy discussion of the book, I've done a little reevaluating." Moreover, "to say I felt more than a trifle silly when these weaknesses [in *Sammy*] were called to my attention is putting it a bit mildly. It is precisely the superficial subjective attitude shown in [the first] review which reflects the dangers of an 'anti-Hollywood' approach, conscious or unconscious." Glenn's new review said exactly the opposite of his first. Before he had called it "*the* Hollywood novel"; now he wrote, "The struggle to form the Guild doesn't emerge in Schulberg's book. Can it then be termed the Hollywood novel?" Before, Glenn had written that the book was "hearteningly free of filth and four-letter words." Now he proclaimed that Schulberg's "conscience…allows him with full knowledge of the facts to show only the dirt and the filth."[51]

Reading the second review, Schulberg felt sorry for Glenn. "They threatened to fire him from his job on the *People's World* and kick him out of the Party," he later said, "unless he did what was demanded."[52] Glenn told Nancy Schwartz, "Ten years later I still wanted to apologize to Budd, but I didn't have the guts." By then, Schulberg had broken with the Party and testified before HUAC, and Glenn used that as an excuse for not talking with him.[53]

Not only were the Reds angered by *Sammy*, but as his father predicted, so were the high-level Jewish producers. Always underplaying their own ethnic background, they feared that Schulberg's negative stereotype of a Jewish producer would do them great damage; it was especially dangerous at a time when anti-Semitism had turned lethal in Germany. Samuel Goldwyn, with whom Schulberg had a writing contract, promptly fired the young novelist. Louis B. Mayer was in a rage, and took his anger out on B. P. Schulberg. "I blame you for this...why didn't you stop him? How could you allow this? It's your fault." Although he himself had asked Budd to suspend publication of the novel, B. P. defended his son. "How could I stop him?" he told Mayer. "It's a free country." Mayer responded, "'Well, I don't care...I think it's an outrage and he ought to be deported.'" B.P. laughed and asked, "'Deported? Where? He was one of the few kids who came out of this place. Where are we going to deport him to? Catalina? Lake Helena? Louis, where do we send him?' And Mayer didn't think it was funny and he said, 'I don't care where you send him, but deport him.'"[54]

Budd Schulberg's closet drama occurred at a time when the American Communists' cry was "Keep America Out of War" and "The Yanks Are Not Coming." Soon the condemnation would extend to President Roosevelt himself. The Communist folk-singing group *The Almanac Singers,* led by Pete Seeger, Josh White, Burl Ives, Woody Guthrie and the screenwriter Millard Lampell, cut an album called *Meet John Doe,* which featured folksy sing-a-long anti-Roosevelt ballads, such as one with the mocking chorus, "I hate war, and so does Eleanor, and we won't be safe till everybody's dead," and "Franklin D., Franklin D., you ain't gonna send us across the sea." The themes of their songs were echoed in the Motion Picture Democratic Committee press releases. In May 1940, its membership—now reduced to a small number of Reds—was told that intervention in Europe's affairs would result in fascism at home.[55]

The Hollywood Reds found new ways to put their considerable organizational and writing skills to work on behalf of the new coalition with the Coughlinite right wing and to promote neutrality toward Nazi Germany. Herbert Biberman became chairman of a new front group, the Hollywood Peace Forum, in which fellow Red John Wexley was vice-chairman and Communist writer Guy Endore secretary-treasurer. The forum printed a well-distributed pamphlet, "Let's Skip the Next War." It was vintage CP propaganda, attempting to give a "progressive" tone to what essentially was advocacy of policies that could only help Nazi Germany.

If America stayed out of war, Endore wrote, every large American city could get its own university and a five-million-dollar public library, as well as hospitals and playgrounds—"all paid for" out of taxes. Herbert Hoover may once have promised "a chicken in every pot." Now the Communist Party was saying "No War for the USA but a House and a Lot for Everyone!"[56]

With the emergence of this kind of propaganda, it was no surprise that Melvyn Douglas and other antifascist liberals soon resigned from the remaining Popular Front organizations. As a result, the Hollywood Reds were increasingly isolated. Tensions that were always brewing in organizations like the Screen Writers Guild now surfaced as guild members objected not only to CP tactics in manipulating and controlling meetings, but to the SWG being forced to take stands on a variety of political matters important to the Party but irrelevant to negotiations with the producers.[57]

Ironically, the guild's strength had led the producers finally to agree to negotiate a contract. But now, because of the Nazi-Soviet Pact, they were in a position to demand that CP members not be present at the bargaining table. Under pressure, John Howard Lawson and Donald Ogden Stewart resigned from the negotiating committee. Stewart was slowly changing some of his views. While he still had contempt for the new liberal anti-Communists, whom he blamed for taking a "panicky retreat...to the safe harbor of 'Communism is the same as Fascism,'" he could not go along with the new American Peace Mobilization Campaign run by the Communist Party. He sadly found himself "reviled by the Right and suspected by the Left."[58]

"The Motherland Has Been Attacked"

For these forlorn and increasingly isolated Hollywood Reds, relief was on its way. On June 22, 1941, Adolf Hitler's army invaded the Soviet Union, thereby ending the alliance of the two totalitarian empires. Donald Ogden Stewart was driving his car when he heard the news on a radio bulletin. "I listened and unexpectedly began to cry," he wrote. "Not with pity for the Russian people: I wept with joy and relief. I was once more on the 'right' side, the side of all my old friends. Now we were all fighting Fascism…. It was one of the happiest nights of my life. I could continue believing in my remote dream, the country where the true equality of man was becoming a reality under the philosophy of Marxism and Leninism and the leadership of the great Stalin."[59]

The beginning of summer was indeed a happy time for Stewart and his wife, Ella Winter (who had previously been married to Lincoln Steffens until his death). War, which they had all worked so hard to avoid, had now been inflicted upon the Russian people and the couple was back at the center of things. "My dinner jacket emerged from its moth balls," Stewart wrote, "and my Hawes and Curtiss dress shirts were shiningly happy in their return to social consciousness." As he dramatically put it, "The clouds lifted and we were fighting beside Roosevelt, Churchill and Stalin for our 'world of the future.'"[60]

On the day of the Nazi invasion of Russia, liberal screenwriter Allen Rivkin had been visiting Sidney and Beatrice Buchman's house in Bel Air. Suddenly, Lillian Hellman came in the door, fashionably dressed all in white. "She was somewhere between ecstatic and furious," Rivkin reported, "and I don't know if she was kidding or serious, but she said, 'The Motherland has been attacked!'"[61]

A few months later, with the attack on Pearl Harbor, the unity between the CP and the rest of America was re-established. With its proximity to Hawaii, the West Coast was immediately affected by the war. Los Angeles had blackouts; the harbor was ringed with barbed wire, and Hollywood stars heard the same air raid sirens that other citizens did.

The film capital mobilized for war. The Motion Picture Academy set up a research council composed of talent from all the top studios to produce training, historical and public relations films for the Army. In addition, 2,700 men and women, about 12 percent of those employed in the film industry, joined the armed forces. Like Communists throughout the country, those in the film colony who were of age to fight volunteered for active duty. Michael Blankfort and Michael Wilson joined the Marines, while Paul Jarrico enlisted in the merchant marine. Ring Lardner Jr., rejected from the services because of his political affiliation, strangely thought that he nonetheless might join the new intelligence agency, the Office of Strategic Services (OSS). But he failed the security check there too. Eventually, he found work in the training film program of the Army Signal Corps.[62] Maurice Rapf had volunteered for all the services and was turned down due to a physical deferment, which he insisted was a euphemism for his political views. (He later admitted lying to a Navy interviewer about being a Communist Party member.) Eventually, he wound up writing for the Industrial Incentive Division of the Navy as well as the Office of Inter-American Affairs under Nelson Rockefeller.[63]

Those Communists who remained in Hollywood had plenty of opportunities to support the war effort. Three days after Pearl Harbor, film colony veterans formed the Hollywood Victory Committee, a clearinghouse for volunteer war efforts by the film community. "Soldiers in greasepaint," film stars and other actors and actresses from stage, screen and radio toured hospitals and USO canteens, as well as appearing for the troops in Europe. Written material was created by the Hollywood Writers Mobilization (HWM), a new Popular Front type group created by old Party stalwarts one week after Pearl Harbor.

For the first time in years, Party members could now join with the rest of Hollywood in fighting a common enemy. Ironically, one of those who had actually joined the Party during the years of the Nazi-Soviet Pact, screenwriter Dalton Trumbo, now found himself a member of a Communist Party that overnight favored war. Trumbo, who had strong pacifist feelings, had written a harrowing antiwar novel, *Johnny Got His Gun*. Its fierce antiwar vision fit right in with the Party program of neutrality during the days of the pact, and the book was serialized in the Party press. But after the German invasion of Russia, Lardner commented dryly, Trumbo suddenly "found his pacifism no longer tenable."[64] Practicing the self-censorship required of a good Communist—unlike "renegades" such as Budd Schulberg—Trumbo remembered his novel, which was taken out of print and not mentioned again until the 1960s, when Vietnam developed as the cause of the Left; then he not only resurrected the book but turned it into a major Hollywood film.

The attempt of Party members to win the trust of their old liberal friends at first made for some awkward moments. As Paul Jarrico admitted, many liberals were still suspicious that Party members "were looking out for the interests of the Soviet Union, not the United States." Jarrico believed that in fact there was no contradiction in serving the interests of both powers, because "the Soviet Union was a vanguard country fighting for a better future for the entire world, including the United States."[65] Isolationists the day before, CP members overnight joined the ranks of full-fledged interventionists.

After Pearl Harbor, the Communist Party essentially remade itself into the left wing of FDR's New Deal coalition. Thus, during the war years, the Party opposed what it considered divisive actions in favor of civil rights for Negro Americans, such as A. Philip Randolph's proposed "March on Washington." It also supported the internment of Japanese Americans on the West Coast and the prosecution of Trotskyists for conspiring to teach and advocate the overthrow of the U.S. government, which had been declared illegal under the Smith Act.

The same kinds of compromises made by the Party nationwide were made in Hollywood. The Screen Writers Guild, in the midst of negotiations with producers on the day Hitler invaded the USSR, was now split over whether they should freeze negotiations and give up demands for wage increases for the war's duration. Communists in the SWG, including John Howard Lawson and Lester Cole, favored the freeze, while non-Communist members opposed it. Ironically, when the Communist guild members went to talk to the studio chiefs, they found that the businessmen all backed a higher minimum wage. SWG board member Harry Tugend recalled, "We were all ecstatic except for the left-wing board members, who sat there, with the freeze proposal in their pockets and egg on their faces."[66]

Some Communists were angry at the compromises

demanded by the Party's wartime chief, Earl Browder. John Bright quit the CP before joining the Coast Guard, as all Party members were ordered to do after enlisting. Attending a Party meeting before departing for duty, he found that the only item on the agenda was the question: "What did you do for the war effort last week?" Bright was stunned. His comrades, he felt, "were talking no differently than Republicans or Democrats." When one bragged that he had sold $75,000 of war bonds in one week, Bright thought: "The Bank of America certainly approved of that." When it came his turn to answer the question, he said that he "had spoken at a meeting in a black church in protest against racial discrimination in the armed forces." The problem was that "this was something that a Party member didn't talk about," because to acknowledge that there was racial prejudice in America could cause divisiveness and possibly compromise unity for victory. His former comrades rebuked him, asking "why I had joined the Party in the first place if I wasn't willing to accept its discipline." Bright responded, "I had joined originally because the Communist Party was eager and willing to do the things that nobody else would do, the unpopular and courageous things." Getting angrier and angrier, he yelled: "I might as well be in some goddamned country club, not sitting around with Communists!"[67]

Bright had a point. Earl Browder soon dissolved the Communist Party and in 1944 transformed it into what was now called the Communist Political Association. Rather than a revolutionary party, the new group defined itself as an organization that would expel any member "who conspires or acts to subvert, undermine, weaken or overthrow any or all institutions of American democracy." At their national convention, the Communists met under giant portraits of FDR, Churchill and Stalin—the latter there as a wartime ally, not as a Communist icon.

The Party again took advantage of the relaxed climate to develop new front groups that would replace the old Popular Front coalitions done in by the Nazi-Soviet Pact. Among them were the Hollywood Writers Mobilization, the Actors' Laboratory Theatre and the People's Educational Center.

Excited by the chance to contribute to the war effort, as well as the chance to make new contacts with established directors, writers and actors, scores of young people who were eager to succeed joined the new fronts. Increasingly, veterans of the New York stage made their way out West, joining the earlier migration of stage people. Director Edward Dmytryk, later one of the Hollywood Ten, observed that at the beginning of the war, "Easterners, primarily men and women from New York, including such theatrical idols as Harold Clurman and Clifford Odets, invaded Hollywood in noticeable numbers. To us natives, they were definitely a political breed, activists of a type we had rarely seen. They seemed to live much closer to reality, and whatever their political affiliations, their dramatic theories were based on Marxist philosophy. Their ideas flooded our arid community, and some of us began to realize how unsophisticated we really were."[68]

Arriving in Hollywood, Group Theatre alumni and other radicals already in the film capital created a new organization, the Actors' Laboratory, in 1941. The majority of actors enrolled in "the Lab" were there to hone their skills, studying technique with masters like Morris Carnovsky. But the organization's secret domination by the Party allowed its cadre to use the group as a vehicle for raising their students' political consciousness, as well as for recruiting those they considered good candidates into the Party. Both the instructors and the Lab's leadership engaged in such recruiting.

Actor Larry Parks, who became an overnight star with his portrayal of singer Al Jolson in *The Jolson Story* (1946), later told HUAC that from 1941 to 1945 he was a member of a CP cell with Carnovsky and Lee J. Cobb, among others. Parks too came into the Party through the Actors' Lab, although he defended the organization as "the finest of its kind" in the training of actors.[69]

In a recent documentary accompanying the fiftieth anniversary re-release on DVD of the classic film *High Noon*, Lloyd Bridges, Larry Parks' best friend during the 1940s, is interviewed. He refers to what he calls the "terrible" years in which people like him were falsely accused of being Communists. "I thought after *High Noon* my future would be pretty rosy," Bridges says, "but anyone who was liberal in those days or who did anything to help humanity suffered." Acknowledging that he was part of the

Actors' Lab, Bridges states casually that "there were apparently quite a few Communists in that organization so I suppose that was one of the reasons I was put on the [black]list."[70]

Not only were there "apparently" a few Communists in the Actors' Lab, but Lloyd Bridges was secretly one of them! In addition, Bridges *asked* to appear before HUAC during its Hollywood hearings in 1951, and he freely named his fellow members— including his friend Larry Parks, who had shielded Bridges in his own testimony. Glad to receive his full cooperation, HUAC heard Bridges' testimony in a private executive session, never acknowledging that he appeared or informing the public of his cooperation. Moreover, Bridges had already voluntarily gone to the FBI in April 1951 and *told the bureau about his CP membership* and his desire to testify before HUAC: "I have worked with these people as directors and as actors and I felt that I was pretty sure in my mind who most of the Communists were."[71]

"I have a great sympathy and feeling for those who are suffering from injustices," Bridges told HUAC in his secret testimony, admitting that the CP "appealed to me to the extent that I listened to what was said." He said that he had been recruited by his mentor Roman Bohnen, under whom he had studied at the Actors' Lab. "We should try and be more socially conscious," Bohnen admonished. "It would give us something as actors that would bring to our role what we otherwise might not do."

Bridges asked his wife for advice about joining the CP. "How can you get hurt by it?" she replied. "There's no law against it.... Russia is our ally right now.... At least they put up the strongest fight against Fascism and Nazism and that is certainly something you want to fight against. You can't do that as an individual, but as an organization you can." With this support and encouragement, Bridges told Bohnen he would give membership a try. Bridges received a Party card bearing his name. He lasted in the Party, according to his testimony, for only a year and a half, going to only two formal meetings. Nevertheless, he felt "elated" at belonging, and although his interest ultimately wore off, he didn't leave the Party because he was loath to hurt his friends' feelings and because he worried that leaving might affect his status in the Actors' Lab.

Bridges also told HUAC in his voluntary appearance that

members of the Party in the Actors' Lab were required to keep their CP membership secret. But despite this injunction, Bridges told the committee that he could tell more or less who were members of the Hollywood Party by the way they talked and acted, and he knew that all the Actors' Lab leaders were members. In a grand Hollywood version of having his cake and eating it too, Lloyd Bridges became the only actor who testified as a cooperative witness before HUAC yet managed to wear the public mantle of an innocent victim of the blacklist who did not cooperate!

Another Party front was the People's Educational Center, where the Party screenwriter Robert Lees taught his craft. The group "was considerably more Marxist than the earlier League of American Writers School had been," he recalled. Indeed, the PEC became his main Party assignment, where he taught students that "political consciousness" must inform their writing.[72]

The PEC moved its operation into an abandoned school building on Vine Street, just north of Hollywood Boulevard. This put the school in what was then the center of Hollywood. Director Edward Dmytryk taught an orientation course in filmmaking. When he started at the PEC, he had not as yet joined the Party. After being invited to a meeting with twenty other men and women at director Frank Tuttle's home in 1944, he signed up. The man he called the Party's "chief salesman," screenwriter Alvah Bessie—best known for the screenplay of *Objective Burma*—made the pitch. By the evening's end, "the air was filled with excitement, tinged with a seductive undercurrent of secretiveness, and when the membership applications were handed out, I signed without a qualm." Dmytryk was given a Party card and a membership book, issued in the fictitious name of Michael Edwards. Included was the preamble to the constitution of the Communist Party USA, which promised that members would carry forward "the traditions of Jefferson, Paine, Jackson and Lincoln." There was no mention of Marx, Lenin or Stalin.[73]

The Politics of Wartime Films

The question that later consumed so many congressmen in the House Committee on Un-American Activities and which was widely debated in the 1950s and is still being debated today, is whether Communists managed to sneak propaganda into the movies they worked on. While it was evident that many Hollywood Communists had worked on major motion pictures and often won Academy Awards for their efforts, it was difficult to point to any Communist doctrine they had managed to inject into their films. The examples that HUAC came up with—such as actor Lionel Stander whistling "The Internationale," the Communist anthem, as he entered an elevator in the lightweight 1938 film *No Time to Marry*—were risible. (The tune was not removed because those in charge of the movie didn't know what it was; thus the scene is the great in-joke mentioned in virtually every book written on the blacklist.) Another often-cited example is a line given to a high school coach in the 1939 film *The Spirit of Culver*, written by the novelist Nathanael West (and incorrectly attributed to Lester Cole, who bragged that he had put it in a film): "It is far better to die on your feet than live as slaves on your knees." The line was taken from a speech to the International Brigades in Spain given by the Communist leader Dolores Iburarri, "La Pasionaria." This, of course, was something that only other Reds would notice, and it hardly turned any high school athletes into Communists.[74]

But the common wisdom that Communists were strong organizers in Hollywood though unable to insinuate their politics into the movies they worked on is undercut, for instance, by the 1946 film *Cloak and Dagger*, directed by Fritz Lang and written by Ring Lardner Jr. and Alvah Bessie, making it in effect an all-Communist and fellow-traveler production. It was, as scholar Bernard Dick notes, "a tribute to the Italian Communist resistance, an exaggerated account of Germany's attempt to manufacture an atom bomb, and a plea that the atomic age would not get off to as bad a start as Hiroshima seemed to indicate."[75] The story concerns an atomic scientist, played by Gary Cooper, who is persuaded to leave the Manhattan Project and travel for the Office of Strategic Services to Switzerland, where he is to seek out a dissident female German physicist. Finding that she has been kidnapped by the Gestapo, he goes to Italy behind enemy lines, where he meets the ostensibly Red partisans. He is put in contact with the heroine who becomes his love interest, played by actress Lili Palmer. She tells him: "In this work we're comrades; we share."

The film contains a major propaganda barrage as the Cooper character echoes the postwar Soviet line on the sharing of atomic secrets and voices his objections to even working on an A-bomb. Set in 1942—when such a scientist would in fact have supported the Einstein letter urging bomb production—the film faithfully reflects CP sentiments of the era. In the version of the film screened in advance for the critics, Cooper says at the end, "God have mercy on us if we ever thought we could really keep science a secret…if we think we can wage other wars without destroying ourselves." It was straight Party-line dialogue of the early Cold War. Probably for that reason, the version released to the public by Warner Brothers ran a different end, with Cooper, back in the United States, promising to return to Italy and his romance with the lovely partisan girl. Lardner and Bessie had tried to do what was required by the Party line, but the studio had subverted them.

Hangmen Also Die (1943) was another virtually all-Communist production. Directed again by Fritz Lang, the film was written by the famous Communist playwright Bertolt Brecht with the aid of another Communist, John Wexley, and had a score by their comrade Hanns Eisler. Set in Prague after the assassination of Reynard Heydrich, the Nazi proconsul there, the film heralded the anti-Nazi resistance of the Czech people, despite the mass arrests and executions of many Czechs in retaliation for Heydrich's murder. With the members of the resistance reporting to what is called "the Central Committee," it is implied that the virtuous and selfless leaders are all Communists.

Another 1943 film, the Warner Brothers hit *Action in the North Atlantic*—starring Humphrey Bogart and written by the top Hollywood Communist John Howard Lawson—is unique as a propaganda effort. An ode not only to the merchant marine but to the Communist-run union that represented the sailors on the East Coast, Joe Curran's National Maritime Union-CIO, its most famous scene takes place in the seamen's hiring hall by the docks. When a survivor of a shipwreck, Pulaski (Dane Clark), says that he won't ship out again and that nobody cares about the merchant marine, another survivor raises his fist to strike him.

Ripping off Pulaski's NMU button—to make the point that quitters don't deserve to wear it—the obligatory Irish character O'Hara (played by William Bendix) delivers a speech about solidarity and international responsibility. "So you want a safe job?" he intones. "Go ask the Poles, the Czechs, the Greeks." At that point, O'Hara and his union brothers rush to sign on for a dangerous mission. Chagrined, and thinking about the ideals of solidarity, Pulaski too decides to join up.

The film also portrays the Soviet Union in the most favorable light. It was, as Bernard Dick puts it, an opportunity for Lawson "to show…his support for the Party and at the same time to write a commercially successful movie."[76] The film not only shows how difficult and dangerous it was for the merchant marine to ship war material (Lend-Lease) to the Russian allies, but also implies that in every sense the Soviet Union was America's most noble and worthy ally.

The last part of the film begins with a convoy setting out from Canada in early dawn. Included in the flotilla are a Dutch ship, an American vessel and, of course, one from the Soviet Union. Eventually, U-boats attack the American ship, which has been separated from the others. But at the last moment, Soviet planes arrive and save the helpless ship and crew from Nazi dive bombers. When Pulaski spots the planes, for a moment there is fear that they are German. Then he says "They're ours!" as a close-up shows the Red star insignia on a fuselage. The rescued ship arrives at the port of Murmansk, to be met by hordes of cheering Russian men and women, who greet the seamen with the cry *"Tovarich! Tovarich!"* A sailor, looking confused, asks a crewmate what it means; the other sailor says, "That means comrade—that's good." The first sailor then yells back to the Russians: "Comrade! Comrade!" So *Action in the North Atlantic* is a perfect representation of the wartime Party line: patriotic and pro-Soviet at the same time.

Songs of Soviet Russia

Two of the most notorious wartime films made by Hollywood Communists focus on the Soviet Union itself. The first was *North Star,* with a script by Lillian Hellman and music by Aaron Copland. It depicts a thriving collective farm of happy, healthy Soviet peasants, all of whom look and act like Americans, and who frequently and spontaneously burst into silly songs. The Germans invade; they bomb a group of young people walking to Kiev on a camping trip, after which the men leave to become guerilla fighters. The invading Germans take blood from children for wounded German soldiers, and most of the village people die in battle. Meant to portray the heroism and nobility of the Soviet people, it is a starry-eyed view of the USSR, a film equivalent of the text and photos in *Soviet Russia Today,* a Soviet propaganda publication aimed at America. The film was a box office hit and earned six Academy Award nominations.

Hellman's script, as the film writer Dan Georgakas has explained, represents "a total reversal of reality."[77] Set in the Ukraine, the film starts with Ukrainian peasants dancing happily on their collective farm, which viewers see has brought them all the material comforts and food they need. Youngsters are preparing to move to the cities to assume professional careers. It is a Sovietization of small-town America.

The reality, of course, is that the Ukrainians were among the strongest resisters to collectivization. Farmers broke their tools and killed their animals rather than hand them over to the state. In the mass starvation that followed, Stalin withheld all government assistance, producing a state-sponsored famine. A total of six million people died. In the Ukraine alone, four million peasants lost their lives.[78] When war broke out, many Ukrainians unsurprisingly saw Hitler's invading army not as oppressors but as liberators. Villagers like those in Hellman's film certainly did not become joyous Soviet partisans united in fighting the Nazis.

The second film, *Song of Russia,* was even more egregious. It tells the story of an American conductor (played by Robert Taylor, who was actually a fierce anti-Communist) who goes on a concert tour of the USSR.[79] There he meets a Russian girl, a concert pianist, who asks him to perform in her village, where the musicians happily labor alongside the peasants in the fields. The conductor eventually falls in love with and marries the Russian girl, and soon the two are performing on radio together at the exact moment when the German invasion begins. As in *North*

Star, the thriving Soviet collective farm is destroyed by the invading Nazi army. The film ends with a scene of a Soviet citizen
telling the conductor and his Russian wife to return to America
and tell everyone the "truth" about Soviet Russia.

Written by Communist writers Paul Jarrico and Richard
Collins, from a story co-authored by Party member Guy Endore,
the film featured songs composed for it by Jerome Kern with
lyrics by the Communist lyricist E. Y. (Yip) Harburg. Advisors for
the film included journalist Anna Louise Strong, perhaps the
best-known propagandist for the Soviet Union in the 1940s, who
lived for many years in Russia editing the English-language
Moscow News. The film, as historian Robert Mayhew has pointed
out, was vetted carefully and then approved by Lowell Mellett at
the Office of War Information. Not only did this government
office urge that the film have a pro-Soviet slant, but Mellett submitted the script to the first secretary of the Soviet embassy in the
United States to get his input![80]

In 1947, the Russian émigré and philosopher Ayn Rand
testified memorably about the film before HUAC, saying that she
"found Communist propaganda…in the smiling faces of Russian children." She noted that in the film's first scene, the
conductor is still at home leading an American orchestra in playing the national anthem, which gradually dissolves into the
Soviet anthem, intended to show symbolically the moral equivalence of the two systems. In her testimony, Rand identified other
scenes in the film that contrasted starkly with reality. Soviet peasants visiting Moscow are shown eating in the equivalent of
American five-star restaurants, which, even if they existed, were
reserved for the top Party elite. She pointed out that smiling
Russian peasants are wearing "beautiful blouses and shoes,"
when they were in fact made destitute by the Soviet system. The
peasants drive new tractors, which they own individually and
which they park in their own private garages. They have their
own radios, rather than listening to the one radio in a collective
common room. The village depicted in the film is, as Mayhew
puts it, "a Potemkin village—a façade built to hide the miserable
reality of Soviet peasant life."[81]

Rand testified that she well understood the need for a military alliance with Russia to win the war; if the film had simply advocated that goal, there would be no problem. But, she continued, "if it is to deceive the American people to present…a better picture of Russia than it really is, then that sort of attitude is nothing but the theory of the Nazi elite, that a choice group of intellectual…leaders will tell the people lies for their own good." Acknowledging that MGM chief Louis B. Mayer made an effort to "cut propaganda out," she said he still failed to realize that "the mere presentation of that kind of happy existence in a country of slavery and horror is terrible because it is propaganda."[82]

Ayn Rand was ridiculed and derided for years by journalists like Victor Navasky for her evaluation of *Song of Russia*. But she was completely correct.

5

"A Great Historic Mistake"

THE ONE FILM THAT NOT EVEN APOLOGISTS CAN DENY WAS UNADULTER-ated Stalinist propaganda was *Mission to Moscow*. Made by Warner Brothers in 1943, it was based on the 1941 memoir of the same title by Joseph Davies, U.S. ambassador to the Soviet Union from 1936 to 1938. Davies' book had been a national bestseller, accounting for an amazing seven hundred thousand hardcover copies. Translated into thirteen languages and published in nine countries, it became an international sensation.[1]

When Davies began to put his book together right after the Nazi invasion of Russia, President Roosevelt was pleased that his old friend (they had served together in the administration of Woodrow Wilson) was engaged on the project. Sumner Welles, the undersecretary of state, allowed him to use State Department documents that had been classified as "confidential, " but the book was primarily based on diaries that Davies had kept during his tour in the USSR.

Mission to Moscow was a crash project, appearing in book-stores a scant three weeks after Pearl Harbor. The book's interventionist message could not have been timelier. The Soviet Union, not long ago perceived by the public as a menace, was soon to be an allied power. Americans trying to grapple with this drastic about-face found in the book a rationale for a warm rela-tionship with the USSR. A week before publication, on December 14, an excerpt was printed in the *New York Times Mag-azine*. Roosevelt, in his own personal copy, wrote that "This book will last."[2]

As far as the public was concerned (according to a Gallup poll commissioned by Davies in October 1942), the most important fact in the book was its judgment about the Moscow purge trials that occurred between 1936 and 1938. Accused of plotting with Nazi Germany to overthrow the Soviet government, most of the old Bolshevik leadership, in this travesty of jurisprudence, was found guilty and summarily executed. The Moscow show trials burst on the political world of the Left, as Sidney Hook wrote, "like a bombshell."[3] The defendants had all been among Lenin's original comrades, and until the moment of their arrest were acclaimed as the first heroes of the Soviet Revolution. They had now been charged with the most heinous of crimes: planning to assassinate Stalin under the exiled Leon Trotsky's direction and conspiring with Nazi Germany and Imperial Japan to destroy the Soviet Union. As if such preposterous charges were not enough, the prosecution claimed that during the October 1917 revolution itself, the accused had been secret allies of the British military in its effort to stop Lenin's seizure of power.

Even more shocking and confusing than the charges against them was the fact that the defendants confessed to the crimes of which they were charged—a pattern that was to become the subject of Arthur Koestler's searing novel *Darkness at Noon*. Although there were widespread suspicions at the time, only decades later would proof emerge about how they were drugged and tortured into confessing, and how their families were threatened unless they cooperated. Although the prosecution was unable to present any actual evidence to substantiate the charges, Western Communists and fellow travelers closed ranks, proclaiming that the defendants were guilty and that Stalin had saved world socialism.

In 1937 and 1938, when Davies was still serving in Russia and confiding to his diary, he had a muddled view of the trials. Writing to FDR's aide Stephen Earley in April 1938, Davies opined, "Here there was no issue left—the guilt had already been determined by the confessions of the accused." But he then acknowledged that much in the confessions was not true, although he did continue to believe that many of the defendants had actually been plotting to overthrow Stalin.[4]

Four years later, when he came to write his book, Davies asserted that the trials had proved "a record of Fifth Columnist and subversive activities in Russia under a conspiracy...[involving] the German and Japanese governments that [was] amazing." He now believed that the conspiracy included plans to assassinate Stalin and stage a military uprising led by General Tukhachevsky, all on behalf of the German general staff. The trials, purges and liquidations—which "seemed so violent at the time and shocked the world"—now seemed to Davies "part of a vigorous and determined effort of the Stalin government to protect itself not only from revolution from within but from attack from without." In dealing with the "treasonable elements" at home, Stalin thus "cleansed the country and rid it of treason."[5]

The film of Davies' book would amplify the themes and take the afterthought about fifth columnists as its main argument. This classic of propaganda films was, according to film historian David Culbert, "the most extreme Hollywood attempt to intensify support for the ally least liked by Americans."[6] It focuses directly on the purge trials, telescoping three different trials that actually took place over three years into one giant trial for the sake of dramatic economy. With the prominent actor Walter Huston portraying Davies, *Mission to Moscow* strove for a documentary aura. Culbert accurately calls it "a notorious example of pro-Soviet special pleading"—a film, moreover, that is a "wholesale rewriting of history," with "use of visual innuendo, and [an] explicit appeal to facts known to be *incorrect*."[7]

How did such a film ever come to be made? Who was responsible? The standard answer was that it was ordered up by the government, upon the request of the president himself. In a newspaper interview, Davies said that it was he who had approached Harry Warner about the book, after other film companies had shown interest. If it was to be a movie, he told Warner, "I want you to make it." Warner agreed, and Davies was paid $25,000. This was a princely sum in 1942, far exceeding anything ever paid for a nonfiction film.[8]

When Jack Warner later testified in an open public hearing before the House Committee on Un-American Activities, he told them, "Many charges have been made, including the fantasy of

'White House pressure,' and have been leveled at our wartime production of *Mission to Moscow*." His only goal in making the film was to spur on the Allied victory, much as they had done in films such as *Objective Burma, Destination Tokyo* and *Action in the North Atlantic*. It was no more "subversive activity," Warner claimed, "than the American Liberty ships which carried food and guns to Russian allies and the American naval vessels which convoyed them."[9]

But *Mission to Moscow* hardly resembled the first two movies he cited, both of which dealt with aspects of the Pacific theater campaign against Japan, and neither of which glorified Stalin's secret police and mass purges.

Warner was on even shakier ground when he tried to defend the contents of *Mission to Moscow*. In executive session, HUAC's chief investigator, Robert Stripling, asked him whether the film was "in some ways a misinterpretation of the facts or the existing conditions," and if "certain historical incidents which were portrayed in the film were not true…?" Warner's answer was that Davies had been the ambassador, and the studio "had to take his word that they were the facts." Warner admitted he knew that John Dewey, the eminent Columbia University philosopher and educator, had condemned the film as a tissue of lies; but the studio chief said, "From what I read and heard, [Dewey] was a Trotskyite and they were the ones who objected mostly…."

It was a rare moment. Here was a conservative corporate studio head who had so internalized Stalinist logic that he was unashamed to employ it before Congress to defend the making of his film! In a similar complaint to the White House about opposition from New York intellectuals, Warner appropriated the very language and even the spelling used by Stalin's opponents and by prosecutor Vyshinsky at the purge trials. "I have learned," he wanted FDR to be told, "that there is a mob around New York and in other cities, *called the Trotskyite Bloc*, that objects to MISSION TO MOSCOW." (Italics added.)[10]

"I personally did not consider that film pro-Communist at the time," Warner added in his executive session testimony before HUAC. But not everyone associated with the film felt the same way. The main objections were raised by the film's producer, Robert Buckner. As he explained in a lengthy letter, he was horrified at the film's depiction of the purge trials in Moscow. "I did not believe that the victims of the so-called Purge Trials were guilty as charged," Buckner wrote, "nor did the majority of the foreign correspondents.... I am convinced that Stalin framed them and I read everything possibly available on the subject, before and long after the film was made. In fact I had a rather violent argument with Davies on this subject when time came to film the trial scenes."

Buckner stressed that originally Davies also favored a depiction of at least some "ambiguity" as to the defendants' guilt. But "when time came to shoot the scene and the guilt or innocence had to be made specific, Davies insisted upon the guilt." At that point, Buckner went to Jack and Harry Warner "and told them that a great historic mistake was being made."

According to Buckner, what happened next was both tragic and farcical. After being informed that Warner had already spent one million dollars on the film, Davies whipped out his checkbook. "I will give you the million here and now," he said, "and will take over the negative of the film from you." The studio chiefs gave in. Thereafter, no one would challenge Davies' insistence that "the victims were guilty as traitors and Trotskyites." In addition, Buckner wrote, "Davies inserted the insinuation that Finland was not actually invaded by the USSR." When he told Davies that "the opposite was true," Davies claimed that he had "privileged knowledge."[11]

Buckner had felt the film would be "really a tough baby" but thought it could be achieved "with careful intelligent unhasty preparation."[12] Jack Warner wanted an important playwright to do the script, and he asked Davies to contact his first choice—Robert Sherwood, the famous New Deal author. "The international importance of this great subject," Warner commented, "needs the type of capabilities that Sherwood possesses."[13]

Sherwood, a critic, editor and writer, would have been a perfect choice. His screenplay for *Abe Lincoln in Illinois* led eventually to his employment as a speechwriter for the president. But he was not interested.

Next, Warner Brothers tried Erskine Caldwell, author of

Tobacco Road, who in 1941 had traveled to Moscow with his wife, the *Life* photographer Margaret Bourke, and had written the text for a book of her work, *You Have Seen Their Faces.* Caldwell did a draft of *Mission to Moscow,* but the studio rejected it.[14]

The job then went to Howard Koch, a former Broadway playwright who would gain lasting fame as co-author of *Casablanca* (1942), for which he won an Academy Award. Koch has often been portrayed as a skillful but nonpolitical screenwriter who landed on the blacklist only because of his unfortunate association with *Mission to Moscow.* Later on, for instance, Victor Navasky wrote in his best-selling book *Naming Names* that there had been much hoopla about Communist propaganda in the movies, "but all [HUAC] could come up with was *Mission to Moscow,* which was written by a non-Communist (Howard Koch) at the request of President Roosevelt."[15] This was two falsehoods in one sentence. In fact, Howard Koch was probably a Party member for some time in the 1930s, and if not, he was clearly a fellow traveler of the Communists and the Soviet Union. Many of his correspondents addressed him as "Comrade Koch," and his rhetorical jargon—labeling opponents of FDR as "fascist," for instance—was standard for Party members and fellow travelers.[16]

In his memoir, *As Time Goes By* (1979), Koch many years later noted that he accepted the job on the condition that he had "the right to select his own technical adviser, someone with personal experience in the Soviet Union whose veracity and objectivity I could trust."[17] He turned to his old, openly pro-Soviet friend Jay Leyda, who had been one of the early political pilgrims to visit the USSR and had been faithful to Stalin and his regime ever since.

In a letter written in 1992 to Thomas Staedeli, a Swiss film writer, Koch claimed that he was not a Communist but worked "with them on good causes to make a better world—and also better movies." He made the same analysis of the world situation as most Communists, asserting that it "was simply a class struggle, capitalism taking its stand against socialism."[18]

Koch clarified his perspective on politics in his memoir, where he said that the writers at Warners were all "politically conscious"—that is, they were "involved in the struggle against fascism." (Today we would call them "left-wing.") Two of those he praised as "leading activists," his euphemism for Party members, were Dalton Trumbo and John Howard Lawson. Recalling that on his first day at Warners he was greeted by Lawson with "a handshake and a warm smile," Koch described the most hard-line Stalinist in Hollywood as a man who might "have made sainthood."[19]

Pondering how to draft a new screenplay, Koch certainly thought like a Communist. "By stressing his conservative background," Koch wrote, explaining why he had chosen to emphasize Davies' capitalist commitments in his portrayal, "we might disarm some who would otherwise be skeptical of any report favorable to the Soviet Union." As he thought of how to open the script, his mind drifted to Haile Selassie's speech before the League of Nations in 1936, when Ethiopia was under Mussolini's guns and only Maxim Litvinov, the Soviet foreign minister, pledged Russian military aid. For Koch, this was not only a perfect opening scene but also a perfect example of "collective security against fascist aggression." He noted with satisfaction: "Let the Soviet-haters scream."[20]

In a letter to Jack and Harry Warner, he discussed this and added a postscript about what he hoped would be the film's political influence. The Soviets were "fulfilling my predictions," he put it, and when the war was won, their struggle would have "contributed tremendously to that victory." Americans should understand that "if we win the peace, we will have to work with Russia." His concern was that the movie would "have great and beneficial repercussions far into the distant future" and would help produce "confidence between the Russian people and our own."[21]

Warners decided to send Howard Koch up to Davies' summer home in New York so that Davies could help with the script.[22] In the meantime, they assigned the film to Michael Curtiz, who had directed *Casablanca* and was used to working with Koch.

Koch found that Davies considered himself an equal in the creative process and demanded a full say in the scripting.[23] One of the changes that the former ambassador demanded was that the film include the claim that Finland was not invaded by the

Soviet Union in 1939. Producer Bob Buckner bridled, not realizing that both Koch and Jay Leyda welcomed this falsehood as a propaganda coup and enjoyed being able to attribute its insertion to Davies.

Not content with the fact that a major studio was making his book into a film, Davies watched the filming on the set, sometimes insisting on frivolous changes. He felt that Walter Huston "refused to make himself up to resemble in any way the personality [Stalin] he purports to represent."[24] His wife wanted her role in the drama embellished, demanding that a scene be added with her and Mrs. Molotov visiting a cosmetics factory.

The most significant change made by Davies was the insertion of the prologue that opens the movie. Speaking directly to the theater audience, the real Davies intones that "no leaders of a nation have been so misrepresented and misunderstood as those in the Soviet government during these critical years between the two world wars." The film, he hopes, "will help to correct that misunderstanding...."

The Role of Jay Leyda

Mission to Moscow's apologia for Stalinism was ensured by the presence of Jay Leyda as technical advisor. The activities of this now-forgotten Communist—who had a second career as a Melville scholar later in life—had, according to Clare Spark, "been cited twelve times in the Martin Dies (HUAC) Report of 1944, and in later years, his movements, associations, and labors were of interest to the FBI, the CIA, the NSA, the Department of the Army and Navy, the State Department, and the United States Information Agency."[25] His correspondence, she writes, "reads like a 'Who's Who' of the 1930s pro-Soviet Left."[26]

Beginning in 1933, Leyda had been in the Soviet Union for three years, during which he worked closely with the great Soviet film director Sergei Eisenstein. At different times, Leyda offered different stories about why he left Russia in 1936. His first version was that all foreigners were told to leave or become Soviet citizens because the purge trials had started. Later he claimed that Eisenstein told him he would never make it as a film director and urged him to work instead on film history and research. When

Iris Barry, head of the Museum of Modern Art's Film Department, came to Moscow, he worked as her guide and interpreter. When Barry offered him the job of MOMA's assistant film curator, he immediately asked Eisenstein whether he should accept the offer. Eisenstein urged him to take it, given that the purge trials meant trouble for resident foreigners.[27]

Later on, producer Bob Buckner claimed that he didn't remember Jay Leyda having a significant role in *Mission to Moscow;* but in fact Leyda was decisive in ensuring that the film portrayed Stalin's purges in a light that was acceptable to American audiences. Outside of Buckner's field of vision, Howard Koch and Leyda had a close personal and political association and were regularly in contact about matters relating to the script and the film's direction.

And Leyda was quite pleased with the end result. In a letter to his friend, the radical intellectual and prominent literary Communist Joseph Freeman, he wrote that "even with all the fumbling and mind-changing and personal motives that clogged up its progress," Freeman would be pleasantly surprised by the movie's "final shape." Leyda explained that what was critical was that "the big things in the film" not be "hopelessly lost among the absurdities." What he meant was that the details—that is, accurate costumes, make-up and so on—were of little concern to him, but "the positive accomplishments of the film...fortify me."[28] These accomplishments are well summed up by historians Clayton R. Koppes and Gregory D. Black, who note that while "the film does not turn the Soviet Union into a Western-style democracy...in keeping with the wartime propaganda approach to America's allies, it depicts happy citizens and a benign government to suggest the people really support the state."[29]

In fact, Leyda was little concerned with what a technical advisor would be expected to do. A report to director Michael Curtiz from one of his associates on the film, Al Alleborn, complained that they had no "Technical Man who knows the [troop] maneuvers...wardrobe and costuming of the people." Leyda was not interested in such trifles. His concern was that the film be faithful to Stalin's worldview. That, of course, was precisely why Koch hired him.[30]

Leyda's manuscripts, held at the Tamiment Institute Library

of New York University, contain a version of the script dated November 9, 1942, titled "Suggested Changes—Revised Version." There is also a portion of a script dated February 6, 1943, titled "Changes to 'Mission to Moscow,'" which includes notes written by Leyda to Howard Koch.[31] These manuscripts show how he made his influence felt as "technical advisor."

In vetting the script, he suggested changes that would deeply affect the political content of the film—for example, in the scene where the Ethiopian ruler, Haile Selassie, asks whether he is to be "left deserted and forgotten" as he pleads for aid from the League of Nations against Italian aggression. The final script indicates that the camera should make a "MED. PANNING SHOT over the faces of the French delegates." The reason for this was crucial: "I suggest leaving the camera on the French delegation during this portion of Selassie's speech," Leyda told Koch. "The device we are using throughout the scene is to have Selassie's words point a finger at the various countries that are selling him out. So by having these words over the [face of Soviet Ambassador] Litvinov...we would create the mistaken impression that Russia was abandoning Ethiopia."

On his way to his assignment in Russia, Ambassador Davies first visited Hitler's Germany, where he was received by an official named Schufeldt. The script has Davies telling Schufeldt: "I understand the Stalin regime is firmly entrenched with the Russian people." The German answers: "On the surface—yes. (Mysteriously.) But before very long you may possibly have cause to change your opinion." In his notes, Leyda said, "Let's shift the initiative to Davies...so that he provides the opportunity for Schufeldt's slip." In other words, while the script had Schufeldt hinting that when he gets to Russia, Davies will find out that many Russians are working with the Nazis to overthrow the Soviet regime, Leyda wanted this slip to be attributed to Davies' acumen, and not to the German official, in order to underscore the ambassador's later conclusion that those accused in the purge were indeed working for Hitler.

One of the scenes, which takes place at a diplomat's party at the Kremlin, includes dialogue between a British diplomat, Lady Chilston, the German representatives von Ribbentrop and von

Schulenberg, the Soviet ambassador Maxim Litvinov and foreign minister V. Molotov, the Japanese Shigemitsu, and two soon-to-be-executed Soviet chieftains, Marshal Tukhachevsky and Politburo member Nikolai Bukharin.

The script has Ambassador Litvinov approaching Davies and telling him, "Not all our enemies are outside Russia. They also have agents working in our midst to create havoc and distrust." Davies appears shocked, responding in surprise: "Traitors? Your own people?" Litvinov explains that they too have a fifth column in their midst, just as Franco's forces had in Madrid. The presence at the gathering of both Tukhachevsky and Bukharin (who in fact had already been arrested at this time) was clearly meant to signal that at the very eve of the conspiracy's exposure these traitors had access to Kremlin diplomatic matters at the highest level.

Leyda was also concerned that the "business with Ribbentrop would tip our hand as to the guilt of Bukharin." If the scene was left in, he told Koch, "it would vitiate the dramatic effect of the trials, since we would know Bukharin's guilt and his link with Ribbentrop before it is established in the testimony."[32]

Thus in the film, audiences see Bukharin confessing: "My hope is that this trial may be the last severe lesson in proving to the world the growing menace of Fascist aggression and the awareness and united strength of Russia…. What matters is not the personal feelings of a repentant enemy, but the welfare and progress of our country." The Soviet state prosecutor, the vicious Andrei Vyshinksy, who told the court that "dogs gone mad should be shot," is portrayed not as a stooge of Stalin but as a benevolent, serious jurist. It is Vyshinsky who shames the defendants and gets them to confess. The court finds them guilty and orders each and every one of them to be shot. When fellow diplomats ask Davies what he thinks, he answers: "Based on twenty years' trial practice, I'd be inclined to believe these confessions."

Later, Davies is shown wiring Secretary of State Cordell Hull that "there is no longer any question in my mind that these defendants…were guilty of a conspiracy with the German and Japanese high commands to pave the way for an attack upon the Soviet state." The purges, in other words, were just and necessary to protect the USSR. The film then shifts to Roosevelt giving his famous "quarantine the aggressors" speech, a scene which absurdly suggests that the purge trials had inspired him to stand tough. In reality, the trials of Bukharin, of NKVD chief Yagoda and others took place after the president had given this speech.

Aside from the characterization of the purge trials, one of the most notorious sequences in the film takes place toward the end, when Davies is shown at what appears to be Madison Square Garden addressing a rally for the war effort. One heckler in the audience shouts: "How about poor little Finland?" Davies retorts: "Russia knew she was going to be attacked by Hitler so the Soviet leaders asked Finland's permission to occupy strategic positions to defend herself against German aggression. She offered to give Finland twice as much territory in exchange, but Hitler's friend Mannerheim refused and the Red Army moved in.... [Crowd applauds]."

This is the precise Soviet line justifying their aggressive war against Finland, a war never approved or supported by the Roosevelt administration or any U.S. official. Every ounce of Leyda's energy was spent on seeing to it that the film did the best possible job for Stalin's propaganda apparatus.

The Film's Reception

It is almost impossible to rent or buy a copy of *Mission to Moscow* today. Unless it is scheduled for showing on PBS, the American Movie Channel or Turner Classic Movies, the only way to view it is at the Museum of Modern Art Film Library in New York City, or the archives at the University of Wisconsin.

But in 1943 the film was considered one of Hollywood's major releases. On April 21, Davies wrote to Jack Warner after attending the critical screening at the White House: "I wish you could have been there to have heard the handsome and enthusiastic comments and tributes to the picture as a great historical production."[33] The next day, Warner ran a screening in Hollywood for what he called a "working class audience," reporting to Davies that the comment cards the audience filled out were all positive. "Am more certain than ever," Jack Warner wired, "that the world public is waiting for this important document."[34] A week later, Warner Brothers opened the film with a gala preview showing for an audience of four thousand people in Washington, D.C., with a sampling of the most important Washington journalists, members of Congress and the executive branch, and other important personalities. Warner Brothers announced that the film would have the extraordinary advertising budget of $500,000—an immense sum for a wartime film.

Mission to Moscow was received by the critics as a major accomplishment. Writing in the *New York Times,* critic Bosley Crowther, who had the power to make or break a film, wrote that the movie showed "a boldness unique in film ventures" since it "comes out sharply and frankly for an understanding of Russia's point of view." Crowther predicted, however, that it would "anger the so-called Trotskyites with its visual re-enactment of the famous 'Moscow trials.'" He also noted that the movie ridiculed the prewar British government and the French and Polish envoys to Russia as being "anti-Russian to the core," and that it took shots at prewar congressional isolationists. The film aspired "to convey a realistic impression of fact," relying for its "dramatic impulse upon the urgency of the time." As for the purge trials, Crowther judged them "briefly but effectively played."[35]

Writing for the left-liberal weekly the *Nation,* the literary critic James Agee was sympathetic to the film's political viewpoint, noting that it would likely "hasten and intensify our cooperation with the Soviet Union" and frustrate those who wanted "to win this particular peace by destroying the Soviet Union." But Agee was too sharp to be completely bamboozled. "Through rumor and internal inference," he wrote, "the Stalinists here stole or were handed such a march that the film is almost describable as the first Soviet production to come from a major American studio." It was, he added, a "mismash: of Stalinism with New Dealism with Hollywoodism with journalism with opportunism...all mosaicked into a remarkable portrait of what the makers of the film think that the American public should think the Soviet Union is like." What particularly galled him was the film's apparent claim that "there is no essential difference...between the Soviet Union and the good old U.S.A."

This was not good enough for Dwight Macdonald, the icon-oclastic radical and former Trotskyist, who condemned Agee's review as "doubletalk." He was amazed that Agee could not see that there was "something rotten in the film's thesis."

The real character of the film's pro-Soviet special pleading was apparent in a scene that was shot but eventually cut from the final print. It depicts a meeting between the exiled Bolshevik leader Leon Trotsky and the Nazi foreign minister von Ribbentrop that in fact never happened. Talking with von Ribbentrop in the office of Germany's minister to Norway, Trotsky informs him that the purge trials would never have occurred if he had been managing affairs in Russia. Realizing that time is running out, Trotsky tells von Ribbentrop that they must "strike fast" because his "following in Russia will fall away." Condescendingly, the German replies that Trotsky has overestimated his following and that his chance has passed. When he departs, von Ribbentrop smirks that he has "no more time for an exile's delusions."

The film's message precipitated a major battle. The first shot was fired in a lengthy letter sent to the *New York Times* by the philosopher John Dewey and Suzanne LaFollette, who had been secretary to the Dewey Commission that investigated the charges made against Trotsky. The film, they wrote, "is the first instance in our country of totalitarian propaganda for mass consumption," which falsifies "history through distortion, omission or pure invention of facts." Even worse, the film was presented as "factual and documentary," not as fiction.

The purge trials, Dewey and LaFollette pointed out, were "frame-ups." They catalogued all the film's errors and travesties, including what they called the sabotaging by the Western Communist parties of the Allied cause during the years of the Nazi-Soviet Pact. The film leapt over and ignored "Stalin's collaboration with Hitler" as well as Churchill's direction of British foreign affairs in order to convey the impression that "Stalin's foreign policy has always been democratic and anti-fascist and Britain's one of appeasement." The film's ending, in which isolationist members of Congress are portrayed as deluded and ignorant, was meant to "discredit the American Congress and…represent the Soviet dictatorship as an advanced democracy." Concluding their broadside, Dewey and LaFollette explained that the real danger of the film was that it would deaden Americans to the importance of "moral values" and the truth. The producers had not made a patriotic film, as they claimed, but one that "assailed the very foundations of freedom."[36]

The literary critic and writer Edmund Wilson saw the film as trying to assert that "democratic institutions are inferior to Soviet purges," and the esteemed art critic Meyer Schapiro thought that "one must turn to Nazi propaganda films for a similar technique and indifference to truth." And Dwight Macdonald went further than he did in his *Nation* magazine letter by calling it "the first totalitarian film to come out of Hollywood…that could have been made in Moscow."[37]

Such critiques put the filmmakers on the defensive. Howard Koch did his best to reply. Rather than address the specific criticisms, he argued that he had tried to deal factually with contemporary themes. His intention, he claimed, was not to whitewash the Soviet Union, since he had never had any "preconceptions about the Soviet Union which we were anxious to cover up." He was merely adapting a book whose "brilliant, legalistic fact-finding and reporting gave me the first impression of an objective appraisal that I could trust."

The readers of Koch's exculpation—published in the *New York Times*—had no way of knowing his pro-Soviet leanings or his relationship with the Stalinist Jay Leyda. He asked them to take him at his word that he had tried to tap many "valid sources of information" before writing the script—which claim, we now know, was entirely false. If there were factual liberties taken, he said, it was only because of the demands of making the story coherent within a two-hour time frame, not because of politics or a decision to echo Stalin's propaganda.

As for loading the film "on the side of the Soviet leaders and against the English and French appeasers," Koch responded that the Soviet policy in Spain had been proved correct, while the Western policy of appeasement proved that the Western nations were wrong. In addressing the question of why he did not show "the less favorable internal aspect of the Soviet experiment," Koch admitted a partial failure: the filmmakers foolishly portrayed Davies as "too quickly convinced of the well-being of the Soviet people and the benevolence of their government," although the sentence implies that they might have taken more time to show how Davies' initial judgment was correct. Finally, the critics' argument was not with the film but with history, which Koch judged had been "unkind to their prejudices."[38]

The intense public debate that followed the film's premiere generated a backlash among actors, writers, directors and producers who were not enamored of the Popular Front and the politics of Hollywood's Communists. In the late 1940s, Sam Wood, a fierce opponent of Franklin D. Roosevelt, helped form one of the first conservative anti-Communist groups in the film capital of the world, the Motion Picture Alliance for the Preservation of American Ideals. Wood, a well-known director at MGM in the 1930s, had become something of a right-wing extremist, a man ready to see FDR as a Communist dupe. What helped push him over the edge was *Mission to Moscow,* which also prodded Victor Fleming, King Vidor, Walt Disney, Gary Cooper, Clark Gable and Morrie Ryskind to start organizing. (Later members included Robert Taylor, Adolphe Menjou, John Wayne, Ward Bond and the anti-Communist union leader Roy Brewer.) Their efforts resulted in the creation of the Motion Picture Alliance in February 1944. Thus *Mission to Moscow* became part of the complex back story for Hollywood's darkest hour—the years of the blacklist.

6

The Cold War Begins in Hollywood

UNTIL 1945, THE HOLLYWOOD COMMUNISTS COULD FEEL THAT THEY had been blessed by history. The invasion of Russia and the wartime alliance between the Soviet Union and the United States had rescued them from their isolation and restored their stature in the film capital. The goal of the Communists—protection of the Soviet Union—once again coincided with that of the United States government, which supported military and economic aid to the Soviets as necessary for defeating the Axis. Once denigrated as "Russia firsters," the comrades now appeared to be more red, white and blue than they were Red. To help them prove their patriotism, the Soviets had abolished the Comintern, arm of the international Communist movement; and in the United States, Earl Browder did Stalin one better by abolishing the Communist Party itself. As a "political association" rather than a revolutionary party, the Communists could position themselves as the left wing of the New Deal—FDR loyalists pushing the president to honor his commitments to the common people.[1]

As the war ended, the Party continued to create new fronts to strengthen its influence. Two groups became particularly important. On the East Coast, the Independent Citizens Committee of the Arts, Sciences and Professions (ICCASP) was, according to a lengthy article in *Time*, the brainchild of Jo Davidson, the fellow-traveling sculptor who had created a highly regarded bust of the president. In 1944, Davidson had invited like-minded individuals on the left of the New Deal coalition to his studio for a discussion on how best to support FDR's re-election campaign. The founders signing on included Ethel Barrymore, the critic and scholar Van Wyck Brooks, and Helen Keller, with Davidson as the group's chairman. "We were mostly virgin voices in things political," he told the press somewhat disingenuously, "most of us had been liberals, which meant that we did a lot of yapping and intellectualizing about things but few of us had ever participated."[2]

As the executive director who would run the group on a day-to-day basis, the organizers picked a master publicist, Hannah Dorner, who was most likely a secret Communist Party member.[3] ICCASP then recruited major ex–New Dealers for its leadership. Harold Ickes, the president's top aide and former interior secretary, became executive chairman. James Roosevelt, FDR's son, became national director in 1946. A wide array of major figures in American life, from Albert Einstein to Frank Sinatra, donated their names to the new organization, which had branches in Manhattan and in Hollywood. According to *Time*, "Frank Sinatra is one of its hardest-working speakers. It can call on Gypsy Rose Lee to bare her navel and William Rose Benet to write a script. Lena Horne will sing at any rally and Walter Huston will recite the Gettysburg Address. Fredric March belongs, and so do Eddie Cantor, Charles Boyer, Humphrey Bogart, Edward G. Robinson, Charles Laughton and Robert Young."

Whoever wrote the unsigned piece for *Time* fully understood the power and dazzle of the celebrity culture: "Some men and women whose every instinct rebels against the sound of a politician's voice, are so conditioned that they are unable to resist when their favorite movie star whoops up an issue." Noting that ICCASP was the logical successor to the Hollywood Anti-Nazi League, the Hollywood Committee for Loyalist Spain and what the writer facetiously named the "Steinbeck Committee for Underprivileged Okies," the article implied that the organization was the latest Communist front. It was significant, for example, that the Communist novelist Howard Fast, identified as a writer for the *Daily Worker* and the *New Masses*, produced the group's handouts and press releases. And as the story pointed out, in an aside that would continue to resonate for the next sixty years, "Few stars, male or female, would be caught at a [studio] commissary lunch table without a Cause. Most of them, horrified at the thought of being considered bloated capitalists, favor leftish causes."

One of the ICASSP's first efforts was a rally at Madison Square Garden for FDR's re-election. The featured speaker was Vice-President Henry A. Wallace, whom the president had just booted off the election-year ticket in favor of Senator Harry S. Truman of Missouri. Democratic bigwigs such as party chairman Bob Hannegan were horrified at the headline role afforded the man who would soon be widely identified as a Communist stooge, but twenty thousand people packed the Garden, and large contributors were entertained by Bert Lahr, Joe E. Lewis, Myrna Loy and Ethel Merman at a dinner that raised $40,000.

Meanwhile, several groups on the West Coast—including the Hollywood Democratic Committee, the CIO Political Action Committee and the National Citizens Political Action Committee—joined to form the Hollywood Independent Citizens Committee of the Arts, Sciences and Professions (HICCASP). From the very start, Hannah Dorner, who ran the New York group, intended to create a unified organization that would combine the clout of the West Coast and East Coast organizations. Their work was "a nation-wide job," she wrote to Jo Davidson, and she was "particularly anxious to have a Hollywood-affiliated or cooperating body."[4]

From its beginnings as a vehicle to get FDR re-elected, the group quickly swerved in an anti-American and pro-Soviet direction. By October 1945, Hannah Dorner was trying to get ICCASP to turn against the new president, Harry S. Truman. He showed "no will" to fight with the "reactionary" members of Congress, she told her board, arguing that they had to oppose the "incipient native fascism" coming from the new administration and show the public that there was no longer any "democratic purpose" to American foreign policy.[5] Speaking to HICCASP the following month, John Howard Lawson told members that the United States was starting "to strangle democracy everywhere," and that this was the *sole issue* for the group to stress (emphasis added). Unlike the USA, he told them, the Soviet Union had demonstrated that it had a peaceful policy while the United States was "building up fascist forces in the Far East."[6]

Cold winds from Moscow interfered with the promising growth of ICCASP. In the spring of 1945, at the time of the merger creating a new national group, Stalin announced the start of a new Cold War by proclaiming the United States the world's principal and most dangerous enemy. The change in line was indicated by a seemingly innocuous theoretical article that appeared in the French Communist monthly magazine *Cahiers du Communisme* in April 1945. Purportedly written by the French CP leader Jacques Duclos, it presented the author's judgment that the position on international relations taken by Earl Browder and American Communists—that the United States and the Soviet Union could peacefully cooperate in the spirit of the Yalta conference—was naïve and dangerous.

Most significant was Duclos's firm opposition to the dissolution of the American CP and its transformation into a political association. That step was nothing less than the "liquidation" of an independent Communist presence in the United States, which amounted to a gross revision of Marxism-Leninism. It was predicated on "the concept of a long-term class peace" instead of renewed class struggle and strong opposition to what was certain to be the aggressive posture of a victorious American imperialism.[7]

As we now know, the article—which led to a tumultuous upheaval in the ranks of American Communism, including the expulsion of Earl Browder and the reconstitution of an American Communist Party—was not written by Duclos but came directly from Moscow, with Stalin's personal approval.[8] The document, as Earl Browder himself would later say, was "the first *public* declaration of the Cold War."[9]

The new tough line swiftly spread through the ranks of HICCASP. A June 1945 report to the board, for instance, began by claiming that the problem they faced was that of "reactionary elements" in the government who were using the old Nazi tactics of "divide and conquer."[10]

Now that the leadership of the ICCASP had enshrined opposition to the Truman foreign policy as their primary concern, the alliance with liberals was doomed. One of the first breaking points in the film community came when actress Olivia de Havilland, a liberal member of HICCASP, was ready to deliver a long scheduled speech at a Seattle rally in June 1946. It had been written for her by the Party's most prolific and highest-paid screenwriter, Dalton Trumbo, author of major screenplays including *Tender Comrade, Thirty Seconds over Tokyo,* and *Our Vines Have Tender Grapes.* His friend Ring Lardner Jr. described him as "slight but strong, kind of wiry," sandy-haired with an on-again/off-again moustache.[11] Urbane, witty, volatile, and possessed of boundless energy, Trumbo was a larger-than-life eccentric who stayed up late into the night writing his screenplays while immersed in his bathtub.

Trumbo, who was born in Colorado in 1905, liked to point out that his family had been in America for two hundred years. When his father lost his job and moved the family to Los Angeles, Trumbo dropped out of the University of Colorado after his first year and followed them. Soon afterward, tragedy struck: his father died and Trumbo became the main support of his family. Instead of attending the University of Southern California, which had been his plan, he took a job in the Davis Perfection Bakery, a commercial bakery in downtown Los Angeles, where he worked for the next eight years before being able to make a living as a writer.[12]

In the war years, along with his prolific film work, Trumbo had written speeches for scores of people in the Popular Front coalition, from Katherine Hepburn to Secretary of State Edward Stettinius. Olivia de Havilland was aghast at the draft of the speech he gave her for the rally in Seattle. Trumbo wanted her to condemn what he called "the drive of certain interests toward a war against the Soviet Union" and the policy of an administration that he charged with supporting union busting, anti-Semitism and bigotry against racial minorities.[13]

De Havilland substituted a speech with an almost opposite point of view, underlining the growing differences between the genuine liberals and the Hollywood Communists. From 1932 to 1945, she told her audience, a "coalition of all liberal and progressive forces" made up a sizable majority of the New Deal supporters. But in the postwar era, "reactionary forces have driven a wedge into the liberal coalition" and were trying to make it appear "that the great liberal movement is controlled by those who are more interested in taking orders from Moscow and following the so-called Party line than they are interested in making democracy work." To prove otherwise, liberals would have to distance themselves openly from both Moscow and American Communists.

"We believe in democracy," she told the crowd, "and not in Communism." She reminded the audience that when the CPUSA had endorsed Roosevelt for re-election in 1944, he repudiated their endorsement. Today, she acknowledged, Communists "frequently join liberal organizations. That is their right. But it is also our right to see that they do not control us. Or guide us...or represent us."

Trumbo exploded in a fit of rage when he heard what De Havilland had done. He wrote her a tart letter noting that writers are customarily informed of the rejection of their work by its return to them.[14] Then, turning to Ernest Pascal, HICCASP's treasurer, who along with James Roosevelt had authored the new De Havilland speech, he listed all the points they had eliminated from his draft, which together amounted to a condemnation of the Truman administration for pursuing an anti-Soviet policy. Then he charged that "one-fifth of the speech" De Havilland had given was nothing but "a denunciation of Communism," with no mention of "fascism" and no trace of "my unfriendly references to it." By omitting all his pro-Soviet words, Trumbo charged, the speech had degenerated into an exercise in "Red-baiting."[15]

If it later became obvious that ICCASP (HICCASP in Hollywood) was a Communist front, at the time it looked quite different to the young actor Ronald Reagan, just emerging from the armed forces. He wrote afterward of the period that he was "blindly and busily joining every organization I could find that would guarantee to save the world." He found that "the Communists [were] high on the Hollywood hog" at this time. But like others, Reagan saw them as "liberals, and being liberal ourselves, [we] bedded down with them."[16] With other liberals, he joined HICCASP, which sounded, he quipped, "like the cough of a dying man." When he was asked to fill a vacancy on its board, he felt honored. Attending his first board meeting in July 1946, he was surprised that he knew many of the seventy people present to be Communist Party members.

For years, the organization's legitimacy had largely come from the nominal chairmanship of the group by FDR's son, James Roosevelt. After initially underplaying the worries of some non-Communist members that the group was dominated by the Communist minority, Roosevelt decided to act. When he rose to speak, he expressed his concern that HICCASP "was being accused of being a Communist front organization," and he asked for a statement in opposition to Communism that would reassure the public. According to Reagan, pandemonium ensued. Musician Artie Shaw sprang to his feet and offered to recite the USSR constitution from memory, "yelling that it was a lot more democratic than that of the United States." A prominent screenwriter then jumped up and said, "if there was ever a war between the United States and Russia, he would volunteer for Russia." When Reagan took the floor to chastise them, he was inundated "waist high in epithets such as 'Fascist' and 'capitalist scum' and 'enemy of the proletariat,' and 'witch-hunter,'" and, of course, the ultimate charge: "Red-baiter." His bitterest critics were Party members Dalton Trumbo and John Howard Lawson.

Since the group was sharply divided, a committee representing both sides was appointed to see if some accord could be reached on a statement. As Reagan was leaving the meeting, Dore Schary came up to him and whispered that he should come up to Olivia de Havilland's apartment. When he arrived he found Schary, Roosevelt, De Havilland and about nine others whose mood was surprisingly gleeful. They told him that as a result of the speech Trumbo had written for her, De Havilland had grown increasingly suspicious that HICCASP was controlled by the Communists. When she approached Roosevelt, they had devised a plan to "smoke out" the Communists. They came up with a resolution: "We affirm our belief in free enterprise and the democratic system and repudiate Communism as desirable for the United States."

A few nights later, when the joint committee met and they read their statement, all hell broke loose again. Wagging his finger at Reagan, Lawson shouted, "This organization will never adopt a statement which endorses free enterprise and repudiates Communism! ...a two-party system is in no way necessary or even desirable for democracy!" When Reagan suggested that they let the whole membership decide by secret ballot, Lawson informed him that "the membership [wasn't] sophisticated enough to make this decision." The vote never got to the membership but was sent to HICCASP's executive committee. De Havilland was the liberals' only representative and cast the only "aye" vote for their resolution. Reagan claimed he resigned from the group that evening; the others followed soon afterward.

James Roosevelt resigned as chairman in July 1946, citing poor health. He thought the organization had lost its "character of independence." Its reputation could be restored, he now felt, only if it took a stand "in favor of improvements in our economic system within the framework of private property and private enterprise," and only if the organization stated "affirmatively their opposition to the principles of Communism." This, he insisted, could be done without having to join in "the flood of Red-baiting."[17] What Roosevelt failed to comprehend, of course, was that to the Party and its members, opposing Marxism-Leninism was in and of itself Red-baiting.

Such developments caused Arthur Schlesinger to write about the group in an article that appeared in a July 1946 issue of *Life*. A well-known and highly respected intellectual without any sympathy for Republicans or right-wingers, Schlesinger was a bona fide liberal; therefore his claim that HICCASP was a Communist front hit especially hard. With a September rally scheduled for the Hollywood Bowl, featuring pianist Arthur Rubinstein, actor Gregory Peck, Communist composer and folksinger Earl Robinson and the left-wing senator from Florida, Claude Pepper (fondly referred to by his enemies as "Red Pepper"), the board of ICCASP worried that the article might pose a problem, and publicly responded to the young historian that the organization was not under the control of any group or party and that any relationship to the Communist Party's positions (in an odd word choice) was "coincidental."[18]

But Roosevelt's resignation and Schlesinger's article were not the only problems that ICCASP faced. The national political tide was turning against them. In November 1946, the entire Democratic slate in California, including the candidate for state attorney general, future governor Edmund G. (Pat) Brown, was defeated. The liberal Jerry Voorhis, always a supporter of the Popular Front, was beaten by a returning veteran named Richard M. Nixon. Nationally, the House returned to Republican control and the political Left had good reason to be worried about the future.

The Hollywood Strikes

The collapse of the largest Hollywood Popular Front group only forced the remaining Hollywood Reds to dig in and reassert their newly found hard line. Trumbo complained to fellow-traveling California journalist Carey McWilliams about the plethora of anti-Communist books that were being published, which he said included the novels of James T. Farrell, the Soviet defector Kravchenko's best-selling *I Choose Freedom,* and a favorable biography of Leon Trotsky. Fortunately, he wrote, they had influence only "in the rare intellectual atmosphere of the East Coast," an obvious reference to the group later known as "the New York intellectuals," then grouped around the anti-Communist journal *Partisan Review.* The problem he and his comrades faced in Hollywood was a different one; that of figuring out how to use "art as a weapon for the destruction of fascism...racial bigotry or economic oppression or the drive toward war."

His answer was to treat everyone in the industry as "industrial workers" who had to be organized on a trade union basis. Those in the film trade, he told McWilliams, could not give up the task of trying to use film "for progressive purposes," because if they did, it would be tantamount to abandoning the struggle altogether, giving in to "defeatist reasoning" and handing film over to "the exclusive use of reactionaries and...conscious fascists." But he could still be proud of the many films that "went on the offensive." Trumbo cited those written by himself and other Hollywood Communists and fellow travelers, including on his list *Confessions of a Nazi Spy, Joe Smith: American, Watch on the Rhine, Sahara, The Great Dictator,* and *Action in the North Atlantic.*[19]

The working-class fantasies of Communists such as Trumbo were shared by most of the directors, actors and screenwriters who belonged to the Party. Even though they lived in a far different world from that of the rank-and-file electricians, stagehands, set and costume designers, projectionists and other workers who kept the film industry going, they always talked about extending the hand of solidarity to those they regarded as "real," genuine workers.

The opportunity to latch onto what appeared to be the real thing—a bona fide class struggle in Hollywood—finally took place in March 1945 as the war was coming to an end. Two American Federation of Labor (AFL) unions contested for the right to represent back-lot workers—the International Alliance of Theatrical Stage Employees and Moving Picture Machine Operators of the U.S. and Canada (IATSE), and a left-wing group, the Conference of Studio Unions (CSU). As a result of the latter's strike action, all production was reported paralyzed at Warner Brothers, Twentieth Century Fox and Universal Studios.[20]

On the surface, the only issue was a jurisdictional dispute. Who would represent the workforce: the AFL-affiliated IATSE, the oldest show-business union in the country; or the left-wing CSU, which was attempting to organize the crafts-dominated building trades unions? The upstart union was led by Herbert Sorrell, a pro-Communist militant later described by Ronald Reagan as "a large and muscular man with a most aggressive attitude." Sorrell's goal was to unite all non-IATSE union locals in Hollywood and to establish new locals for unorganized trades in the motion picture business. His CSU broke ranks with other unions by affiliating openly with Popular Front and Communist-led organizations, which in turn lent them support when they clashed with IATSE.

There had been earlier efforts by the CP to organize a labor movement in Hollywood. It was not until this moment, however, that the Communist organizers, led by Sorrell, were strong enough to push the issue. Communists in the Screen Writers Guild immediately pushed to endorse Sorrell and the CSU, and John Howard Lawson, the Party's leader in the film capital, began to call for all-out support for those on the CSU picket line. The guild's official position was that it should not take any such political stance, and the majority of its members argued that the strike was not their fight. Almost evenly divided between centrist liberals and Communists or fellow travelers, the guild's board voted by a narrow margin to cross the picket lines and not honor the CSU strike action.

The Screen Actors Guild (SAG) sent out a mail ballot to its eight thousand members to determine its position. At a mass meeting, representatives of both sides made their arguments.[21] When the vote was finally counted, the SAG voted 3,029 to 88 not to support the strike.

Although the Left had been outvoted, Sorrell refused to turn back. He decided to single out one studio, Warner Brothers, for mass picketing, which he hoped would break the unified resistance of all the studio chiefs to recognition of his group. The result was the "Battle of Burbank." At 7 A.M. on October 5, 1945, seven or eight hundred picketers from the CSU appeared at the studio gates and, according to eyewitness accounts, were "knifed, clubbed and gassed before police reserves restored order." By day's end, reported the *New York Times,* "about a dozen persons were injured, some by fire hoses which swept them off their feet on the glass-littered pavement, some by tear-gas bombs and some by fists or missiles." The report cited one case of a man slugged by a socket wrench welded by a CSU loyalist, and said another man was beaten up by strikers when he tried to cross the picket line. With some of his associates, Sorrell was arrested and held on $1,500 bond, although he insisted that the mass action was a "spontaneous" move by the union's rank and file, and he denied having anything to do with violations of a court injunction against picketing Warner theaters.[22]

Both sides were clearly engaging in violence, and tensions were high. Roy Brewer, head of IATSE, claimed that the Communists were responsible and that Harry Bridges, the longshoremen's union chief and Sorrell's ally, had sent down organized goons from San Francisco to provoke violence. The CSU and the political Left argued that IATSE was a mob-run union and that the mob's goons were responsible for all the violence. Evidently, the class struggle desired by the newly militant Communist Party was now taking place.

A year later, a larger and even more volatile CSU strike

erupted as Sorrell began yet another jurisdictional battle, this time over the issue of who represented workers on set construction and who handled props on sound stages. Again, Sorrell called his legions out on the picket lines, seeking a repeat of the Battle of Burbank. But now, with the Cold War a fact of American life, Sorrell's ties to the Communist Party worked against him. The only support that CSU now had came from the CP and the Communist-dominated HICCASP. On June 18, 1946, at the California AFL's state convention, eight unions demanded that Sorrell be investigated as "an important stooge and tool of the Communist Party's design for the destruction of AFL unions in Hollywood."[23]

On September 26, seven major film studios were again brought to a standstill by a strike of several thousand CSU members, including carpenters, painters and other technical workers.[24] *Time* magazine reported that strikers "scattered tacks in the path of movie stars' automobiles, threw coffee in the faces of picket-line crossers, stoned busloads of rival AF of L workers convoyed through their jeering, milling ranks."

The strike got support from the California Communist Party's labor chief, Phil Connelly, who was on the board of the state's Congress of Industrial Organizations (CIO). But many members of Communist-led unions were not as enthusiastic as their leaders; furious at another strike that meant loss of their paychecks, they rebelled. Communist attorney Ben Margolis acknowledged that the cartoonists, office workers and screen story analysts he represented all wanted to work, but Sorrell responded that they would have to cross his picket lines. According to Margolis, even Harry Bridges tried to persuade Sorrell to back down.[25]

The Screen Writers Guild officially opposed the strike, as it had the previous one, although adamant Communist members, now in a distinct minority, gave the CSU their support. Screenwriter John Bright not only backed the CSU but volunteered to drive Sorrell around, since the union boss's driver's license had been revoked. Others who had "work at home" clauses in their contracts, such as Donald Ogden Stewart, Dorothy Parker and Alan Campbell, were able to support Sorrell and avoid being disciplined. A hard-line Red, Bright was openly chastised by producer Eddie Mannix, who told him bluntly: "Your fucking union isn't supporting the strike. What obligation do you have to support it?" Knowing that he was only making a token gesture, Bright nevertheless stood fast. He was promptly fired by MGM.[26]

The Communists acknowledged afterward that this was the moment they lost control over the Hollywood labor movement. Writing about how he perceived the strike and about its significance, Ronald Reagan, still a liberal Democrat at this point, concluded that the Communists "were the cause of the labor strife, they used jurisdictional disputes as excuses for their scheme…to gain economic control of the motion picture industry in order to finance their activities and subvert the screen for their propaganda."[27] Reagan saw the CP's strategy as being in lockstep with Moscow's postwar hostility toward the United States—the citadel of capitalism.

As a leader and future president of the Screen Actors Guild, Reagan, along with fellow actor and SAG president (1946–1947) Robert Montgomery, persuaded its members to reject their original neutrality. When violence broke out during the 1946 strike, Reagan was among the actors who crossed the CSU picket lines, riding through the chaos in buses hired by Warner Brothers.

It was during this period, two nights before Reagan was to present his case before a large SAG meeting, that his friend and fellow star William Holden called to tell him about a meeting scheduled to be held at actress Ida Lupino's place. Apparently the Party had borrowed her house and invited a group of big-name stars—"a half-dozen innocents"—to hear about the labor dispute. The discussion was led by actor Sterling Hayden, a fairly new Party recruit. (Testifying later about this before HUAC, Hayden said that the Party instructed him to do what he could to secure Screen Actors Guild support for the CSU strike and to undermine the influence of Reagan and Montgomery.)[28]

Deciding in effect to crash the gathering, the two men were warmly welcomed by Lupino, but others in the crowd of about seventy-five assembled on her outdoor patio were "astonished and miffed" at their appearance. Once the meeting began, "the CSU was lauded to the skies, the IATSE was damned, and the

SAG drew faint praise…for trying to be blessed with the peace-makers." Reagan waited for the right moment, then stood up and asked for the floor, where he "confronted one of the most hostile audiences I could ever hope to address." The Screen Actors Guild, he told them, had carefully investigated the issues, and he itemized for them the conclusions he had reached and was going to present to SAG a few days later. Reagan spoke for forty minutes, managing to keep his temper "in spite of interruptions and boos and the customary name-calling." Finally, the actor John Garfield—then one of the biggest screen draws in Hollywood—turned to the crowd and asked "Why don't you listen to him? …He does have information you don't have." The group was clearly surprised, as Garfield was known to be a man of the Left and perhaps a Communist. A few moments later, Reagan saw the Communist actor Howard Da Silva take Garfield to the back of the patio, back him up against a tree and "read [him] an angry riot act, punctuated by a jabbing finger." Reagan always regretted that he and Holden didn't think to invite Garfield to join them for some beers.[29]

Sterling Hayden also let the Party down that evening. He was appointed to convince people to support the strike. Instead, he later admitted, writing of himself in the second person, he had "laid an egg…. Reagan showed up and took over and ground you into a pulp; they all kept looking to you to hold him down but he dominated the whole thing and when it was over they told you right to your face you were pretty weak and the gathering did more harm than good."[30]

The golden era of the Hollywood Communists had come to an end. They had lost influence in their own unions; their mass Popular Front organizations were losing the support of genuine liberals who had once willingly cooperated with the Reds; and they began to be viewed, even in Hollywood, as puppets of Moscow whose patriotism had been a charade.

7

Crackdown: The Case of Albert Maltz

WITH THE INFLUENCE IN HOLLYWOOD IT HAD SOUGHT SO STRENUOUSLY over the past decade now slipping from its grasp, the Communist Party turned inward and tightened its grip on the remaining loyalists. Now that hardliner William Z. Foster had replaced Earl Browder as CPUSA chief, the Party was bent on enforcing orthodoxy among its artists and writers. American Communists did not have available a vast apparatus of state repression as did Stalin in Moscow; so the cultural commissars—V. J. Jerome in New York and John Howard Lawson in Los Angeles—had to rely on bullying, public humiliation and threats of excommunication. While just an echo of the bloody measures carried out in the Soviet Union, these enforcements nevertheless kept many Party members in line.

The most dramatic example of victimization by the new hard line was that of the highly regarded novelist and screenwriter Albert Maltz. A Phi Beta Kappa graduate of Columbia University with a degree in philosophy, Maltz had done graduate work at the Yale University School of Drama and then migrated to New York to become part of the city's radical theater community. As a writer, he tried to combine left-wing politics with his art in the theater, novels and short stories. In 1938 he won the coveted O. Henry Prize for Best Short Story, and until 1941 he taught playwriting in the NYU School of Adult Education. When the war led to a drop in enrollment, Maltz accepted an offer from Paramount Pictures and moved to Hollywood; there he wrote several wartime films, including *This Gun for Hire, Destination Tokyo* and *Pride of the Marines.*

Maltz also scripted a short film on racial discrimination titled *The House I Live In.* It featured Frank Sinatra singing to neighborhood young people the plea for tolerance written by the Communist Party composer Earl Robinson and the Communist lyricist Lewis Meeropol (under the name of Lewis Allen). The song and the film were classic expressions of the wartime alliance between liberals and Communists. Maltz became one of Sinatra's heroes. After seeing *Pride of the Marines,* Sinatra wrote to him saying that he had "never been so emotionally moved by anything—whether it be a film, a book or a story." He had, in fact, been "hungrily awaiting" a vehicle in which he could address America's racial discrimination, and he was humbled to be in a project like *The House I Live In* that a "tremendous amount of Americans" would see and "be made aware of this deplorable problem." He added, in his own distinctive Sinatraese, "You've got to hit 'em right in the kisser with it and, baby, you really did."[1]

Maltz in turn was a fan of Sinatra's. He was thrilled to discover that the star had written an article against racial prejudice for the fan magazine *Modern Screen.* "This is probably the first time in the history of all these movie magazines, that they have ever carried anything like this," Maltz wrote to the singer. He thought that Sinatra's article was so good it would convince people to stop using racial epithets, and that "its importance is incalculable." Moreover, Sinatra was writing for an audience that did not read anything, except perhaps the reactionary Hearst press, which made them "part of the mass base of Fascism." Sinatra, he thought, had the potential to "make democratic ideas a popular, emotionally attractive idea for young people," as though he were organizing a "Youth for Equality" that offset Hearst's "Youth for Christ."

Sinatra's backing of Maltz was a major boost for the Communist screenwriter. Sinatra, he told the singer, would be of great help in the "really sharp struggle" against fascist elements, and he was pleased to have the pop star join him in "the main battleground" in which they would "either win or lose."[2]

Always a committed Communist, Maltz seemed to be the epitome of a Party intellectual: a man who did quality work and also maintained his membership in, and activism for, the CPUSA. Nothing could have adequately prepared him for the storm that ensued when he decided to respond to writer Isidore Schneider's request in the October 1945 issue of the *New Masses,* the Party's literary magazine, for an essay dealing with the relationship between literature and the political situation, between writing for posterity and writing for the moment.

Maltz's "What Shall We Ask of Writers?" appeared in February 1946.[3] Voicing a heretical view, Maltz argued that the problem lay in the Party's concept of "art as a weapon." That might have been useful in the 1920s or 1930s, but continuing adherence to this "shallow approach," as he called it, accounted for the Communists' disappointing artistic output, which had been "restricted, narrowed, turned away from life, sometimes made sterile." Indeed, "art as a weapon" was "not a useful guide, but a straitjacket." To write well, Maltz confessed, he had to "repudiate it and abandon it."

Then Maltz took another step into heterodoxy. Artistic achievement, he said, could not be judged by the politics of an author. Citing Friedrich Engels' statement that Balzac had taught him more about French society than any other writer, despite his royalist and antidemocratic politics, Maltz argued that "writers must be judged by their work and not by the committees they join." As a key example, he cited the work of novelist James T. Farrell, whose *Studs Lonigan* trilogy had been read and admired by a wide array of Americans. Farrell was, to his mind, "one of the outstanding writers in America." Perhaps more than anything else he wrote in his article, this one line was to cause Maltz trouble. As anyone in the political and literary scene of the 1940s knew, Farrell not only had left the orbit of the Communist Party but had become a follower of the exiled and later assassinated Leon Trotsky, joining the Socialist Workers Party, the tiny Trotskyist party in the United States.

Ending his piece by referring to an unnamed "historian"— it was John Howard Lawson—who was having to revise what he had written as a result of the Duclos article published in *Cahiers du Communisme* and the change in party line that it embodied, Maltz asked: "What type of history was this in the first place?"

Had he written this essay during the war, Albert Maltz would have been universally praised by his comrades. But clearly he was not yet attuned to the new era of confrontation.[4] Thus, the cultural commissars who worked out of the Party's main offices in New York City interpreted the article as an act of treason and as a shot across the bow of those in the Hollywood CP who were regarded as New York's enforcers, particularly John Howard Lawson.

While many Party members looked up to Lawson, a good portion of his fellow screenwriters viewed him privately as a compromised man who submitted himself regularly to Party discipline and expected others to do likewise. Richard Collins explained later that when he read Maltz's piece, he interpreted it as a carefully constructed attack on Lawson. Regarding Lawson's attempt to write a history of the United States to which Maltz had obliquely referred, Collins recalled that "no sooner would Lawson get a draft done than some new development in Communist Party policy would occur and he would have to rewrite a part of it, or several chapters...in order to make it conform to the new policy."[5]

Maltz himself had privately criticized Lawson in 1940 when the latter forbade Budd Schulberg to write his proposed novel about Sammy Glick unless it was approved in advance by the Party. Schulberg went to Maltz for help and support. While Maltz sympathized with Schulberg's plight, he had told the young author that he should not buck the Party apparatus.[6]

Maltz's next tiff with Lawson had concerned the demands Lawson had made on Communist director Edward Dmytryk and producer Adrian Scott, who were working on *Cornered,* a film about a Canadian fighter pilot who, after leaving the service, searches for the hideout of an SS officer who has murdered his French bride. Finding him in Argentina, he beats him to death. Scott turned down the first writer's draft of a screenplay and hired the Communist Party writer John Wexley, whom Dmytryk called "a man of extreme leftist leanings." Wexley too turned in a poor and unusable script. The trouble, according to Dmytryk, was that Wexley had "engaged in agitprop," writing "long speeches loaded with thinly disguised Communist propaganda." Dmytryk insisted that someone else be brought in, and the final version was the work of a nonpolitical writer named John Paxton.

When the film was in postproduction, Scott and Dmytryk got a call from Lawson, who said that Wexley had asked him to get in touch with them. They were expecting a simple complaint about screen credit. Instead, they were astonished to be confronted by a committee made up of Lawson, Wexley, Paul Trivers and Richard Collins, "all Communists…who had been picked to hear Wexley's complaint." It was not about screen credit, but about the film's content. Wexley charged that they had emasculated his work, that the film was now "pro- rather than anti-fascist." At yet another meeting, Lawson brought his trio of Party members to demand that Wexley's changes be inserted. But Dmytryk and Scott brought along Maltz, who strongly defended their actions. Maltz realized that what was at stake was basically a question of "the Party's control of its artists." At a lunch meeting, Lawson was "cold, unpleasant and unsatisfactory." He made it clear that for the Party, no such thing as compromise existed. "For the time being," he roared at them, "consider yourselves out of the Party. When you decide that you can accept Party discipline, we'll explore the situation further."[7] Dmytryk and Scott were in effect temporarily expelled; Maltz, however, stepped back into line when confronted by Lawson's tempestuous outburst.

Given his run-ins with Lawson and the cultural commissars and his ultimate submission to their dictates, it is surprising that Maltz ever submitted his essay to the *New Masses*. Perhaps he had convinced himself that things had changed during the war years, and that the day of the hardliners like Lawson and V. J. Jerome had ended. If so, he was soon to be disabused—faced with an assault that surpassed anything he had previously experienced in Communist Party life.

First came a salvo from the Communist writer and self-proclaimed arbiter of theory Mike Gold. Writing in the *Daily Worker*, he declared Maltz guilty of "artistic moralizing." While the best American writers got their ideas and inspiration from Marxism, Gold claimed, Maltz went beyond mere disagreement with this proposition. In singling out Farrell for praise, he had made common cause with "a vicious, voluble Trotskyite…a colleague of Eastman, Eugene Lyons and similar rats" who spread lies and slander on behalf of "war on the Soviet Union." Moreover, Maltz had passed off Farrell's Trotskyism as "a mere peccadillo." By that standard, much better writers—"Nazi rats like Ezra Pound"— should also be "treated respectfully and even forgiven for their horrible politics because they are 'artists.'" Maltz, he concluded, had let the "phony atmosphere of Hollywood…poison him." And he was writing his nonsense just when "the capitalists are plotting…to establish an American fascism as a prelude to American conquest of the world."[8]

Communist screenwriter Alvah Bessie, who had himself bent to Lawson's will and censored his own work (he had wanted to write an honest account of his own experiences in the Spanish Civil War), now piled on, blasting Maltz as "actually anti-Marxist." Indeed, Maltz had inexcusably defended "practically every renegade writer of recent years." He was so blind that he failed to see the need for "*Party* artists…rooted in the working class who realize the truth of Lenin's assertion" that absolute freedom is a "bourgeois or anarchist phrase."[9]

The popular novelist Howard Fast, who alone among the CP literati had written bestseller after bestseller, accused Maltz of favoring the "ideology of liquidation." As Fast saw it, Maltz was calling for "separation from the Communist movement" and was advocating "retreat," a course that could only lead to "artistic death and personal degradation."[10]

As expected, John Howard Lawson also took Maltz to task for expressing his heretical views at a "time of decisive struggle" when the "forces of imperialism" were threatening all the "democratic victories achieved in the Second World War." It was no accident, he suggested, using the jargon of Party members, that Maltz said not one word "about the class struggle."

There would be other attacks in print. But undoubtedly what hurt Maltz the most was the vest-pocket inquisition staged by the Hollywood Party at the home of actor Morris Carnovsky. Writer Leopold Atlas (a Communist screenwriter who later recanted and testified before HUAC as a friendly witness) recalled the arrival of an "intellectual goon squad" from New York City to condemn Maltz—a group that included Mike Gold, V. J. Jerome, Howard Fast, *New Masses* editor and writer Samuel Sillen, along with various hard-line members of the Los Angeles Communist Party.

The proceedings began with Maltz trying to explain what led him to write his article. "Almost instantly," Atlas recalled, "all sorts of howls went up in protest." Only Atlas and Leonardo Bercovici made "small attempts" to support him, but they were quickly shouted down. Alvah Bessie was filled with "bitter vituperation and venom" as he rose up to denounce Maltz. Then came writer Herbert Biberman, his "every accent dripping with hatred." Ironically, all three of those colleagues of Maltz would stand with him a few years later as members of the supposedly united and intransigent Hollywood Ten.

Atlas found the meeting appalling because, as he later told HUAC, Maltz was "a person of some literary stature and...a man of considerable personal integrity" who deserved "some measure of understanding" and consideration. But instead, Maltz was worked over "with every verbal fang and claw at their command; every ax and bludgeon."

After the first round of attacks was over, the struggle session was postponed until a week later. At the next meeting, the Party "completely broke" Maltz. The attacks made him "crawl and recant" as his former "closest friends...treat[ed] him so shamefully, so uncharitably, so wolfishly." As a result of this experience, Atlas realized that he had to leave the Party's ranks, although in Hollywood, to leave meant "professional and economic suicide."[11]

Why didn't Albert Maltz stand up for himself? He later told Victor Navasky that it was his "desire not to be made to become a renegade—my desire not to be expelled from the Party." Maltz considered Party membership to be an "honor" and staying in the Party was a "matter of my personal integrity." Therefore, wanting to remain a Communist, he told himself, "I must be wrong."[12]

Maltz's retrospective apologia for why he did not stand up to defend a moderate, commonsense article about the role of the writer offers a profound insight into the hold the CP had on the Hollywood screenwriters, directors and actors. Their identity lay with the Party and with Communism, not with their careers or their creative work. To break with the Party was to suffer a symbolic death—to be banished from the intellectual family that gave nourishment, and indeed, from history itself.

Letters of Support

The irony was that despite his abject self-abasement, Maltz actually had some support within Party intellectual circles that he might have called upon if he had chosen to make a stand for intellectual freedom. His correspondence reveals that even within the wintry confines of the Party, his article had resonated with those who thought of themselves as writers or artists as well as Communists.

Even the dogmatic Albert E. Kahn, a leading Party writer and later publisher—and a man shown by the Venona decrypts to have been on the KGB payroll—wrote to Maltz saying that his article had "stirred up quite a little tempest," and adding that although he might have formulated his ideas more carefully, "there was much in the article with which I am in hearty agreement." Moreover, Kahn told Maltz that he had "done a real service," since the CP approach to cultural questions was "desperately in need of a thorough reevaluation."[13]

The scholar and psychologist Bernhard J. Stern, an editor of the Party magazine *Science and Society,* wrote to let Maltz know he was hardly "indifferent to the outrageous developments in relation to your article." He was personally "burned up" by Mike Gold's attack, and he added that the "sentiment of many people is on your side." The problem, he acknowledged, was that anyone who supported Maltz would promptly be labeled a "revisionist."[14]

Millard Lampell, a writer and member of the Almanac Singers, wrote to Maltz praising him for raising "issues that damn well needed to be raised." Lampell said that he, Norman Rosten, Arthur Miller and Walter Bernstein were "gathering for informal discussions" of the article, planning to provide "additional comment" for the *New Masses.* "When you put the match to the fuse," he wrote, "the light took."[15]

Yet even as he was receiving this support, Maltz was doing all he could to approach top CP leaders directly in order to placate them. He appealed to the legendary ex-Wobbly and then CP leader Elizabeth Gurley Flynn, but got nowhere.[16] He even sent an unctuous letter to Mike Gold, trying to assure his accuser that he had always been identified "by desire and by act with the labor movement" and had worked with those struggling against "reaction and Fascism, for peace, for a decent, rich future for humanity"—in other words, with the Party and its program.[17] To *New Masses* editor Isidore Schneider, whose request for a discussion on the relation between the arts and politics had started the whole mess, Maltz wrote that he had never envisioned that such a "fury of rage and misinterpretation" would result from his article, especially since he had shown it in advance to twenty-five Party comrades in Hollywood, all of whom had given it their "warm approval." Speaking with bitter irony, he said it was his "misfortune not to have several of [these] readers tell me that I was ripping the heart out of Marxism." Groveling to Schneider, he now proposed writing a second article, this one affirming Marxism as "the lodestone of writers today."[18]

It even occurred to some of Maltz's supporters that perhaps their best path would be to leave the Party, owning up to the fact that it was essentially totalitarian. Shepard Traube, a New York stage director who had directed the Broadway hit *Angel Street* in 1940, and had then gone to Hollywood, where he directed *Street of Memories,* was furious after he read the diatribes by Howard Fast and *New Masses* editor Joe North and the "tripe" by Mike Gold. Traube let Maltz know that not all Party writers were as "stupid...as the lads" who attacked him. Fast, in particular, he held to be "contemptible": more of a "pamphleteer" than a novelist, he was the writer who could "most profit from your piece"—that is, benefit by following Maltz's advice.

Like Maltz, Traube knew that "men with bad politics can be good writers" and that men with good politics had to "perfect themselves as writers." His first instinct he admitted, was "fuck it, let's quit these fools." But Traube said he would try to avoid such defeatism; he would stay on to help improve the Communist movement and "win the middle class in America to the socialist program." That goal would be subverted by the "sectarian mood" taking over the Party, and he feared that more "decent people, honest, open-minded non-Party people" would desert as they became "alienated by the control of Communist blocs within what have been united front organizations."[19]

That of course is precisely what happened in HICCASP and the other front groups. The only ones actually able to say "fuck you" were independent non-Party people like Ernest Hemingway. When Mike Gold blasted Hemingway for painting a nasty portrait of the French Communist leader André Marty in *For Whom the Bell Tolls*, Hemingway responded: "Tell Mike Gold that Ernest Hemingway says he should go fuck himself."[20]

In all, the archive of letters that Maltz received offers an accurate, detailed and complex portrait of intellectual and cultural life in the postwar Communist movement. Almost all his correspondents endorsed his article and supported his analysis. Sidney Elliot Cohen, a partner in Louis B. Boudin's famous law firm, said that at a party he attended of twenty people, "all of whom were either Communists or fellow-travellers," everyone supported Maltz and found the attacks on him both "unwarranted" and "extremely offensive."[21] Yet all of them, and Maltz himself, found it necessary to capitulate entirely to those they privately considered Neanderthals and complete fools.

Finally, Maltz received a conciliatory letter written by one of his fiercest accusers, the *New Masses* editor Joe North. It was meant as a signal to Maltz that there was a way out that would allow him to remain a member in good standing of the Communist Party. It had been a mistake to publish his piece as they did and then attack him, North conceded. The *New Masses* editors should have asked him to reconsider his arguments and submit a different article; it was their fault that they hadn't indicated to him how he was approaching literature "from a bourgeois-liberalistic slant." Moreover, North confessed, the prevalence of the editors' own Browderite "revisionism" had led them to make such a mistake. Therefore he hoped that Maltz would now write a piece that "would recognize the errors involved."[22]

Maltz took the bait. While his defenders were waiting to see the outcome of the Party's campaign against him, he wrote a *mea culpa*. For those who hoped that he would stand his ground, the second article cut the ground out from under them. He began by acknowledging that many had thought his article would result in "the paralysis and liquidation of left-wing culture." For this and other reasons, he admitted that he now had second thoughts about the piece. Telling readers that he had received letters protesting the attacks on him, Maltz now asked his defenders to reconsider their response, just as he had: "[M]y critics were entirely correct in insisting that certain fundamental ideas in my article would...result in the *dissolution of the left-wing cultural movement*." (Italics added.)[23]

Continuing, Maltz wrote that he had moved from "half-truths to total error." The Party hacks, in other words, were right to have condemned him. He reiterated that "from the left-wing cultural movement in America...has come the only major, healthy impetus to an honest literature and art." Any errors it made were "small" compared with its major contributions. In short, he had "presented a distorted view of the facts, history and contribution of the left-wing culture to American life."

Apologizing for what he now admitted was an "unprincipled" attack on the Left, Maltz claimed he would no longer entertain any wrong ideas. He had, he realized, written an article that was "the result of a one-sided nondialectical approach." Trying only to criticize a "mechanical" connection between art and politics, he had actually severed the organic tie between the two. He now understood that fascists, and by implication Trotskyists, could not "produce good art"; this could only come from "writers who love the people." Fascism had produced not one work of art in twelve years, he noted, and when a writer such as Celine turned pro-fascist, he condemned himself to "the artistic sterility of the Fascist," just as the Americans John Dos Passos and James T. Farrell had done. Having a few weeks earlier praised Farrell, he now said that he had characterized him wrongly owing to his "lax" thinking, a result of falsely separating art from politics.

For the Communist Party leaders in Hollywood, Maltz's self-abasing apologia—his retreat into Party lingo and groupthink—was still not sufficient. A public recantation was needed. That took place a day after publication of Maltz's piece in the *Daily Worker,* at a meeting in Hollywood advertised as "Art: Weapon of the People." Chaired by Party screenwriter Waldo Salt, the panel included John Howard Lawson, Sam Sillen, Dalton Trumbo and Carlton Moss, an African-American writer and documentary filmmaker. Maltz launched into his ritual humiliation by restating on stage what he had just committed to print.

Maltz could finally breathe a sigh of relief. At last he had satisfied his critics. Samuel Sillen wrote to praise his recantation: All to whom he had spoken had been "deeply impressed by the dignity, honesty and earnestness of your self-criticism." Now they could join together to "create a reinvigorated literary left." And Sillen informed him that Party chairman William Z. Foster had called Maltz's recantation "a milestone in the history of the organization," and that Foster had asked him to "communicate his warm regards and approval of the personal and political stature you revealed."[24]

Even those who previously had praised Maltz now altered their tune, letting him know that they too approved his confession. Bernhard J. Stern, who had written to give Maltz support against the hardliners, now told him: "You displayed rare courage as an intellectual in admitting your errors without acrimony, and your loyalty, integrity and devotion to the movement was manifested in a genuinely sterling fashion."

If Maltz had retreated into dignified silence after humiliating himself, his story would simply have trailed off into melancholy. But a few years after his own inquisition, he enthusiastically joined in an attack on a colleague who was facing what he himself had endured. This time, the victim was Robert Rossen, who had just written, produced and directed what became the Academy Award winner for Best Picture of 1949, the film adaptation of Robert Penn Warren's novel *All the King's Men.* The film was a big financial success, and Rossen received the

Oscars for Best Director, Best Screenplay and Best Producer.

The film centered on the life of a charismatic populist southern politician, Willie Stark (played by Broderick Crawford), who was obviously modeled on Governor Huey Long of Louisiana. It shows Stark trying to pose as a man of the people while maneuvering and stealing his way into the centers of power. Corrupt to the core, Stark swears to serve the poor and the masses but is motivated only by ego and a consuming thirst for total power. A poor man's lawyer at the film's beginning, he has become a corrupt dictator by the end.

While contemporary viewers saw it as a parable on southern politics and the inherent native fascist danger to the New Deal posed by FDR's populist opponent, the Communist Party leadership feared that viewers would interpret the story as a parable not about Huey Long, but about Joseph Stalin. Soon after the film opened, Rossen was attacked by Party commissar John Howard Lawson.

The assault on Rossen was held, with eerie symbolism, in the Hollywood home of Albert Maltz. Who better to lead the attack on a Party screenwriter than one who had tried to protest, had recanted and been cut down to size? Maltz, Lawson, Herbert Biberman and Alvah Bessie led the tirade against Rossen, during which, as Ed Dmytryk recalled, "Bob's comrades were...giving him hell for dramatizing how power corrupts." At first Dmytryk could not follow why they were so furious at Rossen, and then he understood: "Rossen was really getting hell for exposing the evils of dictatorship, the rock on which the Communist Party was founded." What particularly worried them was that the film might be seen as an exposure "of the evils of one-man rule"—in other words, of Stalinism.

Rossen, however, responded far differently than Albert Maltz. A few minutes of being excoriated by his comrades was enough. Standing up and glaring, he shocked the entire room, especially Maltz, when he said "Stick the whole Party up your ass!" and then stormed out of the house—and out of the Communist Party for good.[25] The first time Rossen testified before HUAC (in 1951, during its Hollywood investigations), he invoked the Fifth Amendment: although he told the committee he had given up Communism, he did not testify about anyone else. Called back again in 1953, at a time when the Cold War was in its peak and just after the Korean War, Rossen named fifty people whom he had known to be Communists. The Party was to find that the bitter fruit of reading people out of its ranks was disillusionment and eventual vengeance.

8

HUAC Goes to Hollywood

BY 1947, THE COMMUNISTS' POSITION IN HOLLYWOOD WAS PRECARI-
ous. Following Moscow's line, Party members portrayed the
United States as being on the verge of a fascist takeover master-
minded by Harry Truman, a charge that frayed the damaged
alliance with liberals even more. When the studios named Eric
Johnston, a successful Seattle businessman and former president
of the United States Chamber of Commerce, as their spokesman
and chief lobbyist in Washington, he immediately announced
that Hollywood would support the Truman administration's policy of "worldwide countering of Soviet expansion."[1] Then, on top
of everything else, the House Committee on Un-American Activities announced that it was coming to town.

Originally created as a temporary committee of Congress,
HUAC had made its mark in the 1930s under the chairmanship
of Martin Dies, a Republican stalwart and enemy of FDR's New
Deal. On January 3, 1945, John E. Rankin, a representative from
Mississippi, the most segregated state in the Union, rose from his
seat and put forth an amendment to the House rules making the
Committee on Un-American Activities a standing committee of
the House. After the 1946 Republican congressional victory,
chairmanship of the new committee passed to the Republican
representative from New Jersey, J. Parnell Thomas, a rock-ribbed
conservative who hoped he would be able to use his post to continue the old Republican battle against the New Deal remnants
and their left-wing supporters.

HUAC's first act in Hollywood was a visit to film composer

and German émigré Hanns Eisler. The committee had already investigated his brother, Gerhart, a top Comintern agent assigned to the American Communist Party in the 1930s who had virtual power over its policies and leadership. The American public sat riveted as they read about his sister, Ruth Fischer, who testified that Gerhart was "the perfect terrorist type" and was responsible for the deaths of some of his German friends, as well as his onetime protector in Moscow, Nikolai Bukharin. Convicted of falsifying an exit visa and later of contempt of Congress, Eisler eventually avoided arrest and imprisonment by stowing away on a Polish freighter docked in New York, and then, after his arrival in Poland, moving on to East Germany.

Gerhart's brother, Hanns, was another story. Part of the émigré German film community in Hollywood and a successful composer of film scores, he was, according to HUAC's chief investigator Robert Stripling, a "stout, stumpy, bald, bespectacled man," living "with more ostentation" than his apparatchik brother, who inhabited a $35-a-month apartment in Sunnyside, Queens. "The day I handed Hanns his subpoena," Stripling recalled, "he was sunning himself in a deck chair on the sand in front of his Malibu Beach, Calif., home." Looking at Stripling, Eisler snarled: "I've been expecting you. Now get out of here."[2]

Eisler was an easy target. Although not involved with the international Communist movement at his brother's level, he had never hidden his commitment to the Soviet Union. He had worked in Moscow for Munzenberg's Mezhrabpom film studio in the 1930s, and, as Stripling pointed out, had written one of the most famous Communist marching songs:

> We're coming with Lenin for Bolshevik work
> From London, Havana,
> Berlin and New York.
> ....
> To battle march onward,
> March on world stormers
> Eyes sharp on your guns.
> ....
> Advance Proletarians
> To conquer the world.[3]

The *Daily Worker* announced Eisler's arrival in America by urging an "outstanding reception for this courageous revolutionary musician and composer."

When Eisler appeared before HUAC on September 24, 1947, the committee had assembled a giant file of his Communist activity over the years, as well as the record of prominent American liberals who welcomed him to America and claimed that he was merely a musician with "liberal views."

Testifying in a short executive session, Eisler was evasive and nonresponsive. As a result, HUAC members decided that he was only the tip of the iceberg. They informed Eric Johnston, the studio lobbyist, that they had decided to look at Communism throughout the film industry and received a promise of cooperation. Stripling, however, heard that the studio chiefs had met privately and vowed not to cooperate. He asked Johnston to give him the minutes of the secret meeting, but Johnston refused.[4]

Content to use the services of talented Red screenwriters, the studio heads would have liked nothing more than to keep their employment out of the public eye. But a small group of industry conservatives and anti-Communist liberals were upset with the ample Communist presence and were determined to do something about it. Their guiding light was director Sam Wood, who became HUAC's leading ally in the film capital.

Long before the arrival of HUAC, Woods' Motion Picture Alliance for the Preservation of American Ideals had warned about the threat of Communists in the industry; but the studio chiefs had not taken the matter seriously. Screenwriter Jack Moffitt once wrote in the *Hollywood Reporter* that Ring Lardner Jr., Budd Schulberg and Maurice Rapf controlled the Communist Party in Hollywood. Sam Goldwyn read the article and laughed, saying, "if they're the ones who are running it, we've got nothing to worry about."[5] When the Motion Picture Alliance presented the studio chiefs with their evidence of Communist infiltration of the industry, again using Rapf as an example, Goldwyn again dismissed them: "If this snot-nosed baby is the Red boss in Hollywood, gentlemen, we've got nothing to fear. Let's go home."[6]

Producers might joke, but the relationship of the Reds to

the studio bosses was symbiotic. The studios got the benefit of their talent, while the moguls let the Reds hold their CP meetings as long as they turned out good scripts. Decades later, Ring Lardner Jr. put it this way:

> Nowhere in the world, except possibly the Kremlin, had there been a group of Communists with a higher standard of living or greater community acceptance than the writers who belonged to the Party in Hollywood. One of the unwritten rules of membership, however, had been a polite understanding with our employers that we wouldn't advertise it. Now my colleagues and I—soon to be known as "The Hollywood Ten"—were a hot story, and the studio bosses could no longer engage in what today might be called a policy of "Don't ask, don't tell."[7]

On May 8 and 9, 1947, HUAC members J. Parnell Thomas, John S. Wood, John McDowell and Robert Stripling set up shop at Hollywood's Biltmore Hotel, where they interviewed fourteen friendly witnesses about Communist infiltration of the film industry. Unlike Martin Dies' foray into Hollywood almost a decade earlier, this investigation took place in a climate of suspicion about Stalinism and the emerging Cold War. The committee wisely began with "friendly" stars who favored their investigation. Actor Robert Taylor, one of Hollywood's biggest box office draws and married to leading actress Barbara Stanwyck, was first up. Ironically, he had played a starring role in the notorious pro-Soviet film *Song of Russia*, which he testified under oath he was forced to do by Lowell Mellett, the wartime coordinator of motion pictures for the U.S. government and an assistant to President Roosevelt. Taylor said that Mellett, at a conference with Louis B. Mayer, had delivered an "ultimatum" demanding that he perform in the picture, and that Mellett had prevented him from joining the Navy in 1943 unless he agreed to star in the film. (Mellett replied that the charge was "too silly to deny.")[8]

The next witness was Leila Rogers, the mother of actress and dancer Ginger Rogers, who identified writers Dalton Trumbo and Clifford Odets as Communists. Stripling told the press that she specifically cited the film *Tender Comrades,* written by Dalton Trumbo, in which her daughter refused to speak lines in the script such as "Share and share alike—that's democracy."[9] Rogers dropped the story in her future testimony when it was pointed out to her that the line was not exactly a smoking gun proving subversive content.

The next day, Adolphe Menjou, a dapper character actor who had assiduously studied Communist doctrine, testified that Hollywood was "one of the main centers of Communist activity in America" and was targeted because movies were "our greatest medium of propaganda." Following him was Jack Warner, the first studio chief to break ranks with his colleagues and cooperate with HUAC. Outraged by the 1945 and 1946 strikes backed by the Communists, Warner, whose studio had the most left-wing reputation in the industry and had produced *Mission to Moscow,* wanted to cover himself. He gave the names of writers he knew to be Communists, such as Odets, and testified that he had dismissed them, although he actually had not.

"We now have hundreds of names, prominent names," J. Parnell Thomas told the press after the first session of the committee, and expressed his hope that the industry would "clean house if it will have the will to do so."[10]

The threat was clear: If Hollywood did not act against the Communists, then the committee would take an even closer look. The industry responded by condemning the Communists but denying that they were allowed to function freely. "Undoubtedly" there were Communists in Hollywood, Eric Johnston told the committee. "But we neither shield nor defend them," and "want to see them exposed." As for propaganda, Johnston argued that any attempts made by the Reds to inject it into films had "failed miserably," and that the studios would "never permit them to succeed," since "we abhor and detest communism."[11]

But HUAC no longer trusted the studios' word. The committee's chief investigator, Robert Stripling, saw their task as exposing attempts to make Hollywood the center of a plot to "communize the country." The committee's focus in the May hearings was mainly on left-wing screenwriters and their efforts to influence the Screen Writers Guild and the content of films. According to Stripling, the committee believed that the studio heads had not made any real effort to remove Communists from the industry, but rather had permitted them "to gain influence and power" and successfully inject propaganda into films.[12]

The moguls, who initially had felt confident that they could ward off the investigation, now found themselves under attack both for the content of the films they produced and for the Communists they hired to work on them. They were also aware that many of the HUAC members were virulently anti-Semitic, and they realized, as historian Neal Gabler writes, that the "tautology of Jew and Communist would ultimately destroy not only the Hollywood Reds but the executives themselves."[13] (This was precisely what Harry Warner had prophesied back in 1934, when he warned Maurice Rapf and Budd Schulberg that if they remained Communists they would "bring anti-Semitism down on the heads of all the movie people.")[14]

The moguls were also worried that their close relationship with FDR during the war years would now backfire, as a new Republican majority moved to take revenge. They knew that J. Parnell Thomas had once testified before the Dies Committee and argued that the New Deal was either pro-Communist or playing into the CP's hands. Despite their fears, however, their first response was to hold firm and hope that the turbulence would pass.

In June, Eric Johnston put forth his own proposal to the studio heads. First, they should insist upon an open investigation by the committee. Second, they should not employ any suspected Communists in jobs where they could influence film content. Third, they should hire James F. Byrnes, President Truman's former secretary of state, to represent them before HUAC. The chiefs agreed to numbers one and three, but stood firm on not allowing any committee to dictate whom they could hire.

The moguls were accustomed to controlling their own kingdoms, as RKO executive Dore Schary revealed: "The men who had fashioned the studios—Mayer, the Warners, Cohn, Laemmle, Zanuck—were *padrones* with passionate pride of possession. Each stage, light bulb, chair, prop was theirs to own and cherish. Contract players, writers, directors, producers were members of the household staff to be pampered when the service was superb, tolerated if it was fair, and penalized or discharged if found incompetent, rebellious, or insubordinate."[15]

These *padrones* were not about to allow any congressional committee to challenge that power

But HUAC kept turning up the pressure. Committee member H. A. Smith informed MGM vice president Eddie Mannix that he would be subpoenaed to appear in Washington if MGM did not fire Communist screenwriter Lester Cole immediately. One week before Cole was due to testify before HUAC, studio head Louis B. Mayer called him into his office and told him, "You and Trumbo are a coupla the best writers we got.... I don't want to lose you." Cole responded that he had the law on his side. "I don't give a shit about the law," Mayer retorted. "It's them goddam commies that you're tied up with. Break with them. Stick with us. With me.... Dough means nothing. We'll tear up the contract, double your salary.... Just make the break." Cole, according to his account, politely declined Mayer's offer and thanked him. "You're nuts!" the studio chief yelled. "Goddam crazy commie! Get out !"[16]

J. Parnell Thomas announced that he would hold the Hollywood hearings in Washington in the fall. Forty-three subpoenas were issued, twenty-four of which were the so-called "friendlies," a list that included many of those who had testified at the earlier closed sessions. Nineteen on the list were uncooperative left-wingers, the "unfriendlies," who had previously been listed by the anti-Communist Motion Picture Alliance: Herbert Biberman, Lewis Milestone, Robert Rossen, Edward Dmytryk, Irving Pichel, Larry Parks, Alvah Bessie, Bertolt Brecht, Lester Cole, Richard Collins, Gordon Kahn, Howard Koch, Ring Lardner Jr., John Howard Lawson, Albert Maltz, Samuel Ornitz, Waldo Salt, Dalton Trumbo and Adrian Scott.

These subpoenaed unfriendly witnesses, "the Nineteen," now had to formulate a strategy. They had one thing in common. Virtually all of them were either members of the Communist Party, fellow travelers of the Party, or self-proclaimed "progressives" who saw the Party as the vanguard of the political Left. Any strategy they devised had to fit in with the CP's current policies, which included not revealing their membership in the Communist Party, even though it was not illegal.

Their defense was dictated by their lawyers' affiliations. They were the Communist Party lawyers Ben Margolis, Martin

Popper and Charles Katz; the former attorney general of California, Robert Kenny; and a noted establishment counsel, Bartley Crum.

The presence of the last two non-Communists was meant to show that the team was independent. In fact, however, Robert Kenny was the quintessential fellow traveler. (Dorothy Healey, who in those years was the Party's Los Angeles chairman, recalled that Kenny was "always willing to work with Communists around issues of common concern" and never hid his willingness to do so.)[17]

Bartley Crum, a nominal Catholic and registered Republican, was a firm believer in civil liberties and a naïve advocate of the Popular Front. Perhaps the most accurate description of his politics comes from his daughter, who wrote that "he was a Republican corporation lawyer with a reputation for espousing radical causes."[18] (He would later become a founding member of one of the last front groups, the Progressive Citizens of America, an alliance of left-wing liberals and Communists who tried to rally the public in support of a 1948 presidential bid by Henry A. Wallace.) In 1946, President Truman had appointed Crum to the international commission called the Anglo-American Committee of Inquiry into Palestine. He became an advocate for the creation of a Jewish state and upon his return from Palestine wrote his best-known book, *Behind the Silken Curtain*.

Adrian Scott had just finished reading this book and suggested to Eddie Dmytryk that they hire Crum to represent them before the House committee. Crum agreed. They told him that they had once belonged to the Party and had left it. But when they tried to gain the support of Dore Schary, who had them under contract at RKO, they told a different story. At a meeting with Schary after he had agreed to appear before the committee as a "friendly" witness, Scott and Dmytryk assured him that "they had never been members of the Communist Party." A few days later, Scott and Dmytryk asked Schary to meet with Charles Katz, another lawyer working for the "unfriendlies," whom Schary correctly believed to be "an active supporter of the Communist Party." Katz wanted to know what he would be saying to HUAC. Schary answered that he would defend those called, criticize

HUAC, and argue that there had been no Communist propaganda inserted into any of their films. After much prodding, however, Schary drew away, fearing that Katz and the Party were "attempting to use" him.[19]

Returning from San Francisco with Crum's agreement to represent them, Scott and Dmytryk joined the other subpoenaed men at a meeting held at the home of actor Edward G. Robinson. In addition to Crum, the lawyers present included Ben Margolis, Charles Katz, Martin Popper and Robert Kenny.

Initially, the group agreed to work together and share all costs, which included newspaper ads, transportation to and lodging in Washington, D.C., plus expenses and fees of the legal representatives. At the first meeting, they made what Dmytryk later called a "disastrous mistake," agreeing that "all decisions would be affirmed unanimously." Dmytryk and Scott would not have concurred had the proposal come from Party members like Lawson or Cole, but the suggestion was made by actor Larry Parks, who was not known as a Communist. Parks showed up at the meeting acting "skittish" and reluctant to cooperate with the others. When he stood up and made the proposal, all present wanted to ease his apprehensions, so they voted for his resolution. Years later, Parks told Dmytryk that he had been urged to advance the resolution by Dalton Trumbo at a private meeting, and that Lawson and Margolis had come up with the strategy.[20]

The group considered its options. They could take the Fifth, but then it would be assumed they had something to hide. Crum suggested that "everybody simply tell the truth," because if one was open about his politics and beliefs, he could not be accused of conspiracy or subversion. He was backed by Alvah Bessie, a hard-line Red who was proud of his membership in the Party. But Crum was argued down by Margolis, by the other Party lawyers, and by Trumbo and Lardner, who believed that answering any of HUAC's questions would imply that the committee had legitimacy.[21] They finally agreed on a set of goals in fashioning a defense: not losing their livelihood by being blacklisted, not going to jail, not discussing their political beliefs, and not giving the committee any names.

They decided that their best defense was to invoke the First

Amendment and claim that HUAC was violating their freedom of speech by inquiring into their political affiliations. Their attorneys said there was a chance they would be cited for contempt of Congress and sentenced to a prison, and would have to wage a lengthy political and court battle to avoid serving time and paying heavy fines. But they were optimistic that they would win before a liberal Supreme Court.[22]

Robert Kenny then came up with an idea that proved to be ruinous. Ring Lardner recalled that Kenny told them: "I want you not to refuse to answer a question but say you're trying to answer it in your own way." Lardner thought this made them appear "weasely and abrasive in the eyes of some liberals who supported our position but not our way of expressing it." It would have been better to make a "simple and straightforward refusal" that would have been "more dignified and effective."[23]

During their five-day train ride from Hollywood to Washington, D.C., Crum, Kenny and Margolis worked with the witnesses on their statements and drilled them on what to expect when they testified. Crum urged the Nineteen to be "dignified," his daughter recalled, but Margolis, the CP lawyer, "exhorted the men to 'stick it to 'em'."[24] Many of their statements reflected the Party's current worldview: that American fascism was imminent and that war between the United States and the Soviet Union was inevitable. To the hard-line Party members among the Nineteen, refusing to cooperate with HUAC was simply "fighting another form of fascism."[25]

Appearing before the committee and raising a ruckus with fierce denunciations and loud grandstanding was something Party stalwarts like John Howard Lawson and Herbert Biberman looked forward to. Both men were ready to strike a heroic pose, believing that HUAC was no more valid in America than the Ku Klux Klan.

In Washington, Dmytryk and Scott tried to lobby members of Congress. When even a sympathetic liberal such as New York's Emmanuel Cellar, then chairman of the House Judiciary Committee, responded negatively, they again discussed the possibility of testifying about their past membership in the Party while denying any present involvement. Dmytryk and Scott told Bartley

Crum about this idea and found him to be enthusiastic and supportive. But when Crum raised the issue with the other lawyers and the rest of the Nineteen, they reminded him that they had all taken a "pledge of unanimity"[26]

Dmytryk learned by accident that the Party members among their group were meeting separately. He happened to be standing with Scott near the main conference room at their lawyers' hotel when they heard familiar voices. After two more similar episodes, Dmytryk realized that these were meetings for Party members only, at which those who had left its ranks were not welcome. On that particular day he overheard that Howard Koch had asked why he should risk his own freedom on behalf of Party members when he was not one. He wanted to testify openly and honestly, and the Party group was concerned that Koch's feelings might sway Scott and Dmytryk, so they were kept segregated. And just in case Koch wavered, his girlfriend was enlisted to put pressure on him, threatening to break off their relationship if he deserted the Nineteen.

The Party group met daily, and all major decisions—both procedural and positional—were made by the Party "fraction" among the Nineteen. Any concerns about the decisions raised by the non-Communist Crum were dismissed, as the weight of the four Party lawyers and fellow traveler Robert Kenny left him and his two clients helpless.

The subpoenas issued to the Nineteen caused an uproar in Hollywood even before they were delivered. Under the auspices of the Hollywood Independent Citizens Committee of the Arts, Sciences and Professions (HICCASP), supporters had held a "Thought Control Conference" in July at the posh Beverly Hills Hotel, chaired by Nineteen member Howard Koch and dedicated to FDR's memory. The keynote was delivered by John Cromwell, chairman of the New York–based Arts, Sciences and Professions Council. It was in many ways a farewell party for the old pro-Communist Left, with the entire left-wing community of California participating. Consistent with the new Party line, speakers drew a parallel between America at that historical moment and Nazi Germany in the early days of the Third Reich.[27]

When the subpoenas were finally served, there were mass

rallies. The official Henry Wallace political action group, the Progressive Citizens of America, held a meeting on "Cultural Freedom and Civil Liberties" in New York City, at which Robert Kenny called HUAC itself an unconstitutional committee. HUAC's activities, left-wing lawyer O. John Rogge told the group, were typical of "incipient fascism."

The Liberals

The big question was how the liberals would react. Philip Dunne, John Huston and Billy Wilder began an organization called "Hollywood Fights Back," changing its name to the "Committee for the First Amendment" (CFA) after conferring with the "unfriendlies," who promised that they planned to conduct a clear-cut constitutional defense, rather than wage a political war. The CFA's purpose was to build an ad hoc group of people in and out of the movie world to protest the procedures of the House committee and to head off censorship and a blacklist.

The first efforts of the CFA were sponsoring two radio broadcasts in favor of the Nineteen and flying movie stars, including Humphrey Bogart and Lauren Bacall, to Washington for HUAC's first set of Hollywood hearings.[28] Bacall recalled an early meeting held at the home of Ira Gershwin, at which Judy Garland, Burt Lancaster, John Huston, Danny Kaye, Gene Kelly and others were present when the CFA's first call to action was drawn up. "I became very emotional about it," Bacall later wrote, adding that her first reaction "should have clued me in as to how cause-prone I could be." Hearing Adrian Scott on the phone from Washington talking about HUAC's excesses, she turned to Bogie and said, "We must go." Hers was a response of pure emotion: "How dare that bastard Thomas treat people this way? What was happening to our country? He must be stopped."

Before they took off, the group met at Dave Chasen's Hollywood restaurant, then a choice hangout of the celebrity crowd. Bacall was excited to be part of a group whose members were all "doing the same thing for the same reason—pure in thought and purpose, on a crusade." Bogart released his own statement to the press:

This has nothing to do with Communism. It's none of my busi-

ness who's a Communist and who isn't. We have...the FBI who
does know these things. The reason I am flying to Washington
is because I am an outraged and angry citizen who feels that
my civil liberties are being taken away from me and that the
Bill of Rights is being abused...nobody in this country has any
right to kick around the Constitution...not even the Un-American Activities Committee.[29]

The hearings got under way in the nation's capital on October 20, 1947. A long line of spectators waited to gain entry to the
Caucus Room of the Old House Office Building, which was fitted
with a battery of newsreel cameras and blazing lights, set up to
photograph the proceedings. "The illusion was sharp and shad-
owless," the Nineteen's official historian, Gordon Kahn,
reported. "Loudspeakers for the public address system...
amplified every whisper in the hearing room." On the first day,
ninety-four members of the press sat at their tables ready to
report. The committee's chairman, J. Parnell Thomas of New Jersey, arrived at 10:20 A.M. A "short, red-faced man," Kahn wrote,
with a round face and a sparse amount of hair, Thomas had small
hands and feet, "and his general appearance could be described
as natty." He was so short that he had to sit on a phone book to
appear as tall as his colleagues, covering the book with a red silk
pillow. In contrast, his chief investigator, Robert Stripling, was a
tall, pale Southerner who appeared to be "the calmest man in the
room."[30]

First to testify were three producers, Jack Warner, Sam
Wood and Louis B. Mayer, all of whom favored making the Communist Party illegal. When it came to his turn, Warner, who
fancied himself a public speaker, began with a forceful opening
statement, which the committee allowed him to deliver. Freedom
could not be won by curtailing anyone's liberties, the producer
warned. Furthermore, there existed "no positive guide to determine whether or not a person is a Communist," and existing laws
offered "no clear-cut definition on that point."[31] When asked by
the committee if the Motion Picture Association might act as a
source for identifying subversives, Warner replied that he didn't
think it would be legal to "have the Association or any men band
together to obstruct the employment of any other man. I don't

believe the Association would have anything whatsoever to do with that type of operation. I would not be party to it and neither would any of the other men, from my knowledge of them."[32] Lest the committee think he sanctioned Communists, he hastened to add that he and his brothers would be happy to establish a fund "to ship to Russia the people who don't like our American system of government and prefer the communistic system to ours."[33]

Next came Louis B. Mayer, the elegantly dressed and slow-moving head of MGM who was one of the highest-paid executives in America. He told the committee that his attorneys had informed him that if a studio attempted to fire an employee because he was a Party member, it would have to prove the allegation or be liable for damage suits. Since they hired thousands of people, it was simply impossible for them to "be responsible for the political views of each individual employee." Like Warner, the MGM chief said he was waiting for Congress to pass new legislation that regulated the employment of Communists in private industry.

A commitment to political freedom for dissenters was made clear in the testimony given before HUAC by two past presidents of the Screen Actors Guild (SAG), Robert Montgomery and George Murphy, and by its current president, Ronald Reagan. They told the committee how they had successfully curtailed Communist influence in their guild. In contrast to other so-called "friendlies," Reagan took a moderate position. The single best way to fight Communism, he told HUAC, was "to make democracy work." The most effective means of countering the Party would be to "expose their lies when we came across them," oppose their propaganda, and in the case of the SAG, prevent them from "trying to run a majority of the organization with a well-organized minority." Reagan believed that the country should not "compromise" democratic principles; and therefore he opposed outlawing the Party on ideological grounds. "As a citizen," he said, "I would hesitate to see any political party outlawed on the basis of its political ideology. We have spent one-hundred seventy years in this country on the basis that democracy is strong enough to stand up and fight against the inroads of any ideology"[34] Reagan, who had actually given names of those he thought might be Communists in his private testimony to the FBI, did not do so in public before HUAC.

At first, the film industry's response to the House committee and the hearings was largely negative. Samuel Goldwyn of MGM was forced to sit the entire week at his tenth-floor suite at the Sherry Netherland Hotel, waiting to hear when he would be called to testify. He felt like a "caged animal," he told the press, and was furious about being tied up by a subpoena and being forced to wait. Goldwyn proclaimed the investigation a "flop" and a "disgraceful performance" that was hurting the motion picture industry and doing "untold harm to America abroad."[35] His words were echoed by industry representative Eric Johnston, who said that HUAC was spreading "a damaging impression of Hollywood...all over the country."[36]

On October 26, the chartered plane of the Committee for the First Amendment (CFA) arrived in the nation's capital. The stars were met by the press and posed for pictures in front of the plane. After settling into the Statler Hotel, producer/director John Huston told the waiting press that they "had not come to attack anybody, nor to defend the unfriendly witnesses. We just wished to fight the growing voluntary censorship in Hollywood."[37] The CFA's plan was to march to the Capitol and present a petition signed by five hundred of Hollywood's leading lights to House Speaker Joseph Martin Jr. deploring HUAC's attempt to "smear the Motion Picture Industry" and to "curb freedom of expression." Then they were going to attend the hearings, hold press conferences, meet with senators and representatives, and perhaps even see President Truman.

That night they took to the airwaves for a nationwide radio broadcast they called "Hollywood Fights Back." Actress Myrna Loy told the audience, "We question the right of Congress to ask any man what he thinks on political issues." John Huston said that HUAC had only produced one piece of legislation in nine years, and that turned out to be unconstitutional. The program ended with superstar Judy Garland urging that listeners write to Congress in protest.[38] The program was so successful that the CFA bought more radio time for another broadcast a week later, this one to feature George S. Kaufman, Moss Hart and Leonard

Bernstein from New York, and Bogart and Bacall from Hollywood.[39]

Advocates of the old Popular Front were at first delighted.
Even anti-Communist liberals now seemed to be on the same side
as the Hollywood Reds. But Communists were not satisfied by a
defense of their political rights as American citizens; they wanted
their defenders to join forces with them in the campaign against
"incipient fascism." For Party members, what was at stake was
nothing less than the future of America itself. The more people
like Philip Dunne defended their rights while openly criticizing
Communist politics and doctrine, the less they welcomed such
intervention.

Dunne and John Huston met with the Nineteen before they
testified to make sure that their own activities coincided with the
strategy taken by the subpoenaed screenwriters, actors and directors. They suggested to the group that when asked questions,
the Nineteen should say something to the effect that they would
not answer because the information HUAC sought was "privileged" under the terms of the First Amendment. Then they
should convene a press conference, have a Supreme Court justice put them under oath, and answer any and all questions any
member of the press might put to them. Much to Dunne's and
Huston's dismay, the Nineteen refused, deciding instead to pretend "to answer the questions while actually evading them and
indulging in combative political speeches, a ploy which
inevitably—and perhaps deservedly—backfired."[40]

What Dunne and Huston did not realize was that the
unfriendly witnesses and their lawyers, meeting privately, had
actually raised the issue of whether or not they believed in free
speech as a principle. One of their lawyers posed a hypothetical
question to them: What if HUAC asks if you believe in free
speech for Communists? What is your answer? As Dmytryk later
recalled, "there was a chorus of 'Yes!'" Then the lawyer continued: What if they ask you if you believe in free speech for fascists?
As some said "Yes," John Howard Lawson "raised a warning
hand." After much discussion over the next week, a six-to-three
majority still voted in favor of free speech, even for fascists. At
that point Lawson instructed them: "The answer is that you do

not believe in freedom of speech for fascists." As he explained, they were to favor free speech for Communists "because what they say is true," whereas what fascists say "is a lie."[41]

The Hearings

The Committee for the First Amendment carefully timed its arrival and its activities to support the film industry and its representative, Eric Johnston, who had been scheduled to appear as the next witness. The committee changed the schedule and John Howard Lawson testified first, something he wanted to do as the Hollywood Party chief. The actor Sterling Hayden, who traveled to the hearings as part of the CFA delegation, described Lawson's demeanor: "From the center of the second row a powerful figure of a man stands up and shuffles sideways toward the aisle. He steps clear and moves forward; as he goes he gives his pants a sharp hitch and cinches the belt taut."[42] Taking the witness stand, Lawson requested his right to read a statement. He handed it over to committee chairman J. Parnell Thomas, who glanced at it and (as Gordon Kahn reported) "thrust it away from him, aghast." Thomas admonished Lawson: "The statement will not be read. I read the first line."[43]

The sentence that infuriated Thomas slammed HUAC's hearings as "an illegal and indecent trial of American citizens," who were being "pilloried and smeared." The source of the "filth" and "dirt" that was heaped on them, Lawson claimed, came from "a parade of stool-pigeons, neurotics, publicity-seeking clowns, Gestapo agents, paid informers, and a few ignorant and frightened Hollywood artists."

Lawson portrayed himself as an honest writer who tried to be true to his craft, and who understood the writer's "special responsibility to serve democracy" and the "free-exchange of ideas." HUAC, he charged, had one goal: to "stifle ideas." They were now waging a war between "thought control and freedom of expression," between the "people," of which he and other Party members were a part, and "a greedy unpatriotic minority" that feared the people and of which HUAC was a part.

The chairman responded simply by noting that HUAC was

"a Congressional Committee set up by law" and by insisting upon an "orderly procedure." He was not to get one. Lawson only answered questions pertaining to his name and his membership in the Screen Writers Guild, mixing his replies with asides such as accusing the committee of practicing "Hitler techniques of creating a scare." Thomas asked Lawson to make an effort to be responsive. He shouted back: "I am not on trial here, Mr. Chairman. This Committee is on trial here before the American people." Thomas reprimanded him: "You will have to stop or you will leave the witness stand." The appearance quickly ended with a furious Thomas rapping the gavel, and Lawson continuing to shout a political speech in which he claimed he was teaching HUAC "the basic principles of American..." Here he was interrupted by Thomas, who ordered him to step down and said: "Officers, take this man away from the stand."[44]

Next on the list of the nineteen "unfriendly witnesses" was screenwriter Dalton Trumbo. (Eventually, ten of the nineteen unfriendlies would be called to testify at this round of hearings, thereby acquiring the name "the Hollywood Ten.") By all accounts, Trumbo was the wittiest, brightest and most talented of the Communist screenwriters. A man of immense style, Trumbo was, as Kahn put it, "a veritable ring-tailed tiger."[45] Appearing at his hearing with a box full of scripts he had written, along with tins of sixteen-millimeter prints of his movies, Trumbo clearly wanted to show the committee that they were dealing with a man of substance, whose work did not contain Communist propaganda. He did not refuse to answer the questions, but did refuse to answer them in the manner demanded by HUAC. Like Lawson, he also first tried to read a prepared statement; and once again, the chairman declared his statement "not pertinent to the inquiry" and would not allow him to present it.

What Trumbo wanted to say was that the committee itself was testing America's devotion to free speech and democracy. The friendly witnesses who preceded him had engaged in "hearsay" and "slander," and he would not seek to answer them. Most of the committee members were well-known opponents of FDR and the New Deal, he said, while all the unfriendly witnesses were supporters. The latter, Trumbo asserted, were not Communists but Roosevelt Democrats, and right-wing Republicans were attacking them as a way of attacking FDR and his legacy by proxy.

Trumbo proved to be adept at the game of pretending to answer questions while actually stonewalling. Even when investigator Robert Stripling asked him whether or not he was an SWG member—which everyone knew he was—he equivocated about "the rights of American labor to inviolably secret membership lists" and the "freedom of labor" in America. When they finally got around to asking him if he was a Communist Party member, Trumbo answered that he wished "to be confronted with any evidence which supports this question" and to "see what you have." At that point Thomas dismissed him from the stand. As Trumbo was being hustled out, he yelled out for the benefit of the media: "This is the beginning of an American concentration camp."

And so it went with the eight others (in addition to Lawson and Trumbo)—Herbert Biberman, Lester Cole, Edward Dmytryk, Ring Lardner Jr., Albert Maltz, Samuel Ornitz and Adrian Scott. Rhyming on investigator Stripling's name, Maltz, who for some reason was allowed to read his statement, referred to him as "Mr. Quisling," the name of the pro-Nazi president of Norway during World War II. Maltz then accused Stripling and Thomas of wanting to ask about his religious beliefs. When they said they had no such intention, Maltz ignored them, saying, "You are going to insist...that since you do not like my religious beliefs I should not work in such industry." When his turn came, Ring Lardner Jr. replied to the question of whether he was a Communist with what became a famous response: "I could answer it, but if I did, I would hate myself in the morning." Thomas was furious and shouted at Lardner: "Leave the witness chair! Leave the witness chair!" Lardner screamed back: "I think I am leaving by force."[46]

As soon as each witness had finished or had been removed before being allowed to have his say, Stripling or his fellow investigator Louis Russell read out a list of his Communist Party activities, in most cases mentioning the number on their individual CP membership cards. This concise and complete record of Communist affiliations made it appear that the unfriendlies' testimony had little to do with constitutional rights and was only a smokescreen to hide their guilt. Despite their noisy show, it was clear that these people were not FDR liberals defending the New Deal legacy; they actually *were* Communists.

Bertolt Brecht

The last witness to be called before the HUAC hearings came to an end was Bertolt Brecht, the exiled German playwright then living in Hollywood, whose case had been separated from the others. Not yet the cult figure he would become in the 1960s and 1970s, Brecht was already Germany's leading Communist playwright, a dedicated revolutionary who had developed his own style of Marxist theater that would come to have worldwide influence.

Brecht turned in a prize-winning performance. Like the other witnesses, he came with an opening statement that he was not permitted to read aloud. In it, he portrayed himself not as the revolutionary Marxist he was, but simply as an anti-Nazi writer who had fled Germany in 1933, one day after the Reichstag fire. Brecht speculated that HUAC had called him because his poems and plays might have been misunderstood. All his activities, he wrote, "have always been purely literary activities of a strictly independent nature," and that as a foreign guest in America he had carefully "refrained from political activities."

Given that the FBI had thoroughly investigated Brecht and was reporting its findings to Robert Stripling, it is hard to comprehend how the House committee failed to seize on the implications of Brecht's creative output and background. The bureau had commented on his views and activities from 1941 to 1947 in this way: "Subject's writings...advocate overthrow of Capitalism, establishment of Communist State and use of sabotage by labor to attain its ends." Other files described Brecht as a man "looked upon by German Communists as their poet laureate."[47]

The FBI had also noted Brecht's work as a technical advisor on Fritz Lang's anti-Nazi film *Hangmen Also Die*, produced in 1943 and based on a Brecht story. The bureau translated his play *Die Massnahme* (*The Measures Taken*) and correctly described it as a play advocating "Communist world revolution by violent means." Furthermore, the FBI files show, according to the historian of the exiles, Alexander Stephan, that Hoover was trying to get Brecht interned as an enemy alien during the war.[48]

Yet of all the Communists subpoenaed by the committee, only Brecht got away with bamboozling them; he left the witness stand unstained and was actually praised by HUAC members for cooperating. Brecht too was asked the $64,000 question: "Are you now or have you ever been a member of the Communist Party of any country?" Remarking that his "colleagues" considered the question "not proper," Brecht replied that he was "a guest in this country" and wanted to avoid legal questions. Then he stated—falsely—that he was not a member of any Communist Party. When asked if he had written "revolutionary" plays, he answered that he had written works "in the fight against Hitler," whose government he sought to overthrow.[49]

When queried about *Die Massnahme,* Brecht called it an "adaptation of an old religious Japanese play" that discussed adhering to an ideal until death. That ideal was a "religious idea," he asserted, and had nothing to do with Communism. Stripling quoted a 1937 interview, published in Russia, in which Brecht had told a Soviet writer that *Die Massnahme* was his "first play on a Communist theme." Yet apparently the investigator was so charmed by the suave German intellectual that he gave him a pass, even though he must have realized that Brecht was lying.

The playwright cleverly led Stripling along, expressing ignorance about the publication of his plays and poems in Communist magazines, and of what he claimed were faulty translations that changed the meaning of his words. He was only an "independent writer" who thought it best "not to join any party whatever," and who was writing not just for German Communists but for "workers of any other kind," including Social Democrats and Catholics.

He ended his *tour de force* performance with a crowning lie when Stripling read a Brecht poem entitled "Forward, We're Not Forgotten," in which the author proclaims in the name of the workers: "We have a world to gain.... All the world will be our own."

Stripling: "Did you write that, Mr. Brecht?"

Brecht: "No. I wrote a German poem, but that is very different from this."

At that point, Stripling thanked Brecht and dismissed him as "a good example to the witnesses of Mr. Kenny and Mr. Crum."

The next day, Brecht left New York City for Europe, on his way to permanent residence in the grim East German Communist state, the so-called German Democratic Republic. After settling in East Berlin, he was made director of his own state-subsidized theater.

Aftermath

The strategy and testimony of the Hollywood Ten turned out to be a political and public relations disaster. Film industry representative Eric Johnston convened a meeting of top studio executives in New York on November 19 to "consider problems presented by the alleged subversive and disloyal activities of persons connected with the motion picture industry." At a dinner held by a group called Picture Pioneers, Johnston denounced Communism, opposed federal censorship of films, and did his best to defend the movie industry. Trying to put the best face on events, he argued that the HUAC hearings had disproved that Hollywood was overrun by Reds and that Communist propaganda had been put on the motion picture screen. At the same time, Johnston scolded the Ten for refusing "to stand up and be counted for whatever they are" and for "playing into the hands of extremists who are all too willing to confuse the honest progressive with the dishonest Red."[50]

Johnston's efforts were in vain. On November 24, after committee chairman J. Parnell Thomas handed Congress a formal report about their behavior on the witness stand and their refusal to answer questions, Congress voted contempt citations for each of the Ten. Thomas argued that it was "ridiculous" for the Ten and their supporters to claim that Congress had no right to inquire into their political affiliations. Just as Congress was being asked to appropriate billions of taxpayer dollars to "stop the floodgate of Communism from sweeping all of Europe," the chairman told his fellow representatives, "what a paradox if that same Congress cannot inquire into the activities of a Communist conspirator in the United States, whose first allegiance is to a foreign government." The Ten, he reminded them, had not been randomly chosen. Prior investigation had "disclosed that they were Communists or had long records of Communist affiliation and activities."[51] Thomas in effect had let the cat out of the bag: HUAC already knew before beginning its inquiry that the Ten were or had been Communists as a result of FBI information.

The vote had the effect of forcing Johnston and the studio chiefs finally to act. On the 24th and 25th at the Waldorf-Astoria in New York, representatives from virtually the entire film industry met to decide how to handle the public relations crisis. Eric Johnston and Donald M. Nelson, head of the Society of Independent Motion Picture Producers, both promised "not to be swayed by hysteria or intimidation." Their promises were all for show and, as the industry would soon find out, meant very little. With a team of topnotch lawyers there to advise them, the moguls backed the decision of those major studios that had already announced they would no longer employ known Communists.

Attending the meeting for RKO, where he was chief of production, the liberal former screenwriter Dore Schary was dismayed: "A sea change had taken place. Johnston had abandoned his previous posture and, seemingly panicked by what he saw as a drastic change in public opinion, was for a tough policy on the part of the industry. He talked to the seventy or eighty people who were in the room as if we were members of an industry manufacturing secret deadly weapons by employing Communists."[52] According to Schary's account, he alone spoke up against the majority, arguing that the Ten were as yet not proven guilty of anything, and emphasizing that no law existed that made it illegal for an American citizen to be a member of the Communist Party. There was no proof that any of them as individuals favored the overthrow of the U.S. government by force, and since the industry maintained that there had been no Communist propaganda in any of its films, then obviously the Ten could not be guilty of inserting any.

Schary's remarks were met by a stinging rebuke from Eric

Johnston and studio executive Spyros Skouras. Schary got support, however, from the independent producer Walter Wanger, who warned them not to rush "into a maelstrom." The biggest surprise came from Eddie Mannix, MGM's general manager. Formerly a bouncer at an amusement park, Mannix was physically and emotionally a tough man, with what Schary called "a rugged temper, iron fists, and an enormous appetite for liquor and women." Known as an anti-Communist hardliner who had wanted the United States to march on Moscow once Hitler was defeated, he surprised the assembled industry leaders by opposing the firing of the Ten. California state law made it illegal to fire anyone for his ideas, he argued, and he would not break the law. But the former secretary of state, James F. Byrnes, now working for the film industry as chief counsel, assured those present that no government official would "argue with the decision of the industry to get rid of 'Reds.'" One could, he advised, make use of the morals clause of their contracts and fire them for bringing disrepute to the industry. The last word was from Johnston, who threatened to quit his job if the opponents of the blacklist did not come to their senses.

The upshot of the meeting was the passage of the Waldorf Statement. Here the producers agreed not to employ Communists; to fire those members of the recalcitrant Hollywood Ten under contract; and not to rehire them until they had been acquitted in a court, had purged themselves of "contempt of Congress," or had declared under oath that they were not members of the Communist Party.[53]

A few days later, it was all over. Eight of the Ten had been fired—by MGM, Warner Brothers and Twentieth Century Fox. Only Schary at RKO had not as yet acted against Adrian Scott and Ed Dmytryk; and when the RKO board met in Los Angles, Schary announced that he would not execute any order to fire them. RKO's chairman, Floyd Odlum, ordered company president Peter Rathvon to do the firing himself.

As the opponents of the blacklist saw it, no less serious than the actual outcome was the collapse of the liberal opposition to HUAC. With its planeload of movie stars flying into Washington for the hearings, the Committee for the First Amendment had garnered a great deal of publicity and managed to stir up wide opposition to HUAC along with sympathy for the subpoenaed Ten. That sympathy soon evaporated after the country witnessed the demeanor of the Ten during their testimony.

After the hearings, the élan and commitment of CFA members began to fade. In her innocence, Lauren Bacall had believed that they could make the House committee stop its investigations, and that her own speeches were so effective that she might even make a successful run for Congress. But her group was put on the defensive when the press started asking them questions: "We had to admit we didn't know whether any of the witnesses were Communists."

Decades afterward Bacall confessed, "we didn't realize until much later that we were being used to some degree by the Unfriendly Ten, in that our focus was subtly altered to defending them individually and collectively." Bacall did not even realize when she traveled to Washington that most of the ten "unfriendlies" were in fact Communist Party members. Later, as she looked at photos taken in front of their chartered plane, Bacall for the first time noticed the craft's name: "We saw that the name of the plane was the *Red Star.*" She commented, "Coincidence or design?"[54]

Immediately upon his return to Hollywood, her husband, Humphrey Bogart—the CFA's top star—faced intense pressure from fans, friends and journalists. The Ten's stance before HUAC made it appear to many, including some of the CFA actors, that they were in fact defending Communists and Communism, and not the principles of free speech and democracy. Columnists like Ed Sullivan warned Bogart that many perceived him to be a Red.

Bogart and the other CFA members met once again at the Gershwins' house to discuss the outcome of their Washington trip. Angry that the Ten had made him look like an idiot, Bogart shouted at Danny Kaye, "You fuckers sold me out," and stormed out of the CFA meeting. When one last get-together was called, attendance had declined so dramatically that the meeting was held in a small projection room. Billy Wilder told the group, "we oughta fold."[55]

Soon afterward, Bogart was asked to write a new statement declaring that he was not a Communist and had no sympathy for their cause. First, he wrote a letter George Sokolsky, which the right-wing columnist printed in his December 6, 1947 newspaper column. "I am not a Communist," Bogart stated. "I am not a Communist sympathizer. I detest Communism just as any decent American does. My name will not be found on any Communist front organization as a sponsor for anything Communistic." His only concern, Bogart explained, was trying to prevent American citizens from being "deprived of their constitutional rights." Essentially admitting he had been duped by the Reds, he acknowledged that the CFA trip was "ill-advised, even foolish."[56]

Next, an article titled "I'm No Communist" appeared under Bogart's name in *Photoplay,* a popular fan magazine. Here he complained that although the entire liberal press had accused HUAC of violating free speech, once Hollywood actors joined them with the same protest, "the roof fell in on us."[57] While affirming his original goals, Bogart (his biographer writes) again "clearly dissociated himself from the Communists and the Hollywood Ten."[58]

Almost immediately, the Reds who had exulted in Bogart's support began to blast him. Hollywood Ten screenwriter Lester Cole proclaimed that Bogie was "frightened."[59] Harmonica virtuoso and fellow traveler Larry Adler said that Bogart had "caved in in the most demeaning, debasing way, saying that he was duped...and then Gene Kelly reneged, and Danny Kaye...and Frank Sinatra...and those of us who didn't stood out like carbuncles." In a similar vein, the Red screenwriter Alvah Bessie castigated Bogart for calling himself both a dupe and a dope, and accused him of having "provoked a panic that rapidly destroyed the Committee for the First Amendment itself."[60]

Bogart and most of the CFA delegation were equally repelled by HUAC and the Hollywood Reds, and they left the nation's capital feeling that the groups deserved each other. From that moment, liberal support for the Ten crumbled away. People like John Huston retreated to their private lives, while others stopped giving money. The romance was over and would never be the same again.

9

HUAC Returns

THE STUDIOS SURVEYED THE DAMAGE—THE IMAGE OF THE TEN TESTI-fying before HUAC, the contempt citations voted by Congress, all the negative publicity. Fearing for the economic future of the industry, they saw only one way to proceed: fire the Hollywood Ten.

But such a course raised other questions: How would the studio chiefs go about identifying authentic Communists, given that the Party functioned as a secret organization? How would they prevent the blacklist from creating a pervasive atmosphere of fear? How would they guarantee that people put on the list were actually Communist Party members and not merely left-wing dissenters? And finally, how would an ex-Communist or someone falsely suspected of being a Communist go about clearing his or her name?

The producers met with guild leaders to discuss such problems. While none of the latter protested the Ten's dismissal, they were concerned about the Waldorf Statement's "open-ended-ness" and about the likelihood of the guilds being used as political "screening agencies." They wanted some assurance that the criteria used to define a "subversive" would not cause collateral damage to "honest liberals."[1] Still, both the Screen Directors Guild and the Screen Actors Guild passed resolutions requiring that their officers sign non-Communist affidavits.

As the only director among the Ten, Edward Dmytryk was particularly vulnerable. The screenwriters could make a living—although at much lower rates of pay—using "fronts" to sign their names on scripts. This option was not available to directors. A group of Dmytryk's liberal colleagues in the Screen Directors Guild agreed to approach the organization about taking a stand against HUAC, the Waldorf Statement and the blacklist. A special summit was called, and as a vice-president of the guild, Dmytryk was optimistic about the outcome.

His spirits remained high until he got to the meeting and found the legendary ultraconservative director Cecil B. De Mille seated at the executives' table, although he was neither a board member nor an officer. (Dmytryk was later told that information concerning left-wingers was routinely passed on to the FBI by De Mille.) As a vote was taken on the anti-HUAC proposals before the guild, De Mille rose to his feet and screamed, "This is war! This is war!" The guild did not take an anti-HUAC position. Dmytryk drove home through a "bewildering and cheerless Hollywood," aghast at what he called De Mille's "battle against decency and democracy."[2]

Despite such setbacks, the Communist Party members in the various guilds did their best to keep the battle going. When new elections were scheduled for leadership of the Screen Writers Guild in November 1947, the Party gave word to its members to support a so-called "Progressive Slate" whose candidates were pledged to a firm anti-HUAC and anti-blacklist stand. On the slate were some of the leading Communist screenwriters, including Lester Cole, Ring Lardner Jr., Harold Buchman and Hugo Butler. Opposing them was the "all-guild slate," a coalition against Communist domination. It was supported by outgoing Screen Writers Guild president Emmet Lavery, who took the position that the Ten had harmed the guild by linking it with the Communist Party.

Screenwriter Richard Collins decided to vote against the CP-backed slate. One of the original Nineteen, he had found himself suddenly unemployable. Already disillusioned with the Party as a result of the Maltz affair and the Duclos letter, Collins felt he no longer needed or wanted "a master in the Communist Party." Many years later he recalled, "It caused quite a stir when I told them I voted the way I felt." This was his very first "revolutionary" public act against the Party's decrees.[3] When the CP's slate suffered an overwhelming electoral defeat, he interpreted it to mean that "the Left ceased to exist in any organized, meaningful sense in the Screen Writers Guild."[4]

The activist Communists and their dwindling group of fellow-traveling supporters did not give up. But solidarity began to break down. Howard Koch was the first to try to rescue his career. Having previously disagreed with his colleagues on their legal strategy, he now sought to separate himself from their campaign. He took out an ad in a Hollywood trade paper declaring that he had never been in the Party, but also that he would not say so when testifying before HUAC. To clarify his own firm opposition to HUAC, he urged that the studios stand fast and defend themselves "by defending each other."[5]

This was a time of torment for some industry liberals, who engaged in strange personal and political gymnastics to deal with their guilty consciences. At RKO, Dore Schary may have avoided obeying the order to fire Adrian Scott and Edward Dmytryk, but he stopped short of condemning their firing by his superiors and refused to resign in protest, as the Communists and their allies had demanded. He rationalized his position by arguing to himself that "it would be more helpful to remain in the business and fight against the blacklisting," and that his own "resignation would in no way clarify the issue." His explanation did little to mollify right-wing columnists such as Westbrook Pegler, Hedda Hopper and George Sokolsky, who attacked him for being soft on Communists, while the Communists accused him of selling out.

Some liberals still persisted in trying to help. Philip Dunne wanted to resign from Twentieth Century Fox when his friend Ring Lardner Jr. was fired. Lardner and studio chief Darryl Zanuck pleaded with him not to "do anything foolish." He finally relented, claiming that his only defense for earning the "Order of the Chicken" was that to the best of his knowledge, "in no studio did anyone else resign, most notably no member of the Communist Party or habitual follower of its line. In fact, just the opposite happened. The entire industry became demoralized as almost everyone scrambled for cover."[6]

Dunne organized what he called the "Committee of One

Thousand," which he hoped would gain a new and broad support in resisting the blacklist. He fought against the blacklist among the Screen Writers Guild, signed an *amicus curiae* brief on behalf of the Ten, and flew to Washington, D.C., to testify on Dalton Trumbo's behalf at his federal trial. He also gave his own money to help out the suffering families of the dismissed writers.

But most liberals had run out of sympathy. As Dmytryk put it, "many of our less-dedicated supporters were quietly retreating into the safety of their Beverly Hills and Bel Air houses."[7] An embittered Melvyn Douglas, who had been burned by the Communists one too many times, wrote to the chief of an old Popular Front group, the American Veterans Committee, recommending that "liberals not allow themselves to be confused or cajoled into joining hands with the Communists." To commit to such a course, Douglas believed, would be "a serious mistake from the standpoint of both ideology and practical politics."[8]

It soon became clear that the Hollywood Ten could no longer count on much support aside from the Communists and fellow travelers. Whatever good will had once been extended to them had been used up in the HUAC hearings. There were still a few "liberal-chic" fundraisers (as Dmytryk would later characterize them), but such events left a bad taste because of their transparent machinations—presenting the Ten as martyrs and trotting out other Party causes before a collection was taken. Such blatant tactics infuriated potential supporters such as the German novelist and man of letters Thomas Mann, for whom one such evening was enough. "He was willing to lend his name, his prestige and his presence to a fight for freedom of speech and thought," commented Dmytryk. But he was not so willing to front for other causes or individuals supported by the Party.[9]

Early in 1948, the Hollywood Ten went back to Washington, D.C., to stand trial for contempt of Congress. Most received a fine of $1,000 and a one-year jail sentence—the legal maximum for a misdemeanor—but Herbert Biberman and Edward Dmytryk, who appeared before a different judge in the federal district court, received only a $500 fine and a six-month sentence. Apparently the defendants were still confident that when their case came to the Supreme Court, their refusal to testify on

First Amendment grounds would be validated. But they were grasping at straws. As Albert Maltz wrote to his fellow defendants while they were waiting for the case to be heard by the High Court: "We are financially and physically depleted." Their defense fund had only $2,000 left in its coffers, when to carry the appeals through the courts they needed a minimum of $50,000.[10]

In April 1950 the Court voted to deny *certiorari*, refusing even to hear the case. Only Hugo Black and William O. Douglas dissented. The Ten would soon begin their incarceration in various federal prisons throughout the country.

The sting of defeat was mitigated somewhat when J. Parnell Thomas, HUAC's chairman, was accused of padding his own payroll by billing the U.S. Treasury for individuals who were not actually working in his office. Two days before he won election to the House for a seventh term, a grand jury was convened to investigate the charges. Oddly, Thomas invoked the Fifth Amendment and refused to testify. Indicted for conspiracy to defraud the government, he pleaded no contest and received a sentence of six to eighteen months in the federal penitentiary in Danbury, Connecticut.

When Lester Cole and Ring Lardner Jr. went into the Danbury prison yard one day, they saw Thomas, their tormentor, working in the prison chicken coops. Cole recalled the scene: "Atop one of the coops was Thomas, a hoe in hand, scraping chicken droppings from the roof.... He saw me, and...called down, 'Hey, Bolshie, I see you still got your sickle. Where's your hammer?'" To which Cole yelled back, "And I see...you're still picking up chickenshit."[11]

Members of the Hollywood Ten were doing time; but outside the prison walls, the blacklist had taken on a life of its own. Recognizing that the blacklist was now a fact of life, Philip Dunne decided to try to "limit its scope." He worried about the emergence of a "gray list"—that is, a list of "people who could be hired, but just to be on the safe side, better not." At a meeting for presidential candidate Adlai Stevenson, he approached Roy Brewer, chief of the International Alliance of Theatrical and Stage Employees (IATSE), who in 1949 had helped found the

Motion Picture Industry Council, a group that invited the Hollywood unions, guilds and producers to appoint representatives to
its board. After a discussion about the dilemma of false accusations of Party membership, Dunne agreed to help Brewer decide
who was employable in Hollywood and who was not.

It was not long before Dunne managed to obtain clearance
for fifteen people. Other liberals like Dore Schary also worked
with the group in an attempt to minimize the blacklist's damage. Joining him were William Holden, Gene Kelly, Walter
Pidgeon and Ronald Reagan.[12]

"A Poisonous Atmosphere"

In 1951, HUAC announced that it was going to continue the
hearings. The situation in the film capital was now quite different
than in 1947, when HUAC first took on Hollywood. Rather than
inspire resistance, HUAC's new set of hearings "created a mood
of depressed resignation," in one reporter's words. The committee claimed now to be only after individuals, not the movie
industry itself. Industry leaders were no longer ambivalent and
they favored the exposure of so-called Communist sympathizers—a policy they called one of "dissociation." Producers who
had already decided to ban Communists from film employment
extended that ban to all who refused to cooperate with HUAC.

The "indignation, excitement, controversy" of the 1947
hearings were absent this time. The fellow-traveling remnants in
HICCASP held what they hoped would be a mass rally, billed as
a send-off for unfriendly witnesses Gale Sondergaard, Howard Da
Silva, Waldo Salt, Robert Lees, Victor Kilian and Fred Graff, who
had announced that they would not testify and would invoke the
Fifth Amendment. Industry people stayed home in droves.

As the hearings approached, the blacklist had spread
beyond Hollywood, extending into radio and the new medium of
television. Opponents of Communism set up their own private
blacklist and threatened sponsors of shows featuring those they
listed as subversives with boycotts. Two privately published magazines, *Counterattack* and *Red Channels,* applied pressure on the
communications industry.

In Hollywood, the atmosphere became poisonous as previously well-known fellow travelers quickly backed down and cut those who had become tainted. Groucho Marx, for instance, at one time a dependable mainstay at HICCASP and other Popular Front causes, lived a few blocks down the street from Ben and Norma Barzman, two Hollywood Communists who were among the first to feel the pinch of the blacklist. After the first HUAC hearings in 1947, Groucho bumped into Norma while he was taking his new daughter for a walk in her baby carriage. Commenting on the uncomfortably hot weather as he passed by, he added: "Of course—it's doubly hot for you, with two kinds of heat. But don't ask me for anything more than ice cubes, which is as far as my sympathies go."[13]

On a Saturday night in 1950, Gene Kelly's wife Betsy Blair got a call from a friendly Hollywood newspaper reporter. Blair had been part of the Hollywood Communist scene, a believing Marxist who had wanted to join the Party but had been told by higher-ups that because of her husband's star power and fame, it would be better to give quiet support to Communist positions. The journalist told Blair that the next day's issue of *Hollywood Reporter* would feature an editorial attacking a group she belonged to, the Actors' Laboratory, and calling members Gale Sondegaard, Lloyd Gough and Blair part of a "nest of Reds." He also informed her that she was to be replaced in *Kind Lady,* a film for which she had already signed a contract.

Fearing the worst, Blair's agent scheduled a meeting with MGM chief Louis B. Mayer. He immediately chastised her for her naïve and continuing association with Communists. "I don't understand you people," he told her. "You live in the greatest country in the world. I had to talk to Spence [Spencer Tracy] and Kate [Katherine Hepburn] too. What's wrong with you people? You look like a very nice girl.... So what do you want? Don't you appreciate the United States of America?" When Blair responded about the "others" who were not as fortunate as she and Gene Kelly were, Mayer replied, "What do you know about them? If anyone wants to succeed in this country, if they work hard they will. Don't try to change the country...." Blair answered that her mother had taught her that "some things need to be changed."

Mayer sighed: "I knew you were the kind of girl who listens to her mother."

Betsy Blair's ploy worked. She got to keep the part in *Kind Lady,* although Mayer grumbled to the studio's casting director that "Kelly should get rid of his commie wife." Blair would not make another film for four years, and it would be a long ten years before she was allowed to get back on television.[14]

Larry Parks

For those called before HUAC in the second round, one thing had changed: the trial of the Hollywood Ten had taken the option of using the First Amendment off the table. A witness could invoke the Fifth Amendment, as many of them would do, but this gave the appearance of having something to hide. In the public eye, someone who took the Fifth had to be a guilty person cowering behind the Constitution's protection. Individuals who invoked the Fifth Amendment could avoid going to jail and naming their old friends from the Communist movement, but they would definitely be blacklisted.

The ex-Communists faced even more difficult choices. They could clear themselves by testifying before HUAC, thereby finally making it clear that they had broken with the Party and its causes. But to prove their change of heart they had to give HUAC the names of those they'd known while in the Communist Party. It was an agonizing choice for all who were put to the test.

No one suffered more than actor Larry Parks, the first person to testify in the second round of hearings. Parks had joined the Communist Party in 1941. Going to California to pursue his career, he joined the Actors' Lab, where he became part of the Hollywood Red scene. His dynamic appearance in *The Jolson Story* in 1946 marked him as an actor on the road to major stardom. By that time he had left the Party, and when he appeared before the committee it was as a cooperative witness.

Parks took the stance that he would tell them anything they wanted to know about himself, but not talk about others. After a lengthy session, however, he broke down and pleaded with the members not to make him "crawl through the mud to be an informer." But the committee insisted. So Parks, calling himself "the most completely ruined man that you have ever seen," then proceeded to name Morris Carnovsky, Lee J. Cobb, J. Edward Bromberg, Anne Revere and others.[15]

Parks' appearance was so lacerating that HUAC decided to hold many of its subsequent hearings in private executive session, closed to both the public and the press. In these sessions, members of the committee would hear the testimony of those they had called in advance of a public appearance so that they would know what to expect and could better prepare themselves. According to Dmytryk, those who welcomed HUAC's "more accommodating behavior" included Robert Rossen, Elia Kazan, Budd Schulberg, Lloyd Bridges, Isobel Lennart, José Ferrer, Lee J. Cobb, Michael Blankfort, David Raksin and Clifford Odets.[16]

Edward Dmytryk Breaks Ranks

By 1948, Edward Dmytryk's attorney, Bartley Crum, had already left the Progressive Citizens of America. It became apparent to him, according to his daughter, Patricia Bosworth, that the "organization was being dominated by...Communist thinking," and he felt the need to protest against its drive to "forge a third party for the Presidential campaign of Henry Wallace." At the same time, he also dropped his membership in the CP's legal front group, the National Lawyers Guild.[17] Crum told his family that henceforth he would only practice corporate law. There was one exception: he continued to represent Edward Dmytryk, who had decided while he was in prison to break with the Party publicly and take steps to clear himself. This decision would cost Crum. "None of his fellow lawyers ever spoke to him again," his daughter wrote, "...simply because he stood by a client who changed his mind. All he'd ever wanted was for Eddie to feel free to tell the truth."[18]

Dmytryk had resigned cerebrally from the Party back in 1945, when he and Scott fought with John Howard Lawson over the film *Cornered*. Now, sitting in a Washington, D.C., jail waiting to be processed, he became even angrier over the CP's postwar positions. After the Korean War broke out, Dmytryk got into an angry tiff with his prison mate Albert Maltz. Like most Americans, Dmytryk understood that the North Koreans had invaded South Korea, but Maltz denied this view of events. "Who could trust the capitalist press?" he asked Dmytryk. First he needed to hear what Moscow had to say. After meeting with one of the Party lawyers who had just been to New York, Maltz told Dmytryk that "the Americans and the South Koreans had invaded the North" and that "democratic" North Korea was "only striking back."[19]

After two months in the federal prison at Mill Point, West Virginia, to which he had been transferred, Dmytryk made up his mind: "My 'comrades' proclamations of carrying the torch for freedom of speech and thought were proven frauds, and it became obvious the Ten had been sacrifices to the Party's purpose as a pipeline for the Comintern's propaganda.... I wanted out."[20] For Dmytryk, as for Richard Collins, the Korean War was a watershed moment. Their old "comrades" were rooting for the enemy.

During a visit by his wife, Jean, Dmytryk told her his decision to recant. She contacted Crum, who wrote a statement that Dmytryk signed, saying he was not a Communist or a fellow traveler and making it public for the first time that he had not been a Communist when he testified with the other Ten at the HUAC hearings. After his release, Dmytryk was up for a contract with Columbia Pictures. Then one day screenwriter Herbert Biberman, another of the Ten and still a Party member, knocked on his door. Dmytryk was more than surprised, since he had assumed that his prison statement "had permanently removed me from the good graces of the Communists...and the Ten in particular." But here was Biberman, "all smiles and sunshine," asking for Dmytryk's help.

Biberman had with him a petition asking support of parole for the eight who remained in prison. Dmytryk agreed, on condition that his support would only be shown to the parole board and would not be made public and released to the press. Biberman readily agreed. Two days later, Dmytryk found his name splashed on the front pages of *Variety* and the *Hollywood Reporter*, the two major trade papers. Almost immediately, a representative of Columbia Pictures delivered the news: his deal for employment was off.

Biberman's betrayal taught Dmytryk a final tough lesson about the Party: "You know they preach freedom of speech but censor unorthodox opinion; you know they talk democracy but prepare the way for the most inhuman autocracy in modern history. So why do you expect them to keep their word, and why are you still protecting them and the brutal principles they stand for?"[21]

Close to half a million dollars in debt and thoroughly disillusioned, Dmytryk decided that he was now ready to cooperate with the Hollywood anti-Communists and to purge any lingering remnants of his Communist past. Acting on Dmytryk's behalf, Bartley Crum approached the Motion Picture Industry Council and proposed a course of action that would soon become commonplace for those who wanted to clear themselves. First, he agreed to let a well-known Hollywood writer, Richard English, tell Dmytryk's story for the mass-circulation magazine *Saturday Evening Post*. Second, Dmytryk agreed to reappear before HUAC, this time as a friendly witness, whenever HUAC decided to reconvene its Hollywood investigation. Dmytryk's change of heart was a coup for the committee.

When Dmytryk appeared on April 25, 1951, he explained that in 1947 he had still believed that the Soviet Union sincerely sought peace, and that, although he disagreed with the American Communist Party, he did not regard it as any kind of threat. Now, the Korean War had taught him where the Communists really stood. "I had never heard, before 1947, anybody say they would refuse to fight for this country in a war against Soviet Russia," he told HUAC. In addition to Korea, the various spy trials—of Alger Hiss, Judith Coplon, and Ethel and Julius Rosenberg—proved to him that Communists spied against America out of "love of the Party." Dmytryk acknowledged that not all Communists were spies; but he also believed that "a party that encourages them to act in this capacity is treasonable."[22]

When Richard English's article appeared in the May 19 issue of the *Saturday Evening Post*, Dmytryk later remembered, it drove the remnants of the Hollywood Party "into a fury, which, in its vehemence, could only be equaled by the piranha's feeding frenzy.... Nothing but the truth could elicit such a violent reaction." Albert Maltz, who had been in prison with Dmytryk and had served as best man at his wedding, was so furious he wrote and paid for an open letter to Dmytryk that was printed in the center spread of the two Hollywood trade papers.[23]

Writing to the *Saturday Evening Post,* Maltz reiterated the points he had made in his two advertisements. Calling Dmytryk a "deliberate faker and liar," Maltz said that if he was already disillusioned with the Party in 1945 after the fight over *Cornered,* why had he stood with the Ten in 1947 and even gone to jail? Maltz argued that either Dmytryk's "present testimony about the Communist Party is false, and therefore he is a perjurer; or else, in 1947, he self-confessedly was a citizen without principle, honor or sense of public duty." As Maltz saw it, what motivated Dmytryk was only the desire to avoid another term in prison and to be able to resume his career. That is why, he concluded, Dmytryk had become a "commodity for hire," befouling all "with his lies."[24]

Seeing that the Party would try to destroy the credibility of anyone willing to cooperate with HUAC and clear himself, the Motion Picture Industry Council responded to Maltz on June 6, 1951 with its own advertisement in which it accused him of advancing a big lie—the claim that Dmytryk had told him before the original hearings that "progressives" had to go underground. The ad was headlined, "You Can Be a Free Man Again."[25]

Sterling Hayden

Born in 1916 in Montclair, New Jersey, Sterling Hayden grew up to be a rugged, handsome and broad-shouldered man with blond hair and a craggy face. He would make fifty movies during his film career, including a major role in John Huston's *Asphalt Jungle,* in which he portrayed a doomed hoodlum. Later he became a character actor, playing roles in films like *Dr. Strangelove, The Long Goodbye* and *The Godfather.*

Hayden's screen career was eclipsed by this briefer role as a friendly witness before HUAC on April 10, 1951. The aftermath of his post-HUAC appearance, however, took a different turn from that of the other "friendly" witnesses. Hayden turned back to the Left in the 1960s, repudiating his HUAC testimony and becoming a darling of the San Francisco New Left, for which he spoke at meetings of the National Committee to Abolish HUAC and at anti–Vietnam War rallies. As a result of his recantation, Victor Navasky writes, he "won a measure of forgiveness," something that no other friendly witness ever earned.[26]

Why did Hayden agree to be a friendly witness in the first place? After watching Larry Parks testify, Hayden believed that Parks had "consigned himself to oblivion." Hayden, who had belonged to the Communist Party for only a brief six months, resolved not to let himself be put in such a position. Writing of his decision to testify in his 1963 autobiography, Hayden denounced himself as "a real daddy longlegs of a worm when it came to crawling."[27] He explained it this way: "The man who is a hard-core Communist has it all laid out: he goes before the Committee if he has to and tells them to screw themselves. The man who was never in the Party has it easy. All is has to do is say: 'No, I am not now and I never was a member.'" It was different for the ex-Communist: "He's had it."[28]

His memoir, *Wanderer,* is a self-punishing account of how Hayden was lured into a path he willingly repudiated. At the age of fifteen, Hayden had shipped out to sea and continued working on ships for the next seven years, obtaining his master's license at age twenty-one. Unable to buy and operate his own schooner, he found himself broke and moved to New York City. A contact in Boston put him in touch with a Paramount producer, who arranged for Hayden to take a screen test. Looking much like the typical leading man, he passed easily, signed a contract with the studio in 1940, and moved to Los Angeles.

An old friend from seafaring days named Warwick Tompkins had moved to San Francisco, and Hayden renewed the relationship. Tompkins, who had become a devoted Communist, "deluged" him with propaganda. By his own account, Hayden was feeling "restless and dissatisfied" in Hollywood, and Tompkins persistently worked on the young actor to move him into the ranks of the Party. But Hayden, already cast in leading roles in two films, *Virginia* and *Bahama Passage,* desperately wanted to do his part in the war effort and asked Paramount to break his contract.[29]

Enlisting in the Marines, Hayden was transferred to the Office of Strategic Services (OSS), precursor of the CIA. To avoid being identified as a movie star, he called himself John Hamilton. Commissioned as a second lieutenant, he ended up working with the Yugoslav partisans at the port of Bari in Italy. Hayden's dangerous job was to bring the partisans supplies by sea, traveling through the German blockade. He worked with Yugoslavia's Communist leader, Josef Broz Tito, and was greatly impressed by his bravery. Writing to his Communist friend, Hayden said, "Maybe you were not so wrong. These people [the Communists] are doing a magnificent job." Tompkins responded by bombarding Hayden with more Communist literature.

Returning home on leave, Hayden immediately visited Tompkins, basking in "the reflected glory of the partisan movement" and showing off the Order of Merit he had received from the Yugoslavs. Tompkins became his guide to the local Communist movement. Hayden went from meeting to meeting, recounting his wartime exploits. He was taken to the offices of the *People's Daily World,* the West Coast Communist paper, where he met top Party officials.

Back in the film capital and feeling that he wanted to "do something for a better world," Hayden joined HICCASP, the American Veterans Committee and, eventually, the Communist Party. Even though he was a leading man, the Party assigned him to a cell of back-lot workers, and then to one with the Screen Actors Guild, where he was given the job of trying to garner support for the Communist-influenced Conference of Studio Unions (CSU) during the volatile strikes. He failed at this task and in fact, by his own word, was pretty much a failure as a Communist. On an intellectual level, he found Marxist theory irrelevant, boring and hard to grasp. He later told HUAC, "I was constantly told, if I would read forty pages of *Dialectical and Historical Materialism* [by Stalin] I would understand Communism. I never got beyond page eight, and I tried several times."

Knowing that HUAC was readying a second round of hearings, Hayden decided to have his attorney, Martin Gang, send a letter to J. Edgar Hoover stating that he had joined the Party "in a moment of emotional disturbance," but then considered it a great mistake and left its ranks after six months. Hoover replied that while the bureau could not grant any clearances, he suggested that Hayden talk to the Los Angeles FBI office about his membership and Party activities. The FBI listened closely while Hayden spilled all he knew and did not pressure him, although he did not supply them with any names.

The conversation with the FBI did not insulate Hayden from getting the "salmon-colored, mortgage-sized folded thrice" subpoena four months later, asking him to appear before the committee. He panicked. It was one thing to talk to the FBI in private, and yet another to cooperate with HUAC in front of the world. He first tried to work out the conflict with his analyst in therapy. He despised himself for not having the guts to stand up to HUAC, but told his therapist he needed to be employable so that he could pay for therapy. Then he made two predictions: "First I'll end up being a 'cooperative' witness. Second, I'll regret it the rest of my life."[30]

Appearing before HUAC in executive session on April 4, 1951, Hayden told the committee that he had left the Party "in disgust" because of his "dissatisfaction with the narrowness of the people I met in that short period of time," people who differed from "the men and women I had met in the Yugoslav underground." He explained the reasons for his disgust with the Communists:

> Their fight for social justice was and is a sham, a mere façade to attract people like myself who had an honest and sincere desire to do something worthwhile. Their boundless bigotry and their intolerance of opinions which differed from their own were revolting to me. Their absolute conviction and fanatic belief that Russia could do no wrong and their constant criticism of everything American—whether truly faulty or not—convinced me of their insincerity. Their mouthing about freedom . . . turned out to be hollow mockery when I saw their willing submission to Party discipline.[31]

Members of the committee congratulated Hayden. Years later, he gave his final estimate of his performance that day: "Not often does a man find himself eulogized for having behaved in a manner that he himself despises."[32]

Richard Collins

Recruited into the Party by Budd Schulberg in 1937, Richard Collins had quickly become a committed and tireless CP activist, rising to leadership positions in the Hollywood chapter. He stayed in the Party for nine years. Collins sat on the CP's Section Committee, was made a member of the Screen Writers Guild board, and was assigned to work in the leadership of the Committee to Aid Agricultural Workers. His job was to make contact with working people and expand the group's membership. Nominally headed by actress Helen Gahagan Douglas, Collins became her Party liaison on the committee. "I was the one from the Party," he told us, "and Douglas knew it. I was her first man."[33]

Deeply disillusioned by the Maltz affair, Collins was sufficiently alienated from the Party by 1947 that he decided not to run for re-election to the SWG board. When HUAC subpoenaed him along with the other Nineteen, he still did not "have the guts to break with men I knew and liked personally." But when his old friend, the Communist screenwriter Paul Jarrico, asked him for his Party dues, Collins avoided paying them. Unable to get a job and with no further prospects in Hollywood, Collins returned to New York to live with his parents; his father found him work in the clothing industry.[34] When he returned to Hollywood in 1949, Jarrico once again asked him if he was going to return to the Party. This time he gave him a straight answer: No![35]

Collins learned that leaving the ranks of the Party took many steps and was a process that often lasted years. By 1950, he told HUAC in the second round of hearings, "I was beginning to be extremely uncomfortable with my position, which was that I was considered a Communist by almost all of Hollywood, and I was considered a renegade by my ex-associates.... By that time I had made steps to being anti-Soviet, and...I had a real fear that I would be considered, in the event of such a war [with Russia], a friend of the Soviet Union, when actually I was an enemy."[36]

Finally, Collins phoned the FBI and was asked to come in for an interview. He came prepared with a statement saying that he had been a Party member, was no longer one, and wanted them to understand his loyalty to the United States. He would not, however, discuss any of his former associates and would talk only about the inner workings of the Party. In February 1951, Collins got his long-expected subpoena to appear before HUAC. A few days before his appearance, on April 12, his old friend Jarrico contacted him. They sat down to a tense four-hour discussion in which Jarrico tried to convince him that the Soviet Union was devoted to the interests of the world's peoples and was a peace-loving nation.

Then Jarrico made a proposal to Collins: "I think on the basis of fourteen years of friendship, I have the right to ask for your personal assurance that you will not give any names." Collins agreed, on one condition: "If you will give me your personal assurance that in the event of a war between the United States and the Soviet Union, you will do nothing to help the Soviet Union." Jarrico refused, as Collins expected he would, and "since he could not give me this assurance, I would not give him mine, and since we would not lie to each other, we had no further conversation."[37]

Collins later maintained that the studios did not care too much whether one cooperated with HUAC or invoked the Fifth Amendment: "No matter which way you went, you didn't work. ...I think the studios in the main felt they'd be safer not to hire anybody who was involved in it." Anyone who was summoned was seen as tainted.[38] It was a situation reflected in an anecdote involving Harry Warner that made its way through the Hollywood cocktail circuit. Warner apparently fired a writer whose name appeared on a list of front groups. "This is a mistake," the man pleaded, opening a briefcase full of documents substantiating his opposition to the Reds. "The plain fact is that I am an *anti*-Communist." Warner fired back: "I don't give a shit what kind of Communist you are, get out of here!"[39]

Collins had ample reason to justify his cooperation with HUAC; yet like others, he did not want to name former comrades and friends. One strategy was to tell those one cared about that one was going to testify, but assure them that they would not be named. (When Budd Schulberg testified, for instance, he got word to his old friend Maurice Rapf saying that his name would not be mentioned.) Another strategy was to limit the number of names one gave. Collins, who claimed to know virtually everyone who was a member of the Hollywood Party, some three hundred people, named only twenty-six. He came up with this idea while dining with another cooperative witness and friend, Meta Rosenberg, and his attorney, Martin Gang. After much discussion, Collins and Rosenberg ended up with three categories of people they would name: people who had died and could no longer be harmed; those who had been called to appear before HUAC and were already regarded as Communists; and those who had left the Party many years earlier.

Budd Schulberg

Among those Collins named was Budd Schulberg, who by then had himself turned against the Party. His latest novel, *The Disenchanted,* had just been published, and when Collins named him it was major news.[40]

Schulberg responded to the news by sending the committee a telegram offering to testify as a cooperative witness. Since leaving the Party's ranks, he had become convinced that American Communists had inflicted great damage on the cultural scene. They had stifled all artists and intellectuals in their orbit of influence, posed a threat to those who wanted to build a genuine independent American Left, and by their willful ignorance and denial had condoned the deaths of their literary and intellectual counterparts in the Soviet Union.

On the question of which might be the greater menace, HUAC or the Communist Party, Schulberg had little doubt. He believed that it took comparatively little courage to oppose HUAC and the grandstanding members of Congress who made up its ranks. For Hollywood intellectuals, it was a far tougher task to attack the Communists, many of whom worked alongside them in the same industry and attended the same parties.

Schulberg had retained his liberal politics and considered himself a social democrat. (He argued that the Communist Party was actually "a reactionary force in America.")[41] In 1948 he was still enough of a man of the Left that he had supported Henry

A. Wallace's third-party presidential race. To do his part, Schulberg had volunteered to host a gala fundraising party for the Progressive Party at his Pennsylvania farm, which one thousand people ultimately attended. When the event organizers came to see him about details, they told him, "we will take a percentage for our expenses." From their language and method of operation, Schulberg quickly surmised that the Progressive Party's organizers were actually Communist Party members. He recalled that when he had run events for the Party in Los Angeles, he was always instructed to siphon off a percentage for the Party's coffers.

When everyone had left the fundraiser and he was alone with Wallace, Schulberg said to him: "I'm very upset because I know you're not a Communist. But are you aware that you are actually in the hands of the Party?" Wallace responded with surprise. "He was naïve and trusting, and didn't want to believe it," Schulberg later recalled.[42] After Wallace's resounding electoral defeat, Schulberg wrote to him with the observation that "he might have had some chance to win some support from the American people if he hadn't lent himself completely to the line of the Communist Party."[43]

Schulberg was most outraged by the fate of the artists and writers he had met in Russia during his fateful trip there in 1934. One of the tragic victims of Stalin's purges in the arts was the radical theater innovator Vsevolod Meyerhold, who had been so admired by left-wing Americans involved in the radical theater. In 1938, the "liquidation" of the Meyerhold Theatre was announced—it was "alien to Soviet art." Then on June 15, 1939, Meyerhold was forced to attend a public self-criticism session, where he confronted his tormentors: "The pitiful and wretched thing that pretends to the title of the theater of socialist realism has nothing in common with art...." Several days later he was arrested, savagely tortured, and finally shot on February 2, 1940. After his arrest, his wife, the actress Zinaida Raikh, was found dead in their home with her eyes cut out and seventeen knife wounds.[44]

Schulberg told the committee that by 1938 all of the Russian writers he had met "had either been shot or silenced, and after that none of these writers, who were trying to follow their own individual line, were able to function any more."[45] He was so concerned about their fate that along with Arthur Koestler, the ex-Communist European intellectual, he helped found a group called Friends of Intellectual Freedom. Joining him in raising funds and giving political support to this cause were writers Aldous Huxley, Graham Greene, John Dos Passos, James T. Farrell, Richard Rovere and Stephen Spender.

His decision to testify made Schulberg a marked man with his old friends. In the 1960s his old acquaintance Lillian Hellman approached him at a party and proceeded to reprimand him for testifying as a friendly witness before HUAC. "I really felt guilty about all those years I was in the Party," he responded, "when such terrible things were happening to writers like Isaac Babel." To his astonishment, Hellman asked, "What happened to Babel?" He looked at her in disbelief: "What happened to Babel? He was murdered [by Stalin] in 1940." Hellman's ignorant and dismissive reply staggered him: "That's anti-Soviet propaganda."[46]

Talking to Victor Navasky in the 1970s, Schulberg said again that he had no guilt for having talked openly before HUAC. "My guilt is what we did to the Czechs, not to Ring Lardner," he explained. "I testified because I felt guilty for having contributed unwittingly to intellectual and artistic as well as racial oppression." His experience in the American Party, he told Navasky, showed him that the American Communists too were "thought controllers, as extreme in their way as Joe McCarthy was in his." He did not support the blacklist, but he knew that the Reds and fellow travelers clearly "support the deathlist." So while many on the Left attacked him for talking before HUAC, he saw only "their silence," and preferred to be among the "pre-mature anti-Stalinists."[47]

At least one other blacklisted Communist screenwriter, Walter Bernstein, acknowledged the merit of Schulberg's position. Looking back at Schulberg's HUAC testimony in a 1997 interview, he explained that Schulberg had shown how someone could legitimately turn against the Communist Party and yet not grovel, as Bernstein claimed the others who testified had done. Unlike other friendly ex-Communist witnesses, Bernstein thought, Schulberg had approached his testimony "carefully, as literature," and had put together a "brief" to support his position. Although he felt that Schulberg betrayed him personally, Bernstein acknowledged the validity of Schulberg's passionate and hostile response to Soviet repression and bemoaned the fact that because he was so enraged by Schulberg's "informing," he had dismissed what his old friend had to say about Communism and the Soviet Union.[48]

Elia Kazan

If Schulberg was the least ambivalent witness in his public testimony against the Party, Elia Kazan was the most introspective. In his 1988 autobiography, and before that in his 1971 interviews with the French writer Michael Ciment, he offered a complete record of his thoughts about being in the Party, and about how and why he had made the painful decision to turn against it and testify.

Kazan was born Elia Kazanjoglou in 1909, to Greek parents in Turkey. His family came to the United States in 1913. After graduating from Williams College, he moved on to Yale's drama school, where he met his future wife, Molly Thatcher. Unlike Kazan, who for all his success always felt something of an alien, Molly was a consummate insider—a WASP blueblood whose father was a corporate lawyer and whose great-grandfather had been president of Yale. She would urge him on when his moment came before HUAC.

In 1932, Kazan, then twenty-three, took a step that would change his life forever. He met with Lee Strasberg, Harold Clurman and Cheryl Crawford, the directors of the Group Theatre, and became an apprentice at their second summer camp at Sterling Farm. By the summer's end, he had become a full member of the Group Theatre. Visiting his parents in the fall, Kazan found his father sick and demoralized because of the failure of his carpet business. He pledged in his diary to "make the revolution" as a way of getting revenge for what capitalism had done to his family.

He joined the Communist Party cell in the Group, which met

every Tuesday evening, after the performance, in actor J. Edward Bromberg's dressing room at the Belasco Theater. Kazan watched as his friend Clifford Odets, the playwright who had an overnight success with *Awake and Sing,* was promoted by the Party to member-at-large. In order to protect him and allow him what a later time would call "plausible deniability," all records of his role in the CP cell were erased and his Party card was taken away. As Kazan noted, "This was the honor accorded Lillian Hellman and some other glamour intellectuals," who would also be protected from repression when it arrived because their record of Party membership had been erased.[49]

The Party leadership regarded the Group Theatre as a prize. If they could take over and completely fashion the repertoire company, they would score a major triumph in their penetration of American culture. Kazan met with the Party's cultural commissar, V. J. Jerome, who later was to terrorize Hollywood Communists with his edicts and demands. Jerome had a simple task for Kazan and his comrades: "take command of the theatre," using the slogan "all power to the people."

Kazan carried Jerome's message back to the Party cell; they were to "transform the Group into a collective, a theater run by its actors." The proposal meant that the Group would be wrested from the control of its founders and directors, including Lee Strasberg, whose wife, Paula, was a Party member. Much to his own surprise, Kazan found himself arguing against the idea. The members of the Party cell at the Group were stunned, and predictably they voted him down. He was "on the side of the directors, not the 'people,'" they argued, and he was therefore "not a good Communist... [but] an opportunist who'd do anything to get to the top."[50]

A Party cell meeting was called at Paula Strasberg's home, and her husband was asked to leave for the evening. A "leading comrade" was brought in to read Kazan the riot act. He was an organizer from Detroit for the United Auto Workers—a man who, unlike theater people, was a bona fide member of the proletariat. He was there to set the Party cell straight, and he spent his entire presentation attacking Kazan, whom he called a "foreman type" who was "trying to curry favor with the bosses." As the

man droned on, all Kazan could do was enjoy the aroma of pastries being prepared in the bakery beneath the Strasberg
apartment. Eventually, the "Man from Detroit" made it clear that
Kazan would be forgiven, but only after he had acknowledged his
errors and potential treason against the working class. When
Kazan got home in the wee hours of the morning, he instead
wrote a letter resigning his membership in the Communist
Party.[51]

From that experience, Kazan saw what the Party would produce should it ever come to power: a "police state." Yet for years
he maintained the same warm relationship with his former comrades. He still thought like a Communist, and did his part to
prove to them and to himself that he had not moved over to the
side of the reactionaries. He went on the annual May Day parade.
He was still sympathetic to what he saw as "the worldwide movement for the liberation of the oppressed."[52] He accepted the
Popular Front and supported policies favorable to the survival
of the Soviet Union.

When the Group folded, Kazan made his way to Hollywood,
arriving at the time of the Nazi-Soviet Pact, which he rationalized
the same way as hardcore Party members: survival of the USSR
made the agreement necessary and correct. He might feel one
way about the American CP, but the Soviet Union was a different
case: "the one place on earth where socialism was being
attempted." But then, at the pact's end, came the swift change
in position by left-wing intellectuals who overnight went from
criticizing an imperialist war to calling for "a people's struggle"
against the Axis. It was, he wrote, "the beginning of the end of
my attachment to the U.S.S.R."[53]

By the 1950s, Kazan, the leading film director of his generation, had long since made the complete intellectual break with
Communism that so many of the other writers and directors,
even those who had left the Party, had not been able to accomplish. When his subpoena to appear before HUAC arrived, he
was already a committed anti-Communist. He saw nothing wrong
with telling the world what he now regarded as the truth.

When Kazan appeared before HUAC on April 10, 1952, he
created a storm by naming others who had been in the Party with

him when he was part of the Group Theatre cell, between the summer of 1934 and the late winter or early spring of 1936. But Kazan had also testified earlier, on January 14, in a private executive session.

He had one goal, he wrote: to tell the committee "that I'd been a member for a year and a half, that I'd quit in disgust, that the plan of the Party to take over the Group Theatre had failed.... I knew they'd ask me to name the others in our 'cell' and I'd refuse." The committee's director of research, Raphael Nixon, took him first into a waiting room and said that HUAC was "sensitive to the criticism that they smeared people and ruined lives." Then he casually asked Kazan if his friend Clifford Odets had been a Party member. Kazan replied that "I'd cooperate in every way about myself but would not discuss others." Nixon asked Kazan to reconsider. After going for lunch, the committee convened formally, telling him that this was an "executive session" and it would be "kept confidential."

In his executive session testimony, Kazan recounted what the Party demanded of the Group Theatre cell, and told them that V. J. Jerome had "raised hell" and ordered him to "hew to the line," after which he resigned from the Communist Party. When asked to tell who the other Party members were, Kazan refused: "It is a matter of personal conscience." Although he detested the Party, he could not name any names, since his feelings were "based on a good deal of personal encounter." When asked directly about Clifford Odets, he simply said, "I don't want to answer that question." He stressed—obviously much to the committee's dismay—that the "guys who ran the Group Theatre were never members of the Communist Party, to my knowledge."

When the committee asked about actor John Garfield, Kazan called him a "kid from the Bronx" who was definitely not a Communist when he knew him in the Group. Then he proposed an alternative to the line of questioning so far: he would say what he had done while in the Party, and mention that others had been members and that they too regretted their past membership. But he worried that if his appearance were open, "the plans I am working on as a director of a picture in Hollywood would be off tomorrow" because "the pressure groups are so strong."

Emphasizing that he thought HUAC should investigate and that "what you're doing is right," he feared that if he did name names, "I would be out of a job, so to speak."[54]

Kazan's dilemma was that he was caught between two evils—a Party whose ideas he now felt were as corrupt as its "secrecy...tactics...[and] goals," and HUAC, which he also hated. Yet he agreed with his tough anti-Communist wife, Molly, who had had her own run-ins with the Party and who believed that "it was the duty of the government to investigate the Communist movement in our country." Kazan had also spoken with the anti-Stalinist philosopher Sidney Hook, and had been influenced by the analysis in his article and book *Conspiracy Yes: Heresy No,* which developed the argument that the Communist Party was not simply another political party but a tool of the Soviet Union and its secret police. Hook told Kazan that the Party would stop at nothing to control him, would vet his scripts and constantly interfere with his artistic freedom; if he wanted to strike a blow against the Party, he would have to name names.[55]

The more Kazan thought about it, the stronger his convictions became. Certainly he was pressured by the studios, which were hoping he would decide to cooperate so they could keep on having him make films. As an artist, he wanted to continue working. Would it be worth giving up everything that was important to him merely to protect the reputation of the Communist Party? Spyros Skouras, the president of Twentieth Century Fox, urged him to meet with J. Edgar Hoover and his chief aide Louis Nichols. Kazan said he would not, since they would ask him to name old friends in the Party. Later, after the committee leaked news of his executive session testimony to the press, Kazan was pressured by producer Darryl Zanuck, who told him: "Name the names, for chrissake. Who the hell are you going to jail for? You'll be sitting there and someone else will sure as hell name those people. Who are you saving?"

Kazan remembered how the Party had tried to censor him, to change the script of *Viva Zapata!* so the revolutionary position would be more sympathetic; how the Party had treated his friend Albert Maltz; and what had happened to Budd Schulberg when he wanted to write his first novel. He recalled vividly how V. J.

Jerome had sought "unquestioning docility" during the Group Theatre days. He realized that what he had to do was fight "the CP's influence in the arts," and to do this, he had to demonstrate by his actions that he was firmly against them.

Before his second HUAC appearance, in April 1952, Kazan told one of his dearest and oldest friends, Arthur Miller, about his feelings. Miller—Kazan claimed not to know whether or not the playwright was a Party member—argued with him, supporting the Party's position. He was against the Marshall Plan and against the Korean War, and he accused Kazan of being naïve. When Miller bumped into Kazan a few months later after his testimony, Miller snubbed him and went on his way. It would take ten years for them to work together again, and still Kazan never forgave him for that snub.

Kazan also met with Lillian Hellman, whom he then did not know had been a secret Communist Party member. While Miller had at least shown a distant sympathy for Kazan's plight, Hellman "was silent as a coiled snake" and walked out on him rather than remain for a lunch they had planned. She would accuse him, as would others, of selling out for the money. Kazan later wrote, "I did what I did because it was the more tolerable of two alternatives that were, either way, painful...and either way wrong for me."

The most difficult task was talking to his best friend from the Group, the playwright Clifford Odets, who would eventually appear before HUAC as a friendly witness himself. Kazan told Odets that if he did not want to be named, he too would refuse to cooperate, not name names, and give up filmmaking: "I believe we should all of us name all of us, establish the truth of what went on. That would make clear how small the scale was, and this thing would be off our backs. But you are one of my best friends, and I won't even consider that without your permission."

Much to Kazan's surprise, he found that Odets was experiencing the same dilemma; he wanted Kazan's permission to name *him*. They were in agreement. But unlike Kazan, who was fortified by his growing anti-Communism, Odets continued to feel guilty. By testifying and naming names, he would give up his identity as the playwright of the Left, ruining his reputation as "hero-rebel, the fearless prophet of a new world." What gave Kazan strength drained Odets. Afterward, Kazan wished that his friend had not testified; Odets from then on limited himself to rewriting scripts for other Hollywood writers, never doing anything of artistic consequence again.

The last people Kazan spoke with were his old Group colleagues Lee and Paula Strasberg. Paula Strasberg told Kazan to save his career in film, even if it meant naming her. Kazan also received advice he treasured from his friend Budd Schulberg, who took the same course. Later, Schulberg would work with Kazan when he wrote the screenplay for Kazan's masterpiece, *On the Waterfront*. A person in their situation, Schulberg wrote to Kazan, "since he cannot please all his old friends, must settle for pleasing himself."

When Kazan told his wife, Molly, of his decision, she helped him prepare for the storm that would descend after he appeared before HUAC the second time. On April 10 he again testified in a private, closed executive session, but HUAC released the transcript of his testimony to the press the following day. It mirrored his testimony of the previous January, with the exception that this time he gave a complete account, including all the names of those he had known in the Party for the brief time he was a member. He prepared a statement that he handed in at the start, giving his reasons for changing his position, calling it his "obligation as a citizen." Those he named were Lewis Leverett, J. Edward Bromberg, Phoebe Brand, Morris Carnovsky, Tony Kraber, Paula Strasberg, Clifford Odets and Art Smith, most of whom were already known to have been Communists. Kazan had limited his list to the Group Theatre days—carefully avoiding naming anyone he might have suspected or known to be Communists at a later period.[56]

Kazan knew he would now get what the Party felt he had coming: anger, vituperative attacks and unremitting hostility from the left-liberal community. His wife locked herself in her study and typed out a statement on a single page—to be handed in as a newspaper advertisement under Kazan's name—describing the issues leading to his testimony and what his intentions were, and promising that he would be making the same kind of socially conscious films he had always made. Much derided by the Kazan-haters, the statement today reads as a moderate and careful public presentation explaining what motivated him to testify.

It spelled out how America could protect itself "from a dangerous and alien conspiracy and still keep the free, open, healthy way of life that gives us self-respect." Emphasizing that he had "no spy stories to tell," and that at the time he did not understand that the American Party took its orders from Moscow, Kazan explained that it was the Party's discipline and opposition to freedom of speech and art and its dictation of personal conduct that led him to quit in 1936. He also said that what held him back was fear that if he opposed the Communists openly, he would be accused of joining the Right. As a liberal, he stressed that liberalism itself was in danger as long as liberals continued to protect and cooperate with the Communists.[57]

Kazan's statement was hardly the reactionary raving of a mini Joe McCarthy; it was an anti-Communist liberal manifesto. Yet as he anticipated, it only fueled the fire, making him the "target of a well-organized campaign branding my act as shameful."[58] Old friends sent him hostile letters, mostly unsigned. Kazan wrote, "I found I was notorious, an 'informer,' a 'squealer,' a 'rat.' I'd become the star villain for 'progressives;' just as they'd expected me to be the staunchest defender of their position, they now labeled me the most treacherous of traitors." As expected, the *Daily Worker* pointed the way: "One can imagine the chairman of HUAC putting his arms around him and saying, 'This is the greatest moment of your life!' It is the lowest moment of Kazan's life, one which will haunt him forever."[59] The only defense he received was from the anti-Communist liberal historian Arthur M. Schlesinger Jr., who called his ad "a reasonable and dignified document."

John Garfield

John Garfield was the man HUAC really wanted to get. Of all the writers, directors and actors called to appear, Garfield was the closest thing to a major Hollywood figure. In a film career that

began in 1938, he was best known for *Pride of the Marines* (1945);
The Postman Always Rings Twice (1946), and most of all for *Body and Soul* (1947) and *Gentleman's Agreement* (1947). Always appearing as the down-to-earth, gruff but handsome regular guy, he was the first actor who had risen from the ranks of the Group Theatre to reach true stardom.

Referred to as "Julie" by his friends and family, Garfield was born Julius Jacob Garfinkle in 1913, the child of poor Russian immigrants who lived in New York's Lower East Side. His father, a pants-presser and weekend cantor, left the boy with relatives when his wife died in 1920. Growing up rebellious and angry, Garfield skipped school so often that he was shipped to Public School 45 in the Bronx, where Angelo Patri, the school's principal, was known for rehabilitating problem students. Patri took Julie under his wing, encouraging him in boxing and dramatics, and later helped support him when he attended the Heckscher Foundation drama school.

Befriending the young playwright Clifford Odets, who became his lifelong friend, Garfield tried to crack the Group Theatre. They condescended to Garfield as a talented young man who was beneath them because of his scanty education, deficient knowledge of American theater history, and small ambition for anything except acting. Joining the others from the Group who in 1936 began to migrate to Hollywood, Garfield signed a contract with Warner Brothers in 1938. More than any of the others, he became a success there.

In the film capital, Garfield and his wife, Robbe, a dedicated Communist Party activist whom he married in 1935, immediately gravitated to all the popular left-wing and liberal causes. Usually following the lead of his wife, as one biographer writes, Garfield "signed political petitions as easily as he would sign an autograph for a fan."

Because of his wife and his support of her causes, many in the film colony assumed that Garfield too was a Communist. He was prone to blurting out odd statements, such as the popular New York left-wing refrain: "Come the Revolution, we'll all be eating strawberries and cream." He told his friend Robert Whitehead, "You know, I wanted to join the Communist Party. I really did.... I tried. Hell, I'm a joiner. But they wouldn't let me in. Can you imagine that? They thought I was too dumb. They said I couldn't be trusted."[60]

Garfield's troubles began in June 1950, when *Red Channels*, a newsletter privately published by three former FBI agents, included his name on a list of those in the entertainment field with ties to Communist groups and subversive activity. Going through his public record, the former agents tied Garfield to over seventeen different Communist front groups. The influence of *Red Channels*, appearing at the height of the blacklist, was immense. Anyone named there would soon be unemployable. When, for instance, Garfield volunteered to go abroad and entertain American troops fighting in Korea, he found that the Department of Defense would not give him a clearance to perform.

Garfield's agent, George Chasin, tried to get him considered for a role in a movie about impresario Sol Hurok, a role he thought Julie was a natural for. Twentieth Century Fox's manager, Lew Schreiber, kept putting Chasin off. The agent insisted that Fox give Garfield a screen test that the actor would pay for, and that if they hired him, they could get Elia Kazan to direct. Schreiber told him it "would be a waste of Garfield's money and Kazan's time." Garfield was not given a screen test, and Chasin concluded that he was already blacklisted.[61] As it was clear that a blacklist did exist and that he was on it, Garfield became increasingly anxious to prove that he was not a Communist.

On October 13, 1950, he wrote to Dore Schary, MGM's head of production, a hitherto undiscovered letter:

> I wanted to write you this letter a long time ago, but I have been postponing it from time to time thinking that I might see you in person and talk about it....
>
> Will you please not interpret this, directly or indirectly, as any need on my part for a job. Fortunately, I have more demands on me for a long time than I can possibly fill. I don't know if this will always be the case, but it is the case at present and for some time in the future.
>
> I'd like to work in a picture for you. And the terms would be entirely secondary. My schedule is crowded, but the kind of

picture is what is important. That's why, of course, I am talking to you about it. Because I think we think the same on the
subject. It's our democracy. Certainly, it needs improving all
the time, and I am never going to, out of fear of being unpop-
ular, stop "beefing." But it is undoubtedly the best in existence
by far. And it's so much better than all the dictatorships,
including those which pose to be people's governments, like
Russia. I would like to work in a film which has this as a subject matter. It seems to me that this would be about as timely a
picture as one could make, and I think it could be a box office
success. One which calls a spade a spade. One which shows the
wonderful things of our democracy, and perhaps points out
where it can be improved, but also shows the tyranny of countries like Spain and Russia and their satellites....

Although I have been on committees which have had Communists on them, and that may have been foolish because I
know now that committees with Communists on them are frequently dominated and run by Communists, there should be
some way of doing things and expressing one's opinions and
ideals completely independently, where no Communists are
involved. Especially where you do something that shows them
up.

Will you give this some thought and let me hear from you
about it?[62]

This extraordinary letter indicates that Garfield was desperate to avoid the blacklist and to continue working, and was
willing to do what he must in order to achieve that end. Moreover, given his years of readiness to endorse almost any front
group his wife and others asked him to support, Garfield knew
he had to establish that he had gotten off the fellow-traveler's
train when the Cold War began. Later on, after his death, his former comrades would try to depict him as a heroic enemy of the
blacklist and a supporter of the unfriendly witnesses, but this letter reveals that he was against Communist policy and anxious to
appear in anti-Communist films.

Garfield expected to receive a subpoena any day. It finally
arrived in March 1951, in the form of a press announcement by
HUAC. Garfield told the press that he had "nothing to hide,"
and speculated only that he thought they might want informa-

tion from him about the Screen Actors Guild.[63] The next day he hired Louis Nizer, one of the nation's top trial lawyers. "I have always hated communism," he told the media. "It is a tyranny which threatens our country and the peace of the world. Of course then, I have never been a member of the Communist Party or a sympathizer with any of its doctrines. I will be pleased to cooperate with the committee."[64]

Finally appearing before HUAC on April 23, 1951, Garfield denounced Communism as "tyranny" and "dictatorship." He told the committee that the Communist Party was not a legitimate political party such as the Democratic or Republican Party, and that "if the Communist Party was outlawed it would help clear up a lot of confusion on that point." Noting that he had withdrawn his earlier support of Henry Wallace in the 1948 presidential election because he knew that the CP had "captured" Wallace, Garfield tried to fashion himself as the quintessential anti-Communist liberal, a man in Dore Schary's mold. Garfield told HUAC that not only had he never been a Communist, but to his knowledge he had never known any. Asked whether he had ever been asked to join the CP, he answered: "No, if I had been I would have run like hell.... I detest Communism and all it stands for, its suppression of freedom, the destruction of culture, and a threat to the peace of the world."[65]

On the face of it, Garfield's testimony was laughable. Not only did almost everyone in Hollywood know that his wife was a Party member, but, as one columnist quipped, one could not live in New York City and never have known a Communist! Clearly, Garfield was trying to play the committee. "They're out to fuck me," he said to his counsel, Louis Nizer, before taking the stand, "but I'm not going to let them."[66] He knew that HUAC was well aware of his wife's Party membership and his own fellow-traveling. But he assumed they had no proof that he had ever been a Communist.

Strangely, HUAC did not even ask Garfield if he was a married man. It appeared that a deal had been struck behind the scenes: if he was cooperative, his wife would be out of bounds. Ironically, she was furious that he had chosen this path and made it clear that if she had been called, she would have refused to testify.

Garfield told HUAC that he was a liberal, "and I don't think the Communists like liberals." When asked about the violent 1945 strike when the Party was backing the Conference of Studio Unions, Garfield claimed that as Screen Actors Guild members, he and others had "tried in every possible way to stop" the strike, and were at first "impartial" and sometimes opposed to the CSU. By 1946, he told them, he realized that the CSU was the real culprit. He brought along with him minutes of the SAG board from 1945 to 1947, indicating that he had been against the strike and had argued that it was "uncalled for and unwarranted." Toward the hearing's end, Garfield assured the committee that he felt they had a legitimate right to investigate Communism in the motion picture industry, since the Party was a "subversive group."[67]

Garfield made one major mistake when Frank Tavenner, the HUAC counsel, asked him whether he had addressed a meeting in Washington, D.C., during the period of the Nazi-Soviet Pact, attacking what he called the "war drives" going on at the time. Garfield replied, "That is absolutely untrue. I was never in Washington in 1940 and I never made such a speech." Indeed, he said he was "overseas at that time, when the Communists considered the war an imperialistic war." As it happens, easily obtained newspaper reports established that he was indeed in the nation's capital at that time, appearing in a play, and that he had made such an address.

The committee let this pass, but its members went on the attack in other matters. He continued to deny ever being approached to join the Communist Party, or knowing who was and was not a Red. Finally, when one HUAC member asked him if any of the liberal groups he belonged to might have been "used" by the Communist Party, Garfield reluctantly admitted that "they were captured." Confronted with evidence that he had belonged to front groups he now denied ever joining, and that he had often been praised in the pages of the *Daily Worker,* he retorted: "Senator Taft was praised by *The Daily Worker* for his refusal to send troops to Europe. Does that mean he is on their team, so to speak?"

Garfield concluded his appearance by stating "I was glad to appear before you…. I am no Red. I am no 'pink.' I am no fellow-traveler. I am a Democrat by politics, a liberal by inclination, and a loyal citizen of this country." Garfield was dismissed. He was treated as a star by the members, who vied with each other in asking for his autograph and inviting him to dinner. Attorney Louis Nizer was jubilant.

The Communists, as one might have expected, were furious. The *Daily Worker* attacked Garfield as a traitor. When he went to dinner at Club 21 or Toots Shor's, the two big celebrity joints in New York, he found that although he had not named anyone, his old friends like Morris Carnovsky iced him. Moreover, he was now consistently turned down for parts he sought in both film and television.[68]

Unknown to Garfield, the press and the public, HUAC itself was not satisfied. It had convened executive sessions to consider whether he had committed perjury, and it continued to investigate him. The committee was making preparations to call him back.

On May 31, HUAC received testimony from Hede Massing, a confessed former NKVD agent of the Soviet government. Married to Paul Massing after her divorce from Gerhart Eisler, she and her new husband had worked as couriers for a Soviet spy ring run from Paris by Ignatz Reiss, and later they worked with American agents of the Soviets, including Noel Field and Alger Hiss. Her former brother-in-law, composer Hanns Eisler and his wife, Louisa, both knew John Garfield well.

Hede Massing told the committee that Louisa had said cryptically of Garfield, "He is one of us." Massing further testified that Louisa told her Garfield was "a very unstable man, meaning that you cannot count on him, that he is one day this, and one day that." She went on to say: "If I remember right, she always had difficulties with him on political issues, and if I am not mistaken, they played him for a sucker. They played him for money. They didn't say outright he was a dope, but that they implied, or she implied, about him." As for Garfield's claim that he had never known a Communist in his life, Massing found it "fantastic," since it was virtually impossible "not to know that Hanns Eisler was the brother of Gerhart Eisler, and that Hanns Eisler was a Communist for the greater part of his life, being the composer of the greatest Communist anthems in Europe."[69]

Massing's testimony, however, was entirely secondhand. She had met Garfield with her sister-in-law, but had not engaged him in political conversation.

The committee also heard a few days later from the actress Jean Dillow, formerly Jean Carmen, who asked to testify after reading the news reports about Garfield's appearance. Dillow had met Garfield in 1939 when she had a part in his first picture, *Four Daughters.* He only talked about two subjects, she testified: acting and the Soviet Union. Meeting him later in New York City, he told her that he needed to stop at his friend Clifford Odets' apartment, to which he had a key. Once they entered and she saw that Odets was not there, she assumed that Garfield intended her to be another of his conquests.

But to her surprise, instead of seduction, Garfield insisted on giving her literature kept by Odets that presented "a fresh approach to Communism and Russia." Dillow recalled that Garfield "got very enthusiastic...then he started talking about everybody sharing alike." He sounded "like a record." She asked how much of his salary he shared with the Party. Garfield answered, "I don't have to give too much of my salary" because "I do a good job recruiting members." When she asked what he got out of doing all that for the Communist Party, he answered that when the revolution came about, "I will be in favor. I will have a high position in the government."

Dillow added that in 1942 in Chicago, after an opening of Chekov's *The Three Sisters,* there was a party at Ernest Byfield's apartment and all the guests were talking about a Communist Party meeting they had attended. "Soon John had the floor," she said, "and he was really pacing the floor. He was waving his arms and shouting about all the marvelous things Russia gave their people...and the only way of life in the world was the Communist way of life; that this country was going to have it." The actress Paulette Goddard interrupted him, saying, "For God's sake, John, pipe down." When Dillow and Garfield were leaving the party, they bumped into the actress Ruth Gordon, and later

Garfield told Dillow: "She is one of us, Jean. She is a member....
[I]f you want to get anywhere in this business you have got to
change your way of thinking. Everybody who is anybody in this
business is a Communist."[70]

The next day, New York's *Daily Mirror* reported that "Congress was considering a special session to see if Julie was
withholding information." One of HUAC's members, Representative Bernard Kearney, released a statement that "the committee
definitely disbelieves the greater portion of the testimony of
Garfield, especially those portions where he denied ever knowing
anyone who was a Communist." And columnist Victor Reisel, a
preeminent anti-Communist with close ties to the FBI, wrote that
the Justice Department should examine CP card no. 25,192,
which he knew belonged to Garfield's wife, Robbe, and would
prove "why a great star perjured himself."

Meanwhile, Garfield's career was still on hold. Even the Red
Cross cancelled a commercial he had been scheduled to do for
them. He had no major new film contracts; his last movie, *He Ran
All the Way* (1951), had been poorly received, and stress was
affecting his health. To deal with the situation, Garfield decided
to seek the aid of well-known liberal anti-Communists in the New
York Jewish community, especially his old childhood friend
Arnold Forster and his colleague Nathan C. Belth, now working
for the Anti-Defamation League of B'nai Brith in top positions.
The star "was absolutely defeated," Forster told Garfield's biographer. "He was angry, and he was frustrated. He felt that there was
no way he was going to get out of the problem he was in. When
he came to see me I guess it was a last desperate effort."[71]

Forster did his best to help his old friend. The ADL people
urged Garfield to try to gain support from the press. They also
advised him to go public as a strong anti-Communist, and to publish an article that Forster and Belth would help him
write—telling the story of how he was tricked into helping the
Party and its various front groups and causes. The article was to
be called "I Was a Sucker for a Left Hook," a title referring ellip-
tically to the boxing films that Garfield had appeared in. Basically
a rehash of his HUAC testimony, the article was scheduled for
publication in a forthcoming issue of *Look*. But when the editor

Bill Loew had read it over, he sent the piece back to Forster, calling it "slick, unspecific and a special plea," and saying that he
would consider it again after a rewrite.

Garfield took the additional step of approaching the FBI for
an appointment. At a meeting on May 10, 1952, the agents
showed him photos of his appearance at a front group meeting
in Washington, D.C., in 1940. Despite being confronted with the
hard evidence, Garfield strangely continued to deny that he had
been there. The agents then turned to files they had on his wife,
and, according to Forster, showed him cancelled checks made
out by Robbe to the Communist Party, as well as her old Party
membership card. Forster claimed that the bureau told Garfield
that if he would sign a statement admitting that his wife was a
Communist, they would clear him. Garfield looked at the material and replied, "Fuck you!"

Working with Forster to finish his article for *Look*, Garfield
was tense and irritable. He was drinking and smoking heavily,
and going three days at a time without any sleep. Now living at a
room in the Warwick Hotel after tensions with Robbe forced him
to move out of their apartment, Garfield listened to his friend
Clifford Odets' testimony before HUAC on nationwide radio and
heard Odets name mutual old friends as Party members. On May
21, he had dinner with actress and interior decorator Iris Whitney, with whom he was having an affair. He returned to her
apartment, complaining of feeling sick. When she brought him
orange juice the next morning, Whitney found him dead. The
medical records attributed his death to cardiac arrest. He was
thirty-nine years old.

Most of those who have written about his last days have
claimed that the blacklist killed John Garfield. They have revered
him as a hero who stood up to HUAC and the blacklisters, a man
who led the fight against McCarthyism alongside other heroes
like the Hollywood Ten. This picture, as it turns out, is highly distorted. Garfield was a fellow traveler when it led to work and
celebrity; and when the Cold War broke out, he tried his best to
reposition himself as an anti-Communist.

His friend, director John Berry, later said that Garfield knew
that the only way he could regain his self-esteem and his career

was by naming names. "The tension was enormous," Berry said. "The temptation to play ball must have crossed his mind.... I think what happened was, faced with this option, Julius Garfinckle of the Bronx said to John Garfield of Hollywood, 'You can't do this to me.' And John Garfield packed his bags and died. The only way to clear himself was to rat, and he couldn't do that."[72]

But it is equally possible to argue that the Communist Party and its members and fellow travelers were responsible for Garfield's death. Willing to use his name, money and celebrity for their causes during the wartime years, they cared little for what would happen to his career later on. The Party guilt-baited him mercilessly and attacked him as a traitor after his HUAC testimony. Only decades later did they try to transform John Garfield into a martyr killed by HUAC.

Lillian Hellman

Playwright Lillian Hellman began her writing career as a book reviewer in New York City in the mid 1920s. Moving to Hollywood in 1930, she began a new job as a script reader for MGM, where she was paid the lowly sum of $50 per week. By that time she had met her lifelong partner and lover, detective writer Dashiell Hammett.

Returning to New York, Hellman gained success and fame as a stage writer, a career that took off with her first play, *The Children's Hour* (1934). Signing a contract with Goldwyn, Hellman returned to Hollywood, earning $2,500 per week. Her first script, based on her play, was *These Three* (1936), directed by William Wyler. Her best-known drama, *The Little Foxes* (1939), was a hit on Broadway and then purchased by MGM for a film version in 1941. Starring Bette Davis, Herbert Marshall and Teresa Wright, it was nominated for nine Academy Awards.

Hellman began a series of travels to Europe, where she lived in Paris, visited Spain during the years of the Spanish Civil War, and traveled as a journalist to the Soviet Union. Becoming actively involved in the left-wing movement in both New York City and Hollywood, Hellman joined the Communist Party for a few years, and although she quit its ranks, she continued to function as one of the Soviet Union's major defenders. With John Dos Passos and Archibald MacLeish, she wrote the script for *The Spanish Earth* (1937), the documentary used to raise money for the Spanish Republic. Her play *Watch on the Rhine* (1941), which also became a film, was one of the most notable antifascist dramas. Returning to Hollywood during the war years, Hellman also wrote the script for *The North Star* (1943), one of the most blatant examples of pro-Soviet politics in cinema.

Hellman is also remembered for her now-famous 1952 appearance before HUAC. A one-woman brigade against anti-Communism and in favor of resurrecting the glory days of the Popular Front, Hellman stood out as the *grande dame* of the HUAC theater. Her words of defiance—"I cannot and will not cut my conscience to fit this year's fashion"—came to sound like an existential manifesto. In the last years of her life, she was lionized as a culture hero; she toured campuses all over the country, and had a memoir (later revealed to be largely a fiction) made into *Julia,* starring Jane Fonda, one of her ideological heirs.

Hellman's reputation for bravery rests on the widespread belief that unlike other unfriendly witnesses, she declined to invoke the Fifth Amendment when she refused to testify. In fact, she did invoke the Fifth to avoid going to prison, to hide the truth about her own past, and to pretend to be concerned about others.

She always intended *not to testify* and to do anything necessary to avoid an indictment. This is clear from reading the letters that Hellman's attorney Joseph Rauh wrote to her while he was preparing her defense. There was only one course, Rauh wrote Hellman in April 1952—"the one you prefer—to tell the Committee under oath everything about yourself and nothing about anyone else." That course, however, had dangers. The courts did not allow those who invoked the Fifth to pick and choose which questions to answer. HUAC had consistently refused requests of unfriendly witnesses to do just that. Rauh therefore recommended that Hellman write HUAC a letter asking whether she could talk about herself alone and presenting the reasons to the committee.[73]

When Hellman drafted a letter to be presented to HUAC, she at first told the truth. "My own story is simple," Hellman wrote. "I joined the Communist Party in 1938 and left it some time in 1940." Claiming that she was at heart a "maverick," Hellman said that her nature "was no more suitable to the political left than it had been to the conservative background from which I came." Because her experience in Russia convinced her that the Soviet Union did not want war, she joined "peace groups" in which Communists were active. She also freely acknowledged her work in the 1948 Progressive Party of Henry Wallace. All of this, she said, was "a long time ago"—although when she wrote the letter, it was actually only a few years earlier.[74]

A short time later, Hellman rewrote her draft and sent a second version to Rauh. Now she proposed telling HUAC: "I joined the Communist Party in 1938 with little thought as to the serious step I was taking." She did so out of sympathy with Republican Spain and the Soviet Union, and political naïveté. Claiming that she had no real information "about the nature of the Party," she thought its "ultimate aims were humanitarian and idealistic." Had she delivered such a letter to HUAC, of course, Hellman would have come off as a classic dupe. To deal with this, she proposed to add: "I was wrong about the Communist Party," although she had "no bitterness toward the misguided lady who asked me to join." Moreover, Hellman argued, she had differences with the Party and opposed its "glorification" of Nazism during the years of the Nazi-Soviet Pact. Admitting that in the postwar years she joined peace groups in which Communists played a "substantial and often dominant role," she wrote off her actions as the result of being "one of the greatest joiners in history." At the same time, Hellman said she had no bitterness toward those she worked with in the Party and its front groups, "in which I participated freely and knowingly"; she would not "denounce them to protect my own future."[75]

While these two drafts were certainly more honest than her eventual testimony and the letter she actually delivered to HUAC, Rauh made it clear that they were hardly satisfactory: "When you refer to the Communists as people who were going your way, don't you confirm what the House Committee is setting out to prove about you?" The two drafts, he wrote her, would not serve as "a public vindication." Her arguments were "too cavalier," since all American Communists saw membership in the Party as "extremely serious." Next, Rauh gave her advice that she did not wish to hear: "Unless you are willing to state categorically that you were wrong about the Communist Party and to give the reasons why you were wrong, I see no value in any statement."

Clearly, what Hellman was most concerned with—aside from staying out of jail—was not saying anything that would lose her friends on the political Left. She wondered what Hammett would think, given that he had stayed loyal to the Party and had willingly gone to prison rather than cooperate with HUAC.

What Hellman finally did—with Rauh's agreement—was a public relations stroke of brilliance, involving a statement that was fraudulent and filled with evasions, if not outright lies. What Hellman said she was not willing to do was "to bring bad trouble to people who, in my past association with them, were completely innocent of any talk or action that was disloyal or subversive." If she had seen such activity, she assured HUAC, she would have considered it "my duty to have reported it to the proper authorities. But to hurt innocent people whom I knew many years ago in order to save myself, is to me, inhuman and indecent and dishonorable." Claiming never to have been a "political person," Hellman argued that she was upholding "an old-fashioned American tradition," that of "not bearing false witness." These were ideals of "Christian honor" that she trusted the committee would not ask her to violate. She was prepared to "waive the privilege of self-incrimination" and say anything they wanted to know about her, as long as the committee refrained from asking her to "name other people." If they would not, she told them, "I will be forced to plead the privilege of the Fifth Amendment."

She was not indicted, Rauh later said, because she said she was willing to talk about herself, so the committee could not smear her with the accusation that she was a "Fifth Amendment Communist." Nor could they prosecute her, since she made it look as though HUAC had forced her into taking the Fifth. But this explanation—and indeed, the entire case for Hellman's heroism—makes little sense. She did not have to talk about herself precisely *because* she took the Fifth; had she talked about herself without invoking the amendment, she would have forfeited her right against self-incrimination and then would have had to answer all the committee's questions. As Rauh would admit to one of Hellman's biographers, "The fact is, she did have to plead the Fifth Amendment. There was no way out of it, giving the conditions she put up."[76] The more moral position, taken later by playwright Arthur Miller and folksinger Pete Seeger, was to talk about oneself, not invoke the Fifth, and simply refuse to answer questions about others—seriously risking indictment and imprisonment for contempt of Congress.

Rauh's clever strategy, however, paid off. Hellman made it appear that she was not testifying about herself only because of the legal provisions of the Fifth Amendment. ("She was a lay person bewildered by the law," her biographer Carl Rollyson wrote, "a person of conviction and conscience who only wanted to do the right thing.")[77] The committee had put Hellman's letter into the record, but refused to let her read it. Rauh, noting that the committee had accepted her letter, then handed out copies to the press and those attending the hearing as Hellman was testifying. Decades later he explained to her: "I had your letter to the committee mimeographed ahead of time because I had decided to give it out to the press.... I was determined that your plea of self-incrimination was not going to stand naked and ugly while your motivations were so honorable.... The total success of our strategy, of course, was in the press the next day and especially in the *New York Times* of May 22, 1952, whose headline was: 'Lillian Hellman balks House unit—says she is not Red now, but won't disclose if she was lest it hurt others.'"

And of course, Hellman persisted until her death in the claim that she had not been a Communist. Party members were simply "people who wanted to make a better world; many of them were silly people...but that doesn't make for denunciation or furnish enough reason to turn them over for punishment to men who wanted nothing more than newspaper headlines."[78]

As the years passed and Hellman became a celebrated figure in cultural and literary circles once again, she continued to whitewash her past. In 1976—the year *Scoundrel Time,* her memoir of the McCarthy years, appeared—the *New York Times* cultural editor, Hilton Kramer, used it in a seminal article, "The Blacklist and the Cold War." Kramer acknowledged that during the blacklist, "informing became a career in itself, and innocent people *were* smeared and even destroyed by false accusations." But he noted that "less easily recognized" were the "other villains of the tale—the many wealthy Communists in the industry...who denied their true commitments and beliefs, and thereby created an atmosphere of havoc and hazard for the truly innocent." Since Hellman's memoir was at that moment on the bestseller list, Kramer cited the "vicious attacks that anti-Communist liberals and radicals were obliged to endure whenever they attempted to reveal the bloody truth about what Miss Hellman delicately describes as the 'sins' of the Stalinist regime." Who could guess, he asked, that Hellman "was once one of the most vigorous defenders of those 'sins'?" And he pointed to Hellman's signature on a petition attacking philosopher John Dewey, who had chaired a committee of inquiry into the charges made by Stalin against the exile Leon Trotsky in 1936. He quoted *Partisan Review* editor William Phillips, who argued that the Communists were "apologists for the arrest and torture of countless dissident writers in the Soviet Union," and asked, "Could Lillian Hellman not know these things?"[79]

The *Times* was inundated with letters from both supporters and opponents of Kramer's article. One of them came from historian Arthur M. Schlesinger Jr., who wrote favorably about the article and said it should be required reading for anyone under the age of forty. As it turned out, the night before Schlesinger's letter was printed, he was Lillian Hellman's guest at a dinner party she gave at her New York apartment. The next morning, opening the paper and reading Schlesinger's letter, Hellman was stunned. It was not his agreement with Kramer that surprised her, she wrote to Schlesinger, but the way he had nonetheless come to dinner at her home and acted friendly the entire evening! It was not cricket, she scolded, to "sit down next to people in apparent friendship and not tell them that you have publicly embraced their attacker. My regrets."[80] Schlesinger was not one to back down. "You have always known how I felt, and feel, about Stalinism," he replied. Repeating a point he had made in his letter to the *Times,* he told Hellman that one did not have to choose "either Stalinism or McCarthyism," and that one should rather "stand against both."

By 1984, Hellman's reputation was beginning to suffer. Writer Mary McCarthy, appearing on the Dick Cavett television interview program, had stated that everything Hellman said was a lie. Hellman responded by suing her for libel, a case that was in process when Hellman died. Other writers investigated her claims and found that her memoirs were more fiction than fact. And her HUAC appearance was coming in for closer scrutiny. When asked to offer proof of Hellman's "intellectual dishonesty," Mary McCarthy said the obvious: Many other writers and witnesses before HUAC had done what she only pretended to do—that is, testify about themselves and simply refuse to answer questions about others.

Lillian Hellman had been the first of the Hollywood Reds to falsify her past and yet emerge as a hero, for a while, at least. Her later portrayal of the politics of the 1930s, 1940s and 1950s sentimentalized the Old Left, glamorizing their politics and actions to make them out to be the moral exemplars they never were. As the 1950s faded into the past and America became a very different place, the picture she developed came to be widely accepted. This became Hellman's greatest fictional triumph.

☆

10

The Struggle of Dalton Trumbo

IF NOT QUITE THE SCOUNDREL TIME THAT LILLIAN HELLMAN CALLED IT, the decade of the 1950s was nonetheless a dark period in the lives of those who refused to break with the Party. With the blacklist spreading a cloud over Hollywood, its victims had to figure out a way to support their families and carry on with their lives. The consequences included ruined careers, stress-related health problems, divorces and even suicides. But the ordeal also presented some unexpected opportunities.

Dalton Trumbo proved to be one of the most resilient. Smart, well-read and exuberant, he had an instinct for the truth that the others lacked. That instinct, however, was always in conflict with the political lies that bound him to his Communist past. How he handled this tension between truth and loyalty after the fall made him the most interesting of the Hollywood Communists.

When he emerged in 1951 from his ten-month prison stay in Ashland, Kentucky, Trumbo was determined to move forward. Later, he looked back on his prison experience as a "very valuable one," far less depressing than his years laboring in a bakery before he made it as a writer.[1]

The first thing Trumbo did when he arrived in Los Angeles, even before going to his ranch, the Lazy-T, was to contact the King brothers, independent producers of B-movies, who had solicited his services after the blacklist. The brothers had been eager to have "the opportunity to get a fine writer to work for [them] whom [they] could not otherwise afford." Happy to have

Trumbo back, they sent him three original stories and a novel that they thought had movie potential. One of these, *Carnival Story,* was eventually made and released in 1954.[2]

Tumbo's biggest expense and asset was his ranch, and he put it on the market. Because money was still tight, he and his wife decided to follow their friends Jean and Hugo Butler and other blacklistees down to Mexico, where, they were told, things were cheap and there were filmmaking opportunities. But there was no work and soon Trumbo was writing to Michael Wilson, "I am broke as a bankrupt's bastard."[3] He left Mexico and returned to Los Angeles for good in 1954. According to the editor of his letters, Helen Manfull, he had become "an angry man with two dominant aims: to get into the [screenwriting] black market and cultivate it, and to break the blacklist rather than let the black-list break him and his colleagues."[4] A skilled and quick writer, Trumbo found he was able to get a great deal of work, always uncredited and always at a much lower rate of pay than what he had received in the old days. But producers kept him busy, know-ing that they were getting his talent at a bargain-basement price. In his first eighteen months in town, Trumbo wrote twelve low-budget films. He actually had more work than he could handle and farmed out what he couldn't do to other blacklisted writers. (His daughter Mitzi recalled, "At our house, when the phone rang, no matter who they asked for, you never said it was a wrong number, because you never knew what name Dad was writing under that week.")[5]

Trumbo's blacklisted comrades were also forced to strike out in new directions. Anticipating the worst, some Party mem-bers left the country before they could be subpoenaed. This became more difficult as the State Department began to refuse authorization of passports for blacklistees, a practice that was declared unconstitutional by the Supreme Court in 1958. But as Paul Jaricco recalled, people whose passports were lifted after they had made it to France or England were generally well treated by the governments there.[6]

Party members Ben and Norma Barzman hadn't been called during the first HUAC hearings in 1947, but were nerv-ous that the committee would eventually catch up with them.

When fellow screenwriter Bernard Vorhaus suggested that they trade houses to avoid being served a subpoena, it seemed far-fetched, but they decided to give it a try. When the knock came at their door they could honestly say they were not the person being sought. After all, both households had two children—a boy and a girl—an African-American housekeeper and a dog. (The Barzmans got the better of the deal because the Vorhaus's place had a pool and theirs did not.) Finally Eddie Dmytryk proposed that they join him in England, where he intended to direct a film version of a play, *Christ in Concrete,* and have Ben write the script.

The Barzmans arrived in London in 1949. When the film was finished they went to France, eventually forming a film company, Riviera Films. By 1951 they were part of a close-knit community of expatriot Hollywood Reds including John Berry, Jules Dassin, Michael and Zelma Wilson, and Paul Jarrico.[7]

Although they had no remaining Party affiliations after they left America, the Barzmans continued to "feel like Communists." Norma recalled: "Everywhere we went in Europe, people were always warm, welcoming. French intellectuals, whether Communist or not, treated us like heroes.... They believed that by standing up to HUAC we had done something wonderful, and they wanted to do something equally wonderful for us in return."[8] They were thrilled to befriend Picasso, who when first meeting them embraced them and announced, "We are the same."[9]

The Barzmans continued to believe in the Soviet dream long past the awakening of many of their French Communist friends. After Khrushchev's revelations about Stalin's crimes in 1956, they thought "it was wonderful that the Soviet Union could admit to the dreadful things it had perpetrated" and that "it had been pushed into [Stalinism] by the worldwide conspiracy against it." They refused to believe Yves Montand and Simone Signoret when the film stars told them how disappointed they were by their trip to the Soviet Union.[10] It was not until 1968—when the Soviets invaded Czechoslovakia, crushing "the Prague Spring" and dashing their "hopes for Communism with a democratic face"—that the Barzmans allowed themselves to consider the possibility that there were "many things wrong with Communism."[11]

The Barzmans could convince themselves that they had left America on their own terms. Integrating themselves into the foreign film industry, they didn't have to worry about money, and they found interesting projects to work on. Looking back on the experience later, Norma Barzman said: "The truth is, thirty years of exile gave our lives a richness they would never have had.... The blacklistees in Europe remained idealistic, even if their opinions changed."[12] But her husband, Ben, and his friend Joe Losey were bitter. Ben told Larry Ceplair that he never really felt part of the French community; he felt "cheated and victimized," and the "feelings of exclusion, alienation, and uprootedness never really left" him.[13]

Surprisingly, many blacklistees took Norman's position, not Ben's. Architect Zelma Wilson, Michael Wilson's wife, concluded, "I can't say that the Blacklist ruined my life. I had an opportunity to go to Europe and to study the architecture there that I might not have had. I'm not saying I'm happy that Mike was blacklisted, but there are fortuitous things that happen in a lifetime that come out of difficult situations."[14] Paul Jarrico said that although he certainly wouldn't recommend being blacklisted to others, he found it had "many positive aspects," because it allowed him to have experiences he never would have had otherwise: "Apart from Paris and other cities, I had a chance to live in Czechoslovakia...for five months in 1968 during the entire period known as the Prague Spring, so I don't have to get my knowledge about Eastern Europe out of books."[15] Communist screenwriter Allen Boretz returned to writing for the theater after he was blacklisted, eventually ending up in Franco's Spain, where he worked on *El Cid*. While there, he enjoyed the company of Ben Barzman, who was working on a film for Sophia Loren. Boretz was surprised to find that "it was the good life for us, because the bohemians of France had sort of drifted down into Madrid. I enjoyed that part of my life, and so did others who came around to join in it.... I personally felt no repression of any kind. Nobody bothered me in Spain."[16]

Hannah Weinstein, who under her maiden name of Dorner had run the Waldorf Conference and the HICCASP for the Party, moved with her family to England to seek job opportunities. There she formed and ran Dilipa, a TV production company, using the firm to come to the rescue of many of the blacklistees. Her first project starred Boris Karloff and was written by black-listed writers Abe Polonsky and Walter Bernstein. Her next project, the television series *Robin Hood,* turned out to be very successful. The series was shot in England on the grounds of her Foxwarren estate. Ring Lardner Jr. and his partner Ian McLellan Hunter, who had taken a job writing for the Diners Club, headed one group writing the show in New York, while Adrian Scott and Robert Lees worked on it in Los Angeles.[17] The show was sold in both England and the United States, and ran for four years, pro-viding the blacklisted Reds a delicious opportunity to create scripts about taking from the rich to give to the poor.

For some of those who settled or traveled abroad, exile was not a very satisfactory alternative. They missed friends, family and the milieu of America's fast-paced entertainment centers, and many of them returned to the United States. Drawn to the oppor-tunities in television and the theater, a large contingent of blacklistees ended up living in the Upper West Side of New York City. Michael Wilson, Paul Jarrico, Adrian Scott, Albert Maltz and Herbert Biberman joined together to form their own production company, Film Associates, Inc., later called Independent Produc-tions Corporation, which they hoped would enable them to re-establish continuity with their past by making films combin-ing technical excellence with "progressive content."[18]

Trumbo received a letter from Biberman asking for his sup-port and participation in the company. Biberman wanted Trumbo on board as a screenwriter, for which he would receive a nominal fee, deferred against future profits. Trumbo at first declined, citing economic necessity:

> I am, from today on and for some time in the future, not interested in pamphlets, speeches, or progressive motion pic-tures. I have got to earn money—a considerable sum of it—very quickly. I cannot and will not hypothecate two or three months...for any project that doesn't contain the possi-bility of an immediate and substantial sum.... Once I am in a position where the slightest mishap no longer places me in peril, I shall again function as I should like to. But this is well in the future.[19]

Trumbo had second thoughts when Biberman and his associates

managed to raise funds from the International Union of Mine, Mill and Smelter Workers, a former CIO-affiliated union that had been expelled from the labor federation for its control by the Communist Party, to make a film about a strike that the union had been involved in. The film, *Salt of the Earth,* was the chronicle of a strike led by Mexican-American mine workers. With a subplot about the growing feminist consciousness of the workers' wives, it was later seen as one of the first left-wing films to emphasize the twin themes of class and gender. The blacklisted Communists working on this project clearly experienced a momentary euphoria. It was almost possible for them to pretend that they had pushed back time and that the blacklist had never been.

Although the film premiered in 1954 at one movie theater in New York City, the opposition from Roy Brewer and the International Alliance of Theatrical and Stage Employees (IATSE), along with other anti-Communist groups, led to a nationwide boycott by projectionists, and the film could not be shown in theaters. It did not receive major attention until two decades later, during the 1960s, when Hollywood nostalgia for its Communist past suddenly came into vogue. It was finally released in video and the distributors marketed it as "Hollywood's only blacklisted film." Written by Michael Wilson, produced by Paul Jarrico and directed by Herbert Biberman, with Communist actor Will Geer playing a major role, *Salt of the Earth* marked the only time that three of the Hollywood Ten were able to work together on the kind of "progressive" film that the Party always hoped to make during its Hollywood heyday.[20]

Trumbo and "White Chauvinism"

Although *Salt of the Earth* was the only film that the group actually produced, they had other ideas on the drawing board, including one based on the book *Scottsboro Boy,* Communist writer Earl Conrad's account of the life of Heywood Patterson, one of the defendants in the celebrated case. They also wanted to develop a film for Paul Robeson.[21] Both projects were inspired by the burgeoning "Negro Liberation Movement," in which the Party was heavily invested during the 1950s.

The effort to bring themes underlying the Negro Liberation Movement to the screen took place against the backdrop of the Communist Party's most bitter internecine struggle—the so-called campaign against "white chauvinism" that took place between 1949 and 1953. Ostensibly about the Party's relation to the Negro movement, it was in reality something far more radical: a political purge through which hardliners moved to take control of the Party by forcing members to show their loyalty by accusing others of racism, which led to expulsion from the Party's ranks. The Party's behavior was typical of actions taken by organizations under tough external pressure, as their leaders seek to harden the ranks by waging "purification" campaigns.

In what may be the first example of "political correctness" run amok, the Party expelled or brought to trial members whose only sin was using words like "whitewash" or "black sheep," both of which were offered as proof of racism. As Joseph Starobin, the former foreign editor of the *Daily Worker*, explained in his history of the American CP, "Both whites and blacks began to take advantage of the enormous weapon which the charge of 'white chauvinism' gave them to settle scores, to climb organizational ladders, to fight for jobs and to express personality conflicts which, by Communist definition, were never supposed to predominate over political objectivity." It became, as he so accurately put it, an "internal witchhunt."[22]

The Party was turning back to a revolutionary doctrine current before the years of the Popular Front and the wartime alliance with liberals and the New Deal. That doctrine, theoretically sanctified in what became the bible of Communist cadre, *Negro Liberation* by black Communist Harry Haywood, seized on Stalin's theory about the meaning of nationhood. Haywood argued that African-Americans in the Black Belt of the South met Stalin's criteria for a nation, and hence their struggle in America was not for equality but for a nation in southern areas where there was a black majority.[23] The goal would be governmental separation and a "Negro Republic in the Black Belt."[24]

In accordance with the Party's new policy, Biberman informed Trumbo, their new film company would be based on a full partnership with their African-American comrades, not

because they wanted to do them any favors but because they
wanted to be part of "the most active and promising force in our
country." The Negro movement was "the most thrilling, solid,
respectable, promising thing that has taken root in reality in our
country in my lifetime."

Then Biberman returned to New York for further consulta-
tions. Writing to Albert Maltz, with a copy to Trumbo, he told
them what happened when he met with some of the leading
"Negro cultural workers" there. What he thought was a reasonable request led instead to "the very Heavens fall[ing] upon us."
Biberman found, much to his surprise, that they "were too busy
and occupied to spend an instant dealing with people who were
so misinformed as to still consider that they were being 'broad-
minded' in consulting Negro cultural leaders as 'experts' on
Negro material" that was developed by "lily-white artists *for* the
good of the Negro people." White artists could join with them,
he reported, but they would have to admit that "they needed the
Negro people more than the Negro people needed them."

With each sentence, Biberman sounded more and more
agitated. What he had learned from his experience in New York,
he wrote, was "soul-shaking, land-shaking, country-shaking." He
learned about "the poison of chauvinism" and how it was deeply
embedded even in people like themselves. After all, they were
only white middle-class artists, separated from the real struggles
going on in America. After talking with the New York African-
American Communist cultural leaders, Biberman decided that
all their films—including those they thought were favorable to
the fight for civil rights—were in reality patronizing and racist.
Politics meant more than making speeches; it meant working
alongside African-American artists, and learning about them
from their own point of view.[25]

That such a chimerical and unrealistic theory could be resurrected by Communists in America in the 1950s speaks of the
isolated fantasy world in which they lived. But for Trumbo, the
issue had an unpleasant personal denouement involving a
woman named Jean Field, who became a momentary *cause célèbre*
on the Left.

Field had allowed her children to travel to Oklahoma to

visit her ex-husband, Vernon, who had abandoned the family three weeks after the birth of their son in 1940. During the visit, Vernon's father, the assistant attorney general of Oklahoma, brought suit for custody on his son's behalf. The chief evidence was letters Field had written to her children, ages ten and thirteen, that revealed her to be a committed Communist. She wrote that North Korea was a "People's Democracy," that the United States and South Korea had invaded the North, and that the "people's democracy decided they would...unify all of their native land, and drive the foreign [American] imperialists out of their country." The aim of the American invasion was to "draw Russia into war." Indeed, Field closed her letter asking her children to sign the so-called "Stockholm Peace Petition" that was being circulated by the Communist Party, thus helping the people of the world "OWN their countries, economically, politically, in all ways."[26]

Believing that the Oklahoma courts had no jurisdiction over her, Field brought her children back to California. Upon her arrival, she was arrested for kidnapping. She appealed her case, formed a defense committee and sought the aid of the Communist community, which immediately embraced her.

Trumbo stepped into the middle of this drama when he agreed to write a screenplay on the Field case for the Independent Productions Corporation. Because one of the charges against Field was that she had encouraged her son to play with a Negro child, Trumbo decided to center his work on the relationship of a black woman and a white woman sitting in the Oklahoma court room listening to the Field trial.

His colleagues Herbert Biberman, Adrian Scott and Paul Jarrico would judge his work. Unfortunately for Trumbo, they were joined by Jean Field, to whom they ceded a dominant role in judging the script's worthiness. After it was submitted, Biberman called Trumbo to tell him that the group had serious concerns about the script. When Trumbo bridled, Biberman told him he had to take seriously the results of the group's extensive discussions, and especially the "maturity of judgment" coming from Jean Field, who had "deep experience with the issues."

After this prologue, Biberman told Trumbo that he was

enclosing a long criticism written by Field, about which the others were "in agreement in substance."[27] We do not have a copy of the Field critique, but what she said is easily discerned from Trumbo's bitter, thirty-page single-spaced response.[28] What Field had said, and what the entire group apparently agreed with, was that Trumbo was guilty not only of white chauvinism but of "RANK CHAUVINISM." Trumbo did not accept this criticism in the spirit expected of a white Communist—automatically admitting guilt and promising to purge his own compromised attitudes once and for all. Instead, reading Field's comments and getting ready to discuss them in person with his comrades in Los Angeles, Trumbo told Biberman, was "a dreadful experience, and an unfair one, too."

Trumbo's response revealed a shaken man, deeply hurt by the attack coming from those he had always steadfastly defended. He was especially stung by the fact that his old comrades had allowed Field to engage in a witch-hunt in its classic form. Trumbo's script, she apparently claimed in one of her charges, described at one point a Negro boy who was "clean and dressed in his Sunday best." Field castigated Trumbo because this implied that he was "clean only on special occasions," which of course was white chauvinism. Trumbo retorted that he had actually written, "her son is in his best clothes," and later, "polished and dressed in his very best." She had made up words he did not use in order to condemn him. Sarcastically, he asked, "Would it have pleased you if I had written 'dirty and dressed in everyday clothes'?" Or perhaps, he wrote, he should not have attempted to describe Negroes at all.

That Trumbo went on at length—answering each charge of white chauvinism appearing in his script with sometimes turgid, sometimes humorous and sometimes biting comments on the hidden assumptions behind the charges—revealed how tied he still was to the Party. He pleaded with his comrades and tried to turn the charges against him back on them:

> I ask you all to look into your minds and rid yourselves of the self-conscious, uneasy, unsure and patronizing chauvinism which you reveal...by your strange attitude toward Negro children.... Believe me, you must not fear Negroes. You must not

regard them as strange. In many ways they behave remarkably as *you* behave.... Their children get quite as dirty as *your* children.... Their parents take just as much care as *you* in presenting them to the public on "special occasions" as immaculate and well-dressed as possible. They have just as much pride in their children as *you* have in yours. They are *people,* and it is the job of the dramatist...to regard them as such and to present them with the honesty they deserve and so seldom get.

Finally, Trumbo timorously raised the issue of the Party's use of collective criticism and artistic freedom. He lauded the Party's "fine tradition...that whenever a book or play or film is produced which is harmful to the best interests of the working class, that work and its author should and must be attacked in the sharpest possible terms." Acknowledging that Field was operating in "this tradition," Trumbo then argued that she actually had violated Party guidelines, because he had submitted the script to the committee "before production for the express purpose of *preventing* it from being made in a form which would be harmful to the working class." Trumbo went so far as to cite Friedrich Engels as supportive of this "searching and friendly and kind" type of criticism, which is meant to "prevent the work from *needing* to be attacked in sharp and often necessarily unkind terms." Field's report, to the contrary, was "unfriendly, vindictive, envenomed, careless, inaccurate and often inventive," and was not the correct kind of "left wing 'mutual criticism.'"

It must have occurred to Trumbo that he was now getting exactly the kind of criticism that he had watched Albert Maltz endure, except that in his case it came in a time when the Party was basically defunct and irrelevant. He had given Biberman and the Party committee his trust; in return, as he said, they threw "a bucket of filth over me" and caused him "one of the most shameful and serious moments of my life."

The Party's Over

World events—the Soviet invasion of Hungary and the Khrushchev speech to the Twentieth Party Congress revealing Stalin's crimes—and his own obvious frustration and anger at how he had been treated in the Jean Field affair induced Trumbo to quietly leave the Party in the spring of 1956.

He quit, Trumbo wrote to the Communist screenwriter John Bright, because:

> I had long found the meetings intolerably sterile and the consumption of time in relation to results increasingly out of proportion. Add to this my objections to certain persons, my impatience with theoretical discussion, and my perception that ideological differences within the Party more frequently related to power than to ideology. And climax the matter with the XXth Congress which furnished me not the reason but the opportunity to leave.

Trumbo continued with a startling admission of how much of a "bourgeois intellectual" he had been all those years. Referring to the "public agony" displayed by Howard Fast, who quit the Party and wrote a scathing book denouncing Communism and whitewashing his own sordid past in it, Trumbo told Bright that he could not match his behavior "because I never believed in the perfectibility of man nor the perfection of the Soviet Union." Moreover, Trumbo claimed that Khrushchev's revelations did not surprise him:

> My library contains Koestler and Fischer and Orwell and Silone; I am a collector of hysterics like Bullitt and Burnham and Lyons and Levine and Budenz and Chambers; I puzzle politely over Viereck and Fiedler; I have Huxley and Muller and Zirkle on Lysenko, together with the minutes of the 1948 Academy debates than (sic) enthroned him; I haven't neglected Barmine and Krivitsky and Dallin and Simmons and Brzezinski and Haimson and Deutscher, nor Trotsky himself— and I was not surprised.

Trumbo's letter is astonishing. For years, he and the others had denounced opponents of Stalin as anti-Communist or Trotskyite and denied the validity of any of the reports about Stalin's repression and the existence of a secret Gulag. But writing to Bright, still a hard-line Stalinist, Trumbo admits that all the while he had taken a secret pride in actually always knowing the real truth about the Soviet Union.

His departure from the Party was quiet; he told only a few close friends because he didn't want to violate "the long-standing rule of silence among blacklistees...[or to] add to the tribulations or violate the secrecy of those who chose to remain." But his assessment was unflinching: the Party was finished and that all that remained was to "clean up the wreckage."

His critical feelings toward the Party notwithstanding, Trumbo insisted that he would never have changed his stance when confronted by HUAC and proclaimed his "loyalty before a handful of Congressmen who have no right to challenge it." Nor would he have stood before the producers and confessed that for years he had been an idiot.

But Trumbo did not quite say goodbye to all that. He continued to regard the United States as the main villain in the world's drama. As he put it: "All mystique's being madness, it seems clear that the Communist mystique did far less damage to the nation and hence to the world than that of the State Department.... [T]he Communists deluded tens of thousands of Americans, the State Department deluded...scores of millions." And "if those who embraced the Communist mystique could tear themselves from the mourning wall for a glance at the visible world, they would find solace in the fact though they were not more innocent of evil than their opponents, their efforts at least produced immeasurably less of it."[29] But by acknowledging that the Communists were not innocent of evil, Trumbo had at least begun to separate himself from his former comrades.

Trumbo decided to sort out his feelings for himself, in a lengthy single-spaced memo entitled "Secrecy and the Communist Party" that he hoped to publish in the Communist cultural quarterly, *Mainstream,* the direct descendant of the old *New Masses.* Reading it, one is amazed that Trumbo actually entertained the idea that a Communist Party publication would run the article. He tried to sit back and evaluate why and how the CP failed so miserably in Hollywood, despite its widespread influence during the war years. Trumbo's article, until now unknown, reflects the mind of a confused former Communist trying to be honest with himself. He was certain only of one thing: the Party was dead in Hollywood, and perhaps it deserved to have met such a fate. Trumbo's statement is a devastating *J'accuse* in which he charges the Party with using the Ten for propaganda purposes and holds it largely responsible for the blacklist.

"The question of a secret Communist Party," he began, "lies at the very heart of the Hollywood blacklist."[30] He understood well that certain groups, like the NAACP in the South, had a right to organize in secret lest their members be attacked and even murdered by white racists protected by southern law. But the Communist Party was a very different case, since it was "the only organization I know of that has, for over three decades, maintained the secrecy of its general membership regardless of external political circumstances and apparently on a permanent basis."

Trumbo said that if Party members maintained their secrecy, even though at certain times (World War II being an example) others accepted and were even willing to cooperate with them, that secrecy made it appear that the Communists had something to hide, and that they were in fact not candid about their goals and strategies. Trumbo noted the obvious distinction between a secret Leninist group that worked covertly to overthrow a despotic regime like the tsar's in Russia, and a group working for change in America's open political marketplace. It was a distinction the Hollywood Party refused to acknowledge. Trumbo said the CP policy of having "secret members" was a complete disaster. In Hollywood, "they should have all been open Communists, or they should not have been members at all." Communists in the film colony were well paid and lived in a political atmosphere that was *not* oppressive, and yet these same people "dared not publicly reveal" their membership in a legal party to which they voluntarily belonged. Looking back at this recent past, Trumbo wrote, "All we can be certain of is that secret membership did destroy them."

Thinking the issue through, Trumbo came up with ideas in this 1958 essay that he did not dare say publicly until the 1970s. The uncirculated essay was his political testament:

> The moment of choice [for those called to testify] was delayed until the illusion of secrecy collapsed—and by then the qual-

ity of choice was radically changed for the worse. Instead of voluntary choice between party and career, they now faced compulsory choice between informing and the blacklist. The number who chose the blacklist is impressive evidence of the honor and integrity which they brought with them into the Communist Party.

That they were never given an opportunity to face the first and real choice is a tragedy. Whichever decision they at that time might have made, they would have emerged from the past decade with more dignity...than by submitting to a process which has separated them into informers on the one hand, and professional and social exiles on the other. *In a certain sense even the informers can be counted among the victims of a policy which gave them no realistic moment of choice.* [Emphasis added.]

Trumbo also blasted the Communist Party for using the blacklisted screenwriters for its own agenda. In saying this, he provided more evidence of how the Ten were in fact pawns of the Party and were not permitted to wage a fight against the blacklist, which was their primary concern:

From 1948 to the present time, the most prominent of the blacklistees have been exploited for every left-wing cause that came down the pike, regardless of the effect such exploitation might have upon their own anti-blacklist fight. They have consistently been called upon to address public meetings on deportations, the Smith Act, the advancement of The People's World, the Sobell issue, the atom bomb, disarmament, Soviet-American friendship, Harry Bridges...Emmett Till, the National Guardian, and a dozen other just causes.... Whether or not it was right that they should have appeared...is beside the main point...which is: the fact they *did* appear increased rather than diminished their public disrepute, and rendered immeasurably more difficult the winning of their fight.

To Trumbo, he and his colleagues had become mere "adornments" for these causes, "noble losers." Looking over his own record, Trumbo acknowledged freely that he was among those "most to blame" for this.

When Trumbo submitted this article to *Mainstream,* he received a scathing critique from the publication's managing editor,

Charles Humboldt, who was especially bitter about Trumbo's statement that the Russian Revolution was "succumbing to dictatorship." Humboldt replied: "Its *aim* was the establishment of a dictatorship: the rule of the working class." If there was repression, Humboldt argued, it had to be seen in light of the "complex picture of that time." Trumbo failed to consider the "threat of fascist invasion" faced by the Soviet Union and the many "CIA activities in the socialist countries since 1945," which necessitated "security measures" that did not involve suppression of liberty. To bolster his argument, he suggested that Trumbo read the works of the Polish-born historian Isaac Deutscher, whom he incorrectly called "no apologist for Stalin."

Humboldt's rejection of his second thoughts showed Trumbo how far he had moved from the Party's milieu and from the strategy of the Hollywood Ten. In an act that his former comrades would have disdained as "bourgeois individualism," Trumbo allowed his screenwriting pseudonym, Robert Rich, to be placed in nomination for an Academy Award for best screenplay of 1956, which he won for writing *The Brave One.* (When no such writer could be found, Hollywood immediately realized that the nonexistent Rich was most likely Dalton Trumbo.)

"Informers"

In a letter to Guy Endore, a Communist screenwriter who had worked on films such as *Song of Russia* and the popular *Story of G.I. Joe,* as well as editor of two of Hollywood's Popular Front publications, Trumbo sought to clarify his position on how blacklisted writers might be able to return to work. He proposed an unorthodox approach "favoring clearance [from the industry] for those who want it." He did not wish to be misunderstood as sanctioning the act of informing or giving names, although he agreed it had only "ritualistic significance," since everyone already knew all the names. Trumbo admitted that not only was he making a living under the blacklist, but he had "been a happier man since the blacklist than before it." It was not the committee that forced witnesses to inform, Trumbo stressed, "for hundreds of persons have defied it and gone unpunished by authority"; it was the studio chiefs who withheld work unless one appeared and cooperated. Their network, and not HUAC, was "the enforcer," the one "who applies the only lash that really stings."

Outlining in detail his family's own lengthy history from the early days of the Republic, Trumbo noted that his mother was a devout Christian Scientist who always declined to state any of her affiliations on registration forms, and taught him this as a basic right of being an American. That, and not HUAC or the "iron and alien discipline of the Communist Party," made him see informing as "freakish and unnatural." His objection to naming names, Trumbo revealed, was based on the lesson of earliest childhood that we should "bear no tales and...shun the person who does." He saw the informer as a "bondservant of tyranny," and he noted that in the Russian Revolution, as it "succumbed to dictatorship," the informer "throve because he was necessary to the suppression of human liberty."

But Trumbo made one vital exception. Just as he would testify against a friend whom he had witnessed committing vehicular homicide, he noted that "if a man joins the Communist Party and finds treason, espionage and violence afoot, he has no choice but to report everything, including names, to the authorities, exactly as he would report a murder.... He does it to fulfill a legal and moral duty. *He is not an informer; he is a good citizen and patriot.*" (Emphasis added.)[31]

Endore's response must have surprised Trumbo. Not only was he not disturbed about Trumbo's meditation on the issue of informing, he revealed to Trumbo that he had never harbored the "implacable hatred" toward Hollywood friendly witnesses that "pervades most of us." He had even made a point of lunching publicly with an informer the day after he had informed because he "held to the proposition that if I was against the blacklist that blacklisted me, I should also be against all forms of blacklist." Endore wanted nothing less than to "deflate our political importance." He wanted to look back at his past activity and be proud of it, but he felt that he could not. Since Trumbo had raised the issue of espionage, Endore brought up the example of the Rosenberg case. "Someday," he told Trumbo, "I may want to study this case thoroughly…. For the Communist Party would have none of this case for many months. And then, suddenly, they moved in and took it over and made it a case of international importance. The party press that ignored the case for a long long time, began to print reams about it." Asking whether that was good, which he thought it was at the time, he pointed to the obvious: "World attention concentrated on the Rosenberg trial, [and] missed the horror of the Prague trials…. Was that the purpose of the Communist move into the Rosenberg case?" He was no longer willing to "play politics with the lives of others" or to be used "as a decoy, a smoke-screen" by people who had their own motives. "And brother," he concluded, "we've been played."[32]

Like Endore, Trumbo too had continued to socialize with a friendly witness who in the eyes of the Ten had been a major "informer." That man was Richard Collins, who had been in the leading ranks of the Hollywood Party for over nine years and had named people before HUAC. Yet Collins visited Trumbo at his home on a regular basis, where they would spend the evening playing cards, talking and drinking wine. According to Collins, "Dalton Trumbo was my friend forever. He was very open about it. He acted toward me as if nothing had ever happened between us. Other people who saw him would tell me that when my name came up he always defended me and his being friends with me."[33]

At a later date, when Trumbo was having a political fight by letter with Albert Maltz, the latter reminded him of remarks he had made at the memorial ceremony for their old friend Herbert Biberman. At the service, which had been taped, Trumbo praised Biberman because during a trip to Europe, "he'd found there—encountered—someone who had informed on him. And they talked for an hour and a half. And Herbert was *interested* in this man." Trumbo was referring to Edward Dmytryk, whom Biberman had bumped into in a hotel in Spain. But Maltz claimed that they had not spoken for an hour and a half—that the chance meeting took only a brief second and that Biberman had stormed away, having no desire to be friendly with any informer.[34] Whichever version of the Dmytryk-Biberman encounter was correct, it's clear that Trumbo regarded such a friendly chat with an "informer" as a positive thing.

Yesterday's Cause

The time had arrived, Trumbo strongly felt, for the blacklisted writers to adopt a new strategy. For most people, he told Alvah Bessie, they were yesterday's cause. They were all but forgotten, except when the Party needed them to advance some pet project. Therefore he made it clear that he would no longer appear at events sponsored by the Communist Party:

> Artists in a mass medium such as motion pictures live public lives, and…they depend upon public approval for their very existence. More than any other group of people in the United States Hollywood artists are dependent upon their public relations…. A restoration of good public relations for Hollywood blacklistees is the sina quo non [*sic*] of breaking the blacklist, like it or not. It is not good public relations for me to appear at an event sponsored openly or covertly by the People's World. If it *were* good public relations, you would have no trouble getting Frank Sinatra instead of DT—and probably would have approached him first.[35]

From that point on, Trumbo managed his own public image, making sure that every newspaper story and television and radio appearance was "prearranged" to come out in his favor. By this time, he was advising some of his fellow blacklistees not to turn down economic opportunities even if it meant working with people they considered to be informers. The times had changed, Trumbo wrote to his fellow Ten alumnus, screenwriter and director Michael Wilson. The film industry—and not the Left or the Right—had begun to change the rules that enforced a blacklist, because it recognized that it could no longer carry it out effectively. But to win the fight completely, Trumbo said, they had to "restrain certain die-hard elements of the left from making organizational moves," a reference to the need to keep the Communist Party from carrying on its old fights. The key was to realize that since the industry never admitted there was a blacklist, they could never announce its end—but they could simply change their rules and begin to hire those who had not worked in the past decade. The blacklistees should start saying: "the blacklist is over," and that could convince studio chiefs that it was in fact over.

The worst thing to do was continue to act the martyr. Indeed, Trumbo admitted a once-forbidden truth: that many of those addicted to being blacklisted were "mediocrities." Many who had merely gotten by in the old days would find that when the blacklist came to an end, they would not be able to make it.

The blacklist would be ended not by moral posturing, but by the "competence, ability, craftsmanship" of people like themselves. These skills would oblige the studios to use their names, or to use pseudonyms that all would correctly identify. This strategy, he revealed later in the letter, was precisely what he was relying on to have his name put on the film *Spartacus,* which Stanley Kubrick was then filming.

Trumbo's strategy worked, at least for himself. On January 19, 1960, Otto Preminger announced that he had hired Trumbo to write the screenplay for the film *Exodus.* Thus Preminger was the first to give a blacklisted writer his due credit, outmaneuvering Kirk Douglas and producer Edward Lewis, who had planned to do the same for Trumbo and his screenplay for *Spartacus,* for which he had received $75,000 and 5 percent of the profits. All of this offset the capitulation of Frank Sinatra, who had announced that he was going to use Albert Maltz as a writer for *The Execution of Private Slovik* and then backed down in the face of public criticism by groups such as the American Legion, buying out the contract he had signed.[36]

While Trumbo escaped the blacklist by receiving a credit for *Spartacus,* this success did not open a floodgate for others, though screenwriter Waldo Salt had come to a similar conclusion about the necessity for each blacklistee to struggle in his or her own way to come back.[37]

The process that Salt went through to get work in television illustrates how the clearance process had evolved. Salt had been one of the Nineteen who took the Fifth when he appeared before HUAC in 1951. By 1957, he had decided to forgo collective political activities since, he wrote to Fred Rinaldo, the "whole structure of blacklisting" had already "started to leak at the seams." Moreover, he noted sardonically, "I've switched professions lately, from political hack to writer."[38]

Salt had already gone through the same process as figures

like Budd Schulberg and Elia Kazan had decades earlier. His own disaffection with the Party began with its "cultural absurdities and my own doubts of Communist policy." Like so many, he never officially dropped out but just drifted away as his disillusionment grew and he could "no longer stomach the whole thing." Like other former Reds, Salt didn't want to declare himself a "public anti-Communist" because he felt that "such a position in those times of enforced avowals was as undignified and unpatriotic as the enforced avowals of the Russian writers, artists, musicians, scientists, etc."[39]

In 1963, Salt retained the services of attorney Jerome B. Laurie, who was experienced in the clearance process with the television networks, especially NBC. He advised Salt to draw up an affidavit to submit to the networks. In it, Salt wrote that the Communist Party was "undemocratic and diametrically opposed to the free exchange of ideas." He "felt that the idealistic motives which led me to join...were not shared by the policy makers of the Communist Party, [and] that the totalitarianism in Communist countries and the suppression of civil rights in those countries were the very things that I had always been taught to oppose." The affidavit, he concluded, was an "unequivocal declaration" of his "hostility" to the Party or any group that sought to overthrow American democracy. Acknowledging his own prior reluctance to "air dirty linen in public," he now was willing to reaffirm his "undivided loyalty to this country" and to declare his "anti-Communist convictions."[40]

But Laurie warned him that NBC would not accept his affidavit unless it was also mailed to HUAC. In turn, the committee would then send Salt a letter telling him the affidavit was unsatisfactory because when Salt appeared before them the first time, he did not answer their questions, and therefore in order to clear everything up he would be invited to appear again. But Salt, Laurie stressed, did not have to worry because while the networks were aware of HUAC's reaction, "this does not seem to bother them.... Although this has happened on numerous previous occasions, it has never been mentioned, and clearance has been obtained."[41]

Laurie's prediction proved accurate. Once Salt acted on his

own and issued his apologia, the networks ended the blacklist—without the approval of HUAC. He was hired without having to name names or answer HUAC's questions. Salt was once again able to work. His days on the blacklist were over.

"Only Victims"

For all practical purposes, the blacklist had finally come to an end. Millard Lampell received an Emmy in 1966 for a drama, *Eagle in a Cage;* Waldo Salt won an Oscar for his screenplay of *Midnight Cowboy* in 1968; Carl Foreman received the Laurel Award from the Screen Writers Guild in 1969; in 1975, CBS television ran *Fear on Trial,* a television drama based on the blacklisting of radio commentator John Henry Faulk; and in 1976, the SWG had Carl Foreman present that year's Laurel Award to Michael Wilson, who everyone knew had written *The Bridge on the River Kwai,* although it had been attributed to French author Pierre Boule. That year also saw the release of Walter Bernstein's comedy *The Front,* the first movie about the blacklist, starring Woody Allen and featuring many formerly blacklisted artists, including Zero Mostel, John Randolph, Lloyd Gough and others. Rather than haunted figures, the blacklisted writers, directors and actors were becoming culture heroes in the new *zeitgeist.*

All of this was to be the subject of a speech given by Trumbo on March 13, 1970, when he too became the recipient of the guild's Laurel Award. Many expected to hear a triumphalist vindication of the righteousness of their old cause. They were to be gravely disappointed. In what became widely known as Trumbo's "only victims speech," the leading figure of the Hollywood Ten called for reconciliation and forgiveness. Speaking to younger guild members, he announced:

> To them I would say only this: that the blacklist was a time of evil, and that no one on either side who survived it came through untouched by evil. Caught in a situation that had passed beyond the control of mere individuals, each person reacted as his nature, his needs, his convictions, and his particular circumstances compelled him to. There was bad faith

and good, honesty and dishonesty, courage and cowardice, selflessness and opportunism, wisdom and stupidity, good and bad on both sides; and almost every individual involved, no matter where he stood, combined some or all of these antithetical qualities in his own person, in his own acts.

...It will do no good to search for villains or heroes or saints or devils because there were none; there were only victims. Some suffered less than others, some grew and some diminished, but in the final tally we were *all* victims because almost without exception each of us felt compelled to say things he did not want to say, to do things he did not want to do, to deliver and receive wounds he truly did not want to exchange. That is why none of us—right, left, or center—emerged from that long nightmare without sin.

...I assure you—I assure you most sincerely—that what I have said here is not intended to be hurtful to anyone: it is intended rather to repair a hurt, to heal a wound which years ago we inflicted on each other, and on ourselves most of all.[42]

Trumbo's powerful speech—in which he vented feelings he had been harboring for a decade or more—was an explosive event for those who perversely romanticized the blacklist. Trumbo probably expected this, but he was probably not ready for the gales of argument, hostility and reproach he received from his former comrades. In particular, Albert Maltz objected to the very concept that the blacklist created only victims, the punch line of the speech that others were beginning to quote favorably. After Michael Blankfort, once a close friend of Maltz's who had testified as a cooperative witness before HUAC, also cited Trumbo's words in a speech he gave, Maltz decided to respond. To hear someone he considered an informer praise Trumbo was proof that Trumbo had crossed the line. "The ethic of 'equal victims,'" he charged, "has been ecstatically embraced by all who cooperated with the Committee on Un-American Activities when there were penalties for not doing so."[43]

Trumbo responded in a remarkable forty-one-page letter, in which he tried to clarify his position. Trumbo was obviously more than upset, given that Maltz had threatened to go public with his views and to attack Trumbo in a speech or a newspaper advertisement. He began by letting Maltz know the contempt with which he viewed him: "The challenge of explaining *anything* in a way that can make sense to you, combined with the prospect of persuading you not to publish a critical word about a speech I delivered thirty-four months ago is much too exciting for a man of my diseased temperament to resist."

For Trumbo, it boiled down to a question of where one drew the line. "My line stopped at informers," he explained. "…Your line stopped at everyone…whose testimony before the Committee did not, in some way, resemble ours." Maltz may have wanted Blankfort consigned "to the company of the damned," but Trumbo did not.

Indeed, Trumbo made it clear that he was not consumed with hatred of informers, preferring to save his hatred for HUAC rather than "those who were destroyed by it," which included not only the Ten and the resisters but "the informers themselves." As for heroes and villains, Trumbo further explained how he interpreted these categories. Hero was a category reserved for very great men who would live in future generations' memories. Trumbo did not regard the Ten as belonging to such a group:

> The Ten did not volunteer to perform heroic deeds, they were subponed [*sic*] like all other witnesses and compelled against their wills to take the stand and testify. The best evidence that they appeared unwillingly is provided by their motions to quash the subpoenas that finally delivered them into the Committee's hands…. Once summoned, the Ten *could* have invoked the First Amendment at the outset, and refused to give the Committee anything but their names. Had they done so, their position would have been much clearer than it was and their punishment would have been no greater.
>
> Instead, for legal reasons and with legal advice, they first invoked the Constitution, and thereafter pretended to answer questions which they were determined *not* to answer, and didn't. The tactic was designed to give them two chances to escape punishment…the first, a ruling by the Supreme Court upholding their Constitutional right to refuse to answer; the second, acquittal by jury on the ground that they tried to answer and were prevented by the Committee's harassment and premature dismissals. The position was not taken to clarify or

hasten the Constitutional challenge, it was taken to save the witnesses…from punishment.

As for villains, Trumbo argued that one had to consider the question in the context of those who had been members of the Communist Party and how they conducted themselves when they were compelled to testify before HUAC. When the committee called some out of a group of three hundred who had joined the Party in Hollywood, only sixty became informers. Trumbo stressed that none of them had wanted to, that the evidence indicated they did so "with great reluctance" and acted only out of "fear…and under great pressure." He did not think it an accident that not one informer "gave all of the names he could have had he wanted to."

Trumbo, moreover, revealed his understanding and even sympathy for the motives that led them to inform against former friends. Some did it to avoid financial ruin; others to avoid being outed as homosexual, which if revealed was even more of a disgrace than to have been a Communist; others did so because they had long since left the Party "to avoid constant attempts to meddle with the ideological content" of their writing—clearly a reference to Schulberg and more indirectly to Maltz himself, who had accepted such meddling and capitulated to the Stalinist commissars.

Trumbo ended by quoting something he had written to Maltz earlier:

> In a country which, after a reasonable period of punishment, returns murderers and rapists to society on the humane theory that it is still possible for them to become decent and even valuable citizens, I have no intent of fanning the embers of justifiable hatred which burned so brightly twenty-five years ago.
>
> I confess that among those who turned informer there are two or three…whom I still view with nothing short of horror…. When, however, chance throws me in the same room with one of them…my sense of personal virtue is not large enough to prevent me from recognizing their existence and accepting their recognition of mine if it is offered.[44]

By this time, Trumbo's patience with Maltz was wearing thin: "After 25 years in a state of extreme moral ecstasy, the truth is bound to bewilder. On the off-chance you're not too far gone in self-adulation, a strong dose of the basic facts may bring you around—facts, incidentally, as absent from your letters as virtue from a working pimp's heart."

Ironically, while Maltz may have seen himself as a keeper of the flame that others were trying to extinguish by their revisionism, he himself was not pure enough for one of the remaining ironclad Stalinists among the Ten, screenwriter Lester Cole. Although Cole undoubtedly despised Trumbo for having anything decent to say about informers, what bothered him more was that in the mid-1970s Maltz had announced that he was contributing any Soviet royalties due him to Alexander Solzhenitsyn and other dissidents, who in Maltz's eyes were being "blacklisted" by the Soviet government. Cole wrote to him sarcastically about his "valiant championing of that towering symbol of Czarist humanism and freedom, Solzhenitsyn, who starting with the well-publicized 35,000 rubles you gave him...climbed his way to a six million dollar pinnacle," and was now sitting "on his half million dollar estate in Vermont." The exiled Russian author, who had exposed "alleged" Soviet-era gulags, was in desperate need of a new organization that could be "headed by someone like yourself." Anti-Sovietism, Cole wrote Maltz, has "blinded you to the cruel suppression of human rights" in nations like South Africa, Israel, Chile and Argentina. Like Trumbo, Maltz was now "aiding in the growth of neo-fascism."[45] Of all the Ten, it appeared that Cole was the last holdout. Once having been viewed by others as "the last Stalinist," fellow blacklistee Alvah Bessie now passed that mantle, as he said, "onto the shoulders of L. Cole."[46]

Reading through the sometimes vitriolic, sometimes pathetic, sometimes revelatory letters exchanged between these two major figures of the old Hollywood Ten, it becomes apparent that Dalton Trumbo, as much as Albert Maltz, was finally unable to escape the grasp of American Communism. Hovering over all their fights—about whether informers should be shown any grace, or why they had adopted the legal strategy of 1947, or how to handle the issue politically in Hollywood—stood their relationship to the Communist Party, USA. Both men had long since evolved from the old Stalinist positions they once held; Maltz was supporting Soviet dissidents and had opposed the Soviet invasion of Czechoslovakia; Trumbo had come to view the Communist Party as an unnecessarily secretive and duplicitous organization, whose policies and tactics led to its unfavorable reception by most Americans.

Both men, however, continued to view the Communists as partners in the good fight they all shared. The Soviet Union might have been totalitarian, they now understood, but they nevertheless saw it as being on the "right side of history" and therefore worthy of general support.

Maltz believed what the Party had told him. He thought the United States had started the Korean War and that it had practiced germ warfare. Trumbo knew better; as he pointed out, he had read and collected the works of the greatest anti-Communist and anti-Soviet writers and was proud to have always privately known the truth about the evils of Soviet Communism. Trumbo knew the truth, yet he accepted and parroted the Soviet line on foreign policy, viewing the United States as an "imperialist" power. In his eyes, the U.S. State Department did more damage to the world than all of Stalin's bloody suppression of human rights and his creation of a far-flung and repressive empire.

Where Trumbo shone, and moved head and shoulders over the others of the Hollywood Ten (except for Edward Dmytryk, who had broken completely and become a friendly witness) was in his realization that times had changed, that the Party's campaign for the Ten had failed miserably and the blacklist could only be broken by individual action of the blacklistees, not by a compromised political campaign.

Confused and contradictory, Trumbo at least tried to come to terms with his past and that of the movement he had belonged to and supported for so many years. It was ironic that a few decades later, others still stuck in the mythology of the blacklist would use his words and letters to cast the story in stark tones of black and white.

Conclusion

"It remains my firm conviction that [the blacklist] could not have been imposed if a few misguided souls had not provided the witch-hunters with that fatal linkage. Those who joined the Communist Party, and faithfully followed its twisting line, cannot escape their share of responsibility for the broken careers and bankruptcies, the ruin of reputations, the sleepless nights and heartaches the many had to endure because of the folly of the few."

—Philip Dunne, *Take Two: A Life in Movies and Politics*

THE BLACKLIST HARMED THE CAREERS OF SOME OF HOLLYWOOD'S FINEST talents: actors, writers and directors. Its damage extended not only to Hollywood's Communists but to the well-meaning "innocents" and fellow travelers who joined the Party's many Popular Front causes and organizations. Yet while the Hollywood Ten, among the most committed of the Party faithful, loudly protested this "inquisition" and later wore their appearance before HUAC as a badge of honor, the blacklist also served as a godsend for the Communist Party. By the time HUAC arrived on the scene, the comrades had already worn out their welcome in the film capital as a result of their contortions in support of the USSR. Now, as a result of the investigations, they had a new calling card and a new credibility. HUAC and the blacklist allowed them to depict themselves as men and women committed to a democracy that was under unprincipled attack by racists, anti-Semites and reactionaries. They were now victims rather than supporters of Joseph Stalin—martyrs standing alone against the forces of fascism in America.

Their view was based on a partial truth. Some of HUAC's members, like John Rankin (D-Mississippi), were blatantly anti-Semitic and racist. His and some others' tirades against Jews had helped to stampede Hollywood's studio chiefs into instituting the blacklist. But ultimately HUAC and the Party served each other's purposes: HUAC could easily establish that real Communists were active in Hollywood, while the unfriendly witnesses and the Communist Party could just as easily condemn HUAC members for initiating a "reign of terror."

The Party quickly moved to transform the Hollywood Ten into an asset. The Ten dutifully trudged from one Party event to another, speaking about their plight and serving as opening acts for other causes that the CP wanted to piggyback on theirs. As Trumbo realized, this strategy further dehumanized and marginalized them. It also kept them from re-establishing themselves and ending the blacklist, which the Party had an interest in maintaining.

Although it seemed cartoonish at the time, the Party's portrait of the Ten—as stalwarts for peace and civil liberties when everyone else in the film colony capitulated to the demagogues—remained in place. As the decades passed and the war in Vietnam allowed leftism to stage a comeback in Hollywood, the film world's already romanticized view of Communism and the blacklist became ossified. The Red Decades of the 1930s and 1940s, and the equal and opposite anti-Communist reaction of the 1950s, became Hollywood's Great Moment on the American Political Stage; the moment when filmland was Truly Serious.

It was a sign of the times when the activist filmmaker Tim Robbins produced and starred in *Cradle Will Rock* (1999), a sentimentalized view of the 1930s that glamorized the Hollywood Communists. Around the same time, the actor/activist Richard Dreyfuss, himself a Red-diaper baby, commented that being a member of the Party really wasn't so bad; the problem was only that it "sounds like one thing and really is quite another."[1] For Dreyfuss, the Communists who went to Spain and fought in the Abraham Lincoln Brigade "knew the truth before the rest of the world did" and set the "standard for activism and commitment." He hoped his generation remembered what they stood for, so that "we can work through this present and future chaos."[2]

A new generation of activists, beginning in the Vietnam years with Jane Fonda and her colleagues, built on the events of the past, reiterated them in a new round of endless celebrations, and essentially bought the one-sided caricature manufactured by the Communists and their allies. Fonda herself would glorify Lillian Hellman in the film *Julia* (1977), and as we show in the appendix, the industry would paint the era over and over in the accepted fashion: as a black-and-white story of innocent Red heroes and nasty congressional villains.

Not content with using film to retell the story of the era, Hollywood finally officially repudiated itself in its commemoration of the blacklist's fiftieth anniversary in 2001. The centerpiece of the event was a museum exhibit in Los Angeles, "Reds and Blacklists: Political Struggles in the Movie Industry," setting forth how the studios had collaborated with the McCarthyites to ruin the lives of many talented people. The Academy of Motion Picture Arts and Sciences exhibit had as its goal to "document the complicity of various studios, guilds and unions" in the blacklist, and to show the reaction "to the blacklist of *alleged* Communists in Hollywood" (emphasis added). As blacklistee Norma Barzman approvingly noted of the commemoration, it was "their way of apologizing."[3] Incoming Academy president Bruce Davis added, in case one did not already get the point: "We behaved as badly as anybody."[4] The event was like a perverse variant of the Academy Awards, where the remaining group of blacklistees was officially presented with martyrdom and moral sanctity.

Missing from this political extravaganza, and from most accounts of the era in film and memoir, is the actual context in which the hearings and the blacklist played out: Korea, the disclosure that some Communists had been spies against their own country, the rapidly heating Cold War with the Soviet Union. Also missing were the goals of the Communist Party, how it specifically targeted Hollywood, how it embedded its cultural commissars in the film capital, how it infiltrated the guilds and tried to take over the film industry's labor movement, how it sought to inject its message and its outlook into the films that its writers, directors and actors worked on.

How courageous and how moral were the Hollywood Reds? Could their own version of their past actually be accurate? In most of their recollections, they portray themselves as socially conscious individuals disturbed by the threats to democracy embodied in racism and warmongering, and anxious to counter the paranoia and nativism always ready to break through the placid surface of American life. The truth, as we have shown, is that the Hollywood Communists rigorously followed every twist and turn of the Party line, no matter how nonsensical and immoral. Whether it was the Nazi-Soviet Pact, the invasion of Finland or the purge trials, they stood with Stalin.

The most that the Hollywood Communists seemed willing to concede in looking backward was expressed by Paul Jarrico: "I thought the Soviet Union was a vanguard country fighting for a better future for the entire world, including the United States. That was an illusion.... But the illusion didn't make me disloyal; it made me a fool."[5] Letting themselves off the hook as mere fools rather than collaborators, the Hollywood Communists used the fatuousness of their politics to avoid coming to terms with the real-life consequences of the positions they espoused.

The consequences of their foolishness were of course less lethal for Americans than for their European comrades. Otto Katz, for instance, had been Hollywood's darling when he arrived as Willi Münzenberg's ambassador to the film world and helped create the major Popular Front mass organizations. The darkly romantic Katz was fêted in Hollywood, and he knew everyone who was worth knowing. Lillian Hellman had an affair with Katz, and she patterned a main character in her play and film *Watch on the Rhine* after him. A secret Communist, Katz was introduced to everyone as a straightforward antifascist who had risked his life against Hitler in Nazi Germany and had managed to escape into exile.

In 1952, the same Otto Katz (a.k.a. André Simone) was arrested in Communist Czechoslovakia, where he had become part of the government, and was put to death with the other defendants in the so-called Slansky purge trial demanded by Stalin. A loyal Communist to the end, he was accused of being a "Jewish bourgeois nationalist and a spy," as well as a Trotskyite, Zionist and Titoist working in the service of American imperialism. He was subjected to months of mental and physical torture; his codefendant Eugene Loebl (one of the few to escape death) was shocked to find him looking "as if he were a hundred." The once-handsome Katz was now "skin and bones, his face deathly pale."[6]

Hellman and her Hollywood friends knew that Katz was innocent. Not one of them said a word, although some left-wing European intellectuals protested the sentences and tried to stop Katz's execution.[7] One might contrast Yves Montand's response. France's leading actor and singer had not imagined in 1952 that the Slansky trial was rigged. When he learned the truth, he never forgave those who had deceived him. Seventeen years later, believing that "the truth was the truth," Montand abandoned his "paralyzing doubts" about giving ammunition to the "imperialist" enemy and agreed to make a film from a book by one of the surviving Slansky trial defendants, Artur London's *The Confession*.[8]

Setting the record straight has been no easy task. Revisionism about the Communist experience in Hollywood has taken on a life of its own, always abetted by Hollywood itself. The country saw a dispiriting example of this in 1999, when the Academy of Motion Picture Arts and Sciences finally voted to give director Elia Kazan its "Lifetime Achievement" award. Kazan was then in his late eighties and in poor health; it was the last chance the industry would have to honor him for bringing integrity and art into motion pictures. Previous attempts to honor Kazan by other film groups had always been shut down because his opponents said he could never be forgiven for having testified and named names before HUAC. But finally he was to have his night.

Once again, the announcement of the Academy's decision elicited a chorus of protests. Many of Kazan's critics were angry, not simply because he had been a cooperative witness but because he had dared to say that Communists were wrong, dangerous, and part of a conspiracy. So when the aging director approached the podium, introduced by Robert De Niro, a group of Hollywood's finest—including Nick Nolte, Ed Harris, David Geffen, Sherry Lansing and Richard Dreyfuss—sat stonily while others gave a standing ovation.

Outside the theater, veterans of the blacklist once again manned the picket line. Director Abe Polonsky, writers Bernard Gordon and Norma Barzman, and actors Phoebe Brand, Rod Steiger and John Randolph protested, calling themselves the Committee Against Silence. In a full-page ad they took out in the trade papers, they accused Kazan of being the man who "validated the blacklisting of thousands," the man who alone gave HUAC its credibility.[9] This rejectionism, not Kazan's artistic and personal achievement, became the story of the night.

The tirade against Kazan would be repeated, with even more venom, by the mainstream media when the director passed away in September 2003. The *Philadelphia Inquirer* editorialized that Kazan's reputation was "tarnished by his betrayals" and followed with a news story in which the reporter compared this director, who made liberal films with social themes, to the German director Leni Riefenstahl, who glorified "the perverted ideals of Nazism."[10] No one seemed to recall the moral quandary that Kazan had found himself in when he received his subpoena from HUAC: desiring to avoid being an informer, while at the same time understanding that he could no longer perpetuate the big lie about the supposedly benign nature of Communism or condone the notion that the American Communist Party was simply another political party similar to the Republicans and Democrats.

The Hollywood Communists and those who later glorified them never answered the question raised by Ring Lardner Jr.'s son James. How could his father and his father's comrades have "overlooked all the ghastliness that communism was inflicting [in the USSR] where it was an actual…working experiment?"[11] Instead of confronting this, the admirers and descendants of the blacklisted Communists continue to propagate the myth of their unparalleled heroism. This storyline was first codified by journalist Victor Navasky in his best-selling and continually reissued book *Naming Names* (1980). Navasky made the blacklist a simple "moral detective story," in which the villains and heroes were obvious, and the one criterion to judge individuals by was whether or not they "informed."

Navasky even likens Elia Kazan's decision to become a friendly witness to the decision of "patriotic" Germans who shared the SS view that "Communism was the enemy."[12] Navasky has a simpleminded paradigm: those who named names were morally bankrupt; those who refused to testify were "moral exemplars."[13] There is no ambiguity in his version of the past. No one had a reason to inform. Those who sought to tell the truth about Communism must be condemned as informers, stool pigeons and collaborators.

Navasky (and the Navaskyism that followed) transformed a tale composed of various shades into something morally monochromatic. As filmmaker and critic Richard Schickel put it, "The terms for discussion of the blacklist permitted no deviation from the stark dialectic" that the Hollywood Reds had insisted upon. The accepted narrative turned what "anyone with the slightest degree of objectivity ought to see as an incomplete and highly sectarian view of those occurrences into inarguable gospel."[14]

There are always new evangelists to preach this gospel in novel ways. One of the oddest emerged in 2003, when Christopher Trumbo's play about his father, *Trumbo: Red, White and Blacklisted*, caused a stir in its off-Broadway production. Every few weeks, a different major star would step in to assume the leading role of Trumbo, a task first taken for the opening nights by Nathan Lane, one of Broadway's hottest names. On subsequent weeks the role of Trumbo was played by Richard Dreyfuss, Paul Newman and Alec Baldwin, among others. Today's Hollywood Left could not resist the opportunity to make Trumbo into the kind of hero he himself always denied being. The play, as one reviewer said, shows Trumbo "rewarded in true Hollywood fashion, with quiet triumph and humiliation of his enemies."[15] But it fails ever to mention Trumbo's membership in the Communist Party and his devotion to it. The only time Communism is mentioned is when the actor playing Christopher Trumbo notes that his father explained Communism to his children as a system in which people worked and were provided for "each according to his ability, to each according to his needs." As critic Terry Teachout commented, "Innocent viewers will likely come away supposing that his only deeply held conviction was that it is immoral to inform on your friends."[16]

Those who saw the play heard nothing about Trumbo's growing disdain for his former comrades, his anger at their sectarianism and stupidity, his condemnation of the Communist Party's enforced secrecy, his belief that the Party could be partially blamed for the blacklist's success, and his anger at unregenerate former allies like Albert Maltz. Nor did they learn of his decision to befriend the hated informers, his admission that he always knew the murderous truth about Stalinism, his bragging about how he and his comrades had at least succeeded in stopping the production of anti-Communist films, and his eventual realization that he had been fooled by the Party leadership, an insight that led to his "only victims" speech. The play, in short, was another illustration of John Ford's maxim: when there is a conflict between the truth and the myth, print the myth.

So the Hollywood Communists have had their revenge. The blacklist has come to be thought of almost as the best of times. Memoirs of the period continue to appear, not only by blacklistees but by their children. The dream of socialism might have been corrupted under Stalin (the updated version of the old story goes), the Communist Party in America might have become irrelevant, but its ideas and ideals continue to resonate.

Of course, it is right to condemn the blacklist. It was wrong to deprive artists of their livelihood because of their political views. But its most malicious contribution to postwar history was to obscure forever the truth about Communism in Hollywood. It is our hope that with this book, the true story can begin to be recovered.

Appendix

The Blacklist on Film

MOST RECENTLY, *THE MAJESTIC* (2001) STARRED JIM CARREY AS A screenwriter who once innocently attended a Communist front meeting simply to impress a girl. The hero, a political naïf, later finds himself facing a Kafkaesque congressional inquiry. At the film's end, the Carrey character returns to Hollywood and voluntarily appears before HUAC, making a complete fool of them with his moral passion.

The film's screenwriter, Michael Sloane, told the press "I'm amazed that there are so few movies that deal with the blacklist in any way at all."[1] But *The Majestic* is scarcely a rare anomaly, as Sloane seemed to think. Rather, it is but the latest in a series of films about the blacklist that have become something approaching a subgenre in Hollywood during the past three decades. In all of them, Hollywood Communists, if they are depicted as Reds at all, are shown merely as benign and well-meaning idealists who favor racial equality, peace and basic decency for all Americans. None of the films show anything about what the Communists believed or how they operated.

Guilty by Suspicion (1991) stands out from all the other recent films. It received rave reviews in the press and was seen by a wide movie-going public. Critic Roger Ebert called it a "powerful statement against the blacklist," the *New York Times* reviewer Janet Maslin termed it a "tragic evocation of terrible times," and Peter Rainer of the *Los Angeles Times* said it deserved praise for "dealing with a subject that even today, is highly volatile and controversial."

"It is the first time that Hollywood has ever examined the role it played in what was a black time in America," said its director, Irwin Winkler, echoing all the others who claimed that their film about the blacklist was a courageous innovation.[2] *Guilty by Suspicion* uses fictional characters based on composites of actual people to tell the story of a fictional director, David Merrill, played by Robert De Niro, who is supposedly working at Fox for Darryl F. Zanuck. The legendary producer tells Merrill that if he is to continue making films for him, he must go before HUAC and give them the names they want.

A man of integrity, Merrill realizes that he can't do this. He goes to an attorney named Allan Graff, played by the once-blacklisted actor Sam Wanamaker, who advises him to go before HUAC and cooperate. Graff tells him that if he takes the Fifth, however, "you protect yourself against self-incrimination, but you end up guilty by suspicion." Like characters in other films about this subject, Merrill is portrayed as a political innocent. Indeed, almost all of those accused are portrayed as completely innocent—people who have been singled out in a paranoid time, as one character puts it, because "they were people caring about people."

The Merrill character attends a few meetings in 1939 and 1940 because he wants "peace" and is interested in new ideas; in the 1950s, he marches in a "ban the bomb" rally. These are seen in the movie as inconsequential acts. But 1939, of course, was the era of the Nazi-Soviet Pact, when the Communists were against those urging resistance to Hitler. And in 1951, the only campaign that the CP supported against atomic weapons was the so-called Stockholm Peace Petition, initiated by Moscow, which called for Western disarmament but not for a ban on tests of nuclear weapons, since the Soviet Union was at the time conducting such tests.

Merrill's best friend, played by George Wendt, let an attractive girl take him to a Russian War Relief meeting in the 1940s, when Russia was an ally, and now he too is being forced to name names. The film depicts one actual Communist, a director called Joe Lesser—played by Martin Scorsese and patterned after the real director Joseph Losey—and he too is seen as another innocent victim, a man who was openly a Communist and until the 1950s never had trouble making films.

Director Winkler said that the film is about how the rights of all Americans were trampled upon in those days. Whether the accused were actually Hollywood Reds is irrelevant. "What is important," Winkler explained, "is that an individual is accused and then blacklisted; his rights taken away without due process." The CP was legal, he argued, and people "were skewered for their political beliefs." The Stalinist nature of those beliefs goes unexamined. Winkler also admitted that he originally intended to close the film with Dalton Trumbo's "only victims" speech. He decided against it, he said, because while Trumbo could forgive, he himself could not. (Winkler was not blacklisted; nor has he had trouble making films.)

The Way We Were (1973), directed by Sydney Pollack, begins in the 1930s and ends in the late 1960s, chronicling the love affair between Katie Morosky (Barbra Streisand) and rich golden boy Hubbell Gardner (Robert Redford). It begins with Katie, a Young Communist League crusader in college, being heckled by non-Communist students, among whom is her future husband, Hubbell. Their lives come together and then apart as Hubbell, now a screenwriter, goes to Hollywood, where Katie's past comes up against anti-Communist hysteria and the blacklist. As the film ends, Katie is still on the streets, demonstrating in New York against America's A-bomb policy. Gardner passes her as he comes out of the lush Plaza Hotel, and he realizes what he has lost by losing her commitment.

The Front (1976), a humorous film starring Woody Allen and Zero Mostel, was one long in-joke about the blacklist. Directed by blacklisted director Martin Ritt, the film was scripted by blacklisted screenwriter Walter Bernstein. Acting in the film was a theater troupe of old Hollywood Reds and fellow travelers, including Mostel, Herschel Bernardi, Lloyd Gough and Norman Rose. The film depicts the plight of a TV writer named Alfred Miller (Michael Murphy) who finds himself blacklisted because he was a Communist. Not able to get his scripts into production, he enlists the aid of his friend, bartender Howard Prince (Woody Allen), who becomes his front and sells his work to the network.

Incredulous about what has happened to his friend, Prince says to Miller when he learns that he has been blacklisted, "But you've always been a Communist." That is the extent of what the audience learns of his Party activity.

In *Marathon Man* (1976), Dustin Hoffman plays a Columbia University graduate student obsessed with his thesis about his father, a professor who committed suicide in the 1950s because he had been blacklisted after being called before HUAC and accused of being a Communist. A thriller that depicts the CIA as an evil and corrupt force more interested in amassing power than in defending freedom, the film centers on a plot by ex-Nazis to smuggle diamonds into the country. Its backstory, referred to throughout the film, is about the Hoffman character's Jewish father, who because of his strong liberal conscience became another victim of the witch-hunt.

The House on Carroll Street (1987), starring Kelly McGillis, Jessica Tandy, Mandy Patinkin and Jeff Daniels, is a traditional thriller. The character played by McGillis is fired from *Life* magazine for refusing to name names before HUAC. A blacklisted journalist, she soon uncovers a plot to smuggle Nazi war criminals into the country. But in the paranoia of McCarthyism, no one cares about former Nazis. No one believes her because she has been labeled a Communist. The rhetoric of the film suggests that anti-Communism favors the success of fascism.

Fellow Traveler (1989), set in the waning days of the blacklist, begins with the suicide of an unfriendly witness, Clifford Byrne, played by Hart Bochner. It then flashes back to the relationship he had with a close friend, a blacklisted writer, Asa Kaufman, who is played by Ron Silver. Unable to find work because of the blacklist, Kaufman moves to Britain. Kaufman begins an affair with a late colleague's still left-wing girlfriend and regains his old commitment to Communism. In London, Kaufman writes scripts for the hit TV series *Robin Hood* (which was actually written by blacklisted writers employed by Hannah (Dorner) Weinstein, a pro-Communist producer who had moved from New York to London). His friend's suicide continues to haunt him, and Byrne reappears as Kaufman writes the television series. The film suggests that Byrne had killed himself because of the anti-Communist phobia in America.

One of the Hollywood Ten (2002) glamorizes one of the hardest-line Stalinists among the Ten, screenwriter Herbert Biberman. It depicts Biberman's fiery feud with Edward Dmytryk, who is portrayed as finking on Biberman and thereby ruining his career, while continuing to work himself. (In reality, Biberman and Dmytryk both went to jail as members of the Ten, and Dmytryk only testified later after deciding not to remain loyal to the Party.) Viewers are not given any indication of Biberman's role as a hard-line Communist ideologue. The film has him saying: "I joined the Communist Party to fight fascism, and now they call me a Stalinist." The film also shows Biberman's decision to direct an independent left-wing film, *Salt of the Earth,* which blasts Warner Brothers for its complicity in the blacklist, and is offered as proof of how Biberman fought to realize his Marxist ideals.

Acknowledgments

THIS BOOK COULD NOT HAVE BEEN WRITTEN WITHOUT THE HELP, SUPPORT and advice of friends and colleagues. Special thanks are due to two people. The historian Aileen J. Kraditor kindly read an earlier draft, giving it an unsparing and critical look, and made suggestions and edited some of the chapters. Clare L. Spark, an independent historian and author, shared material with us and provided insights on the life and work of Jay Leyda. She also was kind enough to do research for us at the UCLA Library in Los Angeles, where some archival material we needed was available. We are extremely grateful for their help and support.

We discussed and exchanged ideas and material with many writers and scholars. Among those who generously helped us were the film critic, author and documentary filmmaker Richard Schickel; the writers Stephen Koch and Stephen Schwartz; the editor and journalist Scott McConnell of New York and Washington, D.C.; the writer Scott McConnell (no relation) of Los Angeles; the author and expert on Ayn Rand, Robert A. Mayhew; film historian and author Dan Leab, and the author John Meroney, who shared material and discussed ideas from his own forthcoming book about Ronald Reagan and Hollywood. Eric Fettman at the *New York Post,* an expert on Communism, gave us a great deal of food for thought. Ditto for Arnold Beichman of the Hoover Institute.

Herb Romerstein provided us with a copy of the hard-to-find film *Mission to Moscow.* Our friends Louis Menashe and Harvey Klehr offered suggestions and sent us material. Our friend, the historian Allen Weinstein, discussed ideas and gave us valuable material from his own collections. Thomas Staedeli, a film writer from Switzerland, kindly gave us permission to use and cite the letter written to him by Howard Koch.

We were granted interviews, either in person or on the phone and by e-mail, with Richard Collins, Jonathan Foreman, Elizabeth Frank and Budd Schulberg, with whom we spent a remarkable day at his home on Long Island. We thank them all for their willingness to speak with us.

At various libraries and archives, the staff and archivists offered a great deal of help. John Fox, the newly appointed historian of the FBI, made gaining access to material from their archives much easier to arrange. Our friend John Earl Haynes, head of the American history archives at the Library of Congress, was a major help to us. He identified collections to look at, found material for us, and read some earlier drafts of chapters. Peter Filardo at the Tamiment Library at New York University worked with us on the Jay Leyda Papers and other manuscripts; Charles E. Schamel and his staff at the Center for Legislative Archives, National Archives and Records Administration, Washington, D.C., guided us through the recently released records of the House Committee on Un-American Activities; archivists at the UCLA Library, the University of Southern California film collection, and the theater and film collection of the University of Wisconsin Historical Society offered similar help with their own collections. Archivists at the FDR Library in Hyde Park sent us pertinent material from President Franklin Roosevelt's papers.

Finally, we owe tremendous appreciation to our friend, publisher and editor, Peter Collier of Encounter Books. A brilliant writer himself, Peter edited the manuscript the old-fashioned way—line by line—and put us through the necessary task of rewrites and cutting of extraneous detail. We are forever in his debt. We thank Carol Staswick and Diarmid Cammell at Encounter Books for their careful copy-editing.

Ronald Radosh and Allis Radosh

I would like to thank both the Lynde and Harry Bradley Foundation of Milwaukee, Wisconsin, and the Earhart Foundation of Ann Arbor, Michigan, for awarding me research grants that enabled us to complete work on this book.

Colleagues at the Hudson Institute of Washington, D.C., where I am an adjunct senior scholar, offered support and encouragement.

Ronald Radosh

☆

Notes

Chapter 1: The Romance Begins

[1] Sean McMeekin, *The Red Millionaire: A Political Biography of Willi Münzenberg* (New Haven and London: Yale University Press, 2003), p. 19.

[2] Arthur Koestler, *The Invisible Writing* (New York: Macmillan, 1954), p. 209.

[3] Ibid., pp. 207–8.

[4] Babette Gross, *Willi Münzenberg: A Political Biography* (East Lansing: Michigan State University Press, 1974), pp. 167–68.

[5] McMeekin, *The Red Millionaire*, p. 173.

[6] Willi Münzenberg, "Capture the Film!" *Daily Worker*, July 23, 1925.

[7] Willi Münzenberg, "The Picture and Film in the Revolutionary Movement," *Daily Worker*, August 15, 1925.

[8] Gross, *Willi Münzenberg*, p. 216.

[9] In the United States, secret Party members such as the trade-union leader Harry Bridges and the actor/singer Paul Robeson always denied being members of the Communist Party, until their affiliation was revealed in the late 1980s and 1990s.

[10] McMeekin, *The Red Millionaire*, p. 148.

[11] Koestler, *The Invisible Writing*, p. 382; Stephen Koch, *Double Lives: Spies and Writers in the Secret Soviet War of Ideas Against the West* (New York: The Free Press, 1994), pp. 14–24, for Koch's discussion of Münzenberg and the fronts, to which we are indebted.

[12] McMeekin, *The Red Millionaire*, p. 212.

[13] Gross, *Willi Münzenberg*, p. 270; McMeekin, *The Red Millionaire*, p. 272.

[14] Michael Ciment, *Conversations with Losey* (London and New York: Methuen, 1985), p. 21. Most quotes from Losey are taken from Ciment's interviews with him. Discussion of Losey is based as well on the biography by David Caute, *Joseph Losey: A Revenge on Life* (New York: Oxford University Press, 1994).

[15] "Brief on the Work of the CPUSA Secret Apparatus," January 26, 1939; Archive of the Dimitrov Secretariat of the Comintern, RTsKhIDNI 495-72-42, Moscow.

[16] John Earl Haynes and Harvey Klehr; *Venona: Decoding Soviet Espionage in America* (New Haven, Conn.: Yale University Press, 1999), pp. 60–61.

[17] Elinor Langer, "The Secret Drawer," *Nation,* May 30, 1994, p. 756. Peters ran the Washington, D.C., underground, and had introduced Whitaker Chambers to a Communist named Harold Ware, who with Chambers' aid organized a major Communist cell in the government. When Ware died in an auto accident in 1935, Peters took over the handling of the so-called Ware group. One of the group was John Hermann, who was married to writer Josephine Herbst. It was Hermann, according to Herbst's biographer Elinor Langer, who "introduced Chambers to Alger Hiss."

[18] Losey's contacts with Peters were confirmed by the family of an American Communist doctor, Lewis Fraad. Dr. Fraad, who had been Losey's doctor in New York, evidently saw himself as Losey's "mentor" and brought him closer to the Party as well as introducing him to Peters. At the time, Peters was running the arts project for the Party in New York, and Losey was in the unit he supervised. The Fraad family visited their friend Peters in Communist Hungary, where Peters had been deported, in 1964. Later, Fraad learned that Losey was still in touch with Peters in the early 1970s. Losey was in the process of making a film, *The Assassination of Trotsky,* which starred Richard Burton. Losey told his screenwriter, Nicholas Mosley, that Peters had phoned him to talk about the film. According to Fraad, Losey had asked him to serve as a consultant on the project.

Researching his biography, David Caute discovered letters written by Losey to Peters in July 1971, in which Losey indicated he had tried to find Peters in the mid 1960s when he was in Vienna, but had not had his correct address. Finally traveling to Budapest in 1972 to attend a birthday party for actress Elizabeth Taylor, Losey inquired whether he would be possible to meet Peters discreetly "without any embarrassment to yourselves?" The answer was yes, and after the party Losey once again met with the underground Party chief at his Budapest home. Losey wrote about the visit later to another old friend, the Communist millionaire Frederick Vanderbilt Field. "Our friends are well," he reported, "...not so much changed as one might imagine." And Losey wrote to other old friends who had changed, disparaging the loss of their Communist faith and comparing one unfavorably with Peters. See: Caute, *Joseph Losey,* p. 50, citing Losey to J. Peter, February 9, 1972; Losey to Frederick V. Field, December 29, 1972; in Caute, p. 50.

[19] Clare L. Spark, *Hunting Captain Ahab: Psychological Warfare and the Melville Revival* (Kent, Ohio: Kent State University Press, 2001), p. 334.

[20] Ibid., p. 657.

[21] Jay Leyda to Comrade Marshall, July 2, 1933; "Chronological Correspondence folder for 1933," Jay Leyda Papers, Tamiment Library, New York University.

[22] Leyda to Lincoln Kirstein, November 2, 1933; Jay Leyda Papers, box 2. When he spoke about the *chistka,* Leyda was referring to Stalin's first "cleansing" of the Communist Party, when he eliminated nearly one million so-called "Bolshevik oppositionists" by an internal purge. See W. G. Krivitsy, *In Stalin's Secret Service* (New York: Enigma Books, 2000), p. 159.

[23] Leyda to Margaret Leyda Smith, October 19, 1936, Jay Leyda Papers, box 3.

[24] Interview of Maurice Rapf by Patrick McGilligan, in *Tender Comrades: A History of the Hollywood Blacklist,* ed. Patrick McGilligan and Paul Buhle (New York: St. Martin's Press, 1997), pp. 501–2. The text of their oral history interviews of blacklisted Hollywood figures will be used throughout the book.

[25] Nicolas Werth, "A State Against Its People: Violence, Repression, and Terror in the Soviet Union," in Stephan Courtois et al., *The Black Book of Communism: Crimes, Terror, Repression* (Cam-

bridge, Mass.: Harvard University Press, 1999), p. 167. In 2003, Columbia University historian Mark Von Hagen evaluated Duranty's reporting for the *New York Times* that had earned him his Pulitzer, as well as his later writing. He concluded that Duranty's stories were "very effective renditions of the Stalinist leadership's self-understanding of their murderous and progressive project."

26 Ring Lardner Jr., *I'd Hate Myself in the Morning: A Memoir* (New York: Thunder's Mouth Press, Nation Books, 2000), p. 67.

27 Ibid., p. 79.

28 Ibid., p. 98.

29 Maurice Rapf, *Back Lot: Growing Up with the Movies* (Lanham, Md.: The Scarecrow Press, 1999), p. 2.

30 Ibid., p. 70.

31 Ibid., p. 70.

32 Ibid., p. 72.

33 Sergei Eisenstein, *Immoral Memories* (Boston: Houghton, Mifflin, 1983), quoted in Stephen Schwartz, *From West to East: California and the Making of the American Mind* (New York: The Free Press, 1998), pp. 256–57.

34 Budd Schulberg, "Collision with the Party Line," *Saturday Review,* August 30, 1952; p. 8.

35 Ibid.

36 Alexander N. Yakovlev, *A Century of Violence in Soviet Russia* (New Haven, Conn.: Yale University Press, 2002), pp. 114–16. Yakovlev found this document in previously unavailable Soviet archives. TsA FSB RF, f.3, op.1, d.56, II. pp. 160–63. Soon after the writers' congress, at a time when the American guests like Schulberg were back home, the arrests began. Three major poets—Ovcharenko, Tsvelev and Asanov—were banished from Moscow for "counterrevolutionary attitudes." Kliuyev and Pulin were arrested for writing anti-Soviet verses and sent to Siberia, where they were executed by the NKVD. The great poet Osip Mandelstam was imprisoned for writing a now-famous biting and truthful verse about Stalin and the sycophants who surrounded him. Mandelstam died in a Gulag camp in 1938. Of the 700 writers who met at the First Congress of Soviet Writers in 1934, only 50 were still alive to see the second congress in

1954. In all, about 2,000 literary figures were repressed. About 1,500 of them died in prisons or camps. See: Robert Conquest, *The Great Terror: A Reassessment* (New York and London: Oxford University Press, 1990), p. 297.

[37] Rapf letter to his parents, 1934, n.d., excerpted in Rapf, *Back Lot*, p. 76.

[38] Rapf, *Back Lot*, p. 76.

[39] Ibid., pp. 76–77.

[40] Ibid., p. 77.

[41] Interview of Maurice Rapf by Patrick McGilligan, in *Tender Comrades*, ed. McGilligan and Buhle, p. 503.

[42] Neal Gabler, *An Empire of Their Own: How the Jews Invented Hollywood* (New York: Crown Publishers, 1988), pp. 226–27.

[43] Interview of Schulberg by Nancy Lynn Schwartz, n.d., quoted in Nancy Lynn Schwartz, *The Hollywood Writers' Wars* (New York: Alfred A. Knopf, 1982), pp. 39–40.

[44] Donald Ogden Stewart, *By a Stroke of Luck! An Autobiography* (New York: Paddington Press, 1975), p. 227.

[45] Schwartz, *The Hollywood Writers' Wars*, p. 504. Also see Gabler, *An Empire of Their Own*, p. 227.

[46] Rapf, *Back Lot*, p. 78.

Chapter 2: The Hollywood Party

[1] FBI, "Subject: Communist Infiltration–Motion Picture Industry (COMPIC)," File no. 100-138754, Serial 4, part 1 of 15, p. 22, Freedom of Information Act Files, FBI Headquarters, Washington, D.C.

[2] Ronald Brownstein, *The Power and the Glitter: The Hollywood-Washington Connection* (New York: Pantheon Books, 1990), p. 20.

[3] David F. Prindle, *The Politics of Glamour: Ideology and Democracy in the Screen Actors Guild* (Madison: University of Wisconsin Press, 1988), p. 16.

[4] See, for example, Nancy Lynn Schwartz, *The Hollywood Writers' Wars* (New York: Alfred A. Knopf, 1982), pp. 36–38; Brownstein, *The Power and the Glitter*, pp. 40–46; Larry Ceplair and Steven Englund, *The Inquisition in Hollywood: Politics in the Film Community, 1930–1960* (Garden City, N.Y.: Anchor Press/Doubleday, 1980), pp. 89–93.

5 Neal Gabler, *An Empire of Their Own: How the Jews Invented Hollywood* (New York: Crown Publishers, 1988), p. 324.

6 Ibid., p. 326.

7 Howard Koch, *As Times Goes By* (New York: Harcourt Brace Jovanovich, 1979), pp. 86–88.

8 *Screen Actor,* Summer 1979, p. 10.

9 "Pinks Plan to Stalinize Studios," *Variety,* September 16, 1933.

10 Lester Cole, *Hollywood Red: The Autobiography of Lester Cole* (Palo Alto, Calif.: Ramparts Press, 1981), pp. 122–25.

11 Schwartz, *The Hollywood Writers' Wars,* p. 15.

12 Ceplair and Englund, *The Inquisition in Hollywood,* p. 28.

13 Jeff Lawson, "An Ordinary Life," in *Red Diapers: Growing Up in the Communist Left,* ed. Judy Kaplan and Linn Shapiro (Chicago: University of Chicago Press, 1988), p. 58. The account of Lawson's life is taken from this essay, pp. 54–60.

14 Bernard F. Dick, *Radical Innocence: A Critical Study of the Hollywood Ten* (Lexington: University Press of Kentucky, 1989), p. 46.

15 Lawson, "An Ordinary Life," p. 59.

16 Dave Davis and Neal Goldberg, "Organizing the Screen Writers Guild: An Interview with John Howard Lawson," in *The Cineaste Interviews: On the Art and Politics of the Cinema,* ed. Dan Georgakas and Lenny Rubenstein (Chicago: Lake View Press, 1983), p. 190.

17 Wendy Smith, *Real Life Drama: The Group Theatre and America, 1931–1940* (New York: Knopf, 1990), p. 97. Smith was given access to Lawson's unpublished autobiography, from which the quotation is taken.

18 Harold Clurman, *The Fervent Years: The Group Theatre and Thirties* (New York: Da Capo Press, 1983), p. 93.

19 Davis and Goldberg, "Organizing the Screen Writers Guild: An Interview with John Howard Lawson," p. 192.

20 Mike Gold review, *New Masses,* April 10, 1934.

21 Lawson, " 'Inner Conflict' and Proletarian Art: A Reply to Michael Gold," *New Masses,* April 17, 1934.

22 Clurman, *The Fervent Years,* pp. 133-134.

23 Quoted in Ceplair and Englund, *The Inquisition in Hollywood,* p. 64.

24 Clurman, *The Fervent Years,* p.187.

[25] Ibid., p. 244.

[26] Moore, Jarrico and Healy quoted in Schwartz, *The Hollywood Writers' Wars*, pp. 152–153.

[27] Cole, *Hollywood Red*, p. 75. The account of Cole's life is taken from this memoir.

[28] Dick, *Radical Innocence*, p. 31.

[29] Cole, *Hollywood Red*, p. 138.

[30] Kenneth Lloyd Billingsley, *Hollywood Party: How Communism Seduced the American Film Industry in the 1930s and 1940s* (Rocklin, Calif.: Prima Publishing, 1998), pp. 51–52; Neal Gabler, *An Empire Of Their Own: How the Jews Invented Hollywood* (New York: Crown Publishers, 1988), p. 329.

[31] The material on Lawrence/Robbins comes from the research of Robert H. Hethmon, who is preparing a biography of John Howard Lawson. We would like to thank Mr. Hethmon for sharing this information with us.

[32] Quoted in Schwartz, *The Hollywood Writers' Wars*, p. 92.

[33] Maurice Rapf, *Back Lot: Growing Up with the Movies* (Lanham, Md.: The Scarecrow Press, 1999), pp.121–22.

[34] Interview of Budd Schulberg by Ronald Radosh and Allis Radosh, March 17, 2004.

[35] Quoted in Victor S. Navasky, *Naming Names* (New York: The Viking Press, 1980), p. 244.

[36] COMPIC, Part 1 of 5, "Large Financial Contributors to the Communist Party at an Early Date (1935–1936), p. 18.

[37] John McCabe, *Cagney* (New York: Alfred A. Knopf, 1997), pp. 32–33.

[38] Interview of John Bright by Patrick McGilligan and Ken Mate, in *Tender Comrades: A History of the Hollywood Blacklist*, ed. Patrick McGilligan and Paul Buhle (New York: St. Martin's Press, 1997), p. 143.

[39] FOIA dossier on Louis Gibarti, #61-6629, section 3. Deposition of Louis Gibarti before Special Counsel to the United States Senate Robert Morris Esq. and United States Senators Willis Smith and Homer Ferguson, Paris, August 28, 1951, cited in Stephen Koch, *Double Lives: Spies and Writers in the Secret Soviet War of Ideas Against the West* (New York: The Free Press, 1994), p. 30.

[40] Lincoln Steffens to Sam Darcy, April 19, 1934, in FOND 515-

CPUSA Records at the Russian State Archives of Socio-Political History, ARGASPI, Moscow, Russia Delo (reel) 280. These files are on microfilm at the Library of Congress, Washington, D.C.

[41] Lincoln Steffens to Sam Darcy, April 28, 1934, in ibid.

[42] Sam Darcy to Earl Browder, May 5, 1934, in ibid.

[43] Interview of Lionel Stander by Patrick McGilligan and Ken Mate, in *Tender Comrades,* ed. McGilligan and Buhle, p. 610.

[44] "Film Actor Named in Coast Red Plot," *New York Times,* August 18, 1934, p. 5.

[45] Testimony of John L. Leech, August 16, 1940, House Committee on Un-American Activities (Dies Committee), in "Printed Testimony from Public and Executive Session Hearings, 1938–1944," pp. 1381–91, Record Group 233, Records of the U.S. House of Representatives, Center for Legislative Archives, National Archives, Washington, D.C.

[46] Testimony of James Cagney, August 16, 1940, ibid., pp. 1481–1501.

[47] Cagney quoted in McCabe, *Cagney,* p. 117.

Chapter 3: The Popular Front: 1935–1939

[1] W. G. Krivitsky, *In Stalin's Secret Service* (New York: Enigma Books, 2000), pp. 54, 60.

[2] Harvey Klehr and John Earl Haynes, *The American Communist Movement: Storming Heaven Itself* (New York: Twayne Publishers, 1992), pp. 70–81.

[3] Testimony of Max Silver, May 8, 1951, House Committee on Un-American Activities, Executive Session, Record Group 233, box 51, Records of the Investigative Section, Transcripts of Executive Session Testimony, National Archives, Washington, D.C.

[4] Interview of Lionel Stander by Patrick McGilligan and Ken Mate, in *Tender Comrades: A History of the Hollywood Blacklist,* ed. Patrick McGilligan and Paul Buhle (New York: St. Martin's Press, 1997), p. 609.

[5] Interview of Budd Schulberg by Nancy Lynn Schwartz in *The Hollywood Writers' Wars* (New York: Alfred A. Knopf, 1982), p. 92.

[6] Richard Collins, "Confessions of a Red Screenwriter," *New Leader,* October 6, 1952.

[7] Testimony of Frank Tuttle, May 24, 1951, House Committee on

Un-American Activities, U.S. 82nd Congress, *Hearings Regarding the Communist Infiltration of the Motion Picture Industry* (Washington, D.C.: U.S. Government Printing Office, 1951), pp. 628–29.

8 Testimony of Meta Reis Rosenberg, April 13, 1951, ibid., p. 285.

9 Interview of Frank Tarloff by Paul Buhle, in *Tender Comrades*, ed. McGilligan and Buhle, p. 646.

10 Interview of Abraham Lincoln Polonsky by Paul Buhle and Dave Wagner, in *Tender Comrades*, p. 486.

11 Budd Schulberg, *Writers in America: The Four Seasons of Success* (New York: Stein & Day, 1983), pp. 167–68.

12 Interview of Elizabeth Frank by Allis Radosh, November 28, 2004.

13 Interview of Budd Schulberg by Ronald Radosh and Allis Radosh, March 17, 2004.

14 Quoted in Schwartz, *The Hollywood Writers' Wars*, p. 92.

15 Quoted in ibid., p. 94.

16 Maurice Rapf, *Back Lot: Growing Up with the Movies* (Lanham, Md.: The Scarecrow Press, 1999), pp. 85–86.

17 Interview of Robert Lees by Paul Buhle and Dave Wagner, in *Tender Comrades*, ed. McGilligan and Buhle, pp. 416–17.

18 Ibid., pp. 419–21.

19 Interview of Richard Collins by Ronald Radosh and Allis Radosh, May 4, 2004.

20 Richard Collins, "Confessions of a Red Screenwriter," *New Leader*, October 6, 1952.

21 Philip Dunne, *Take Two: A Life in Movies and Politics* (New York McGraw Hill, 1980), p. 119.

22 Testimony of Frank Tuttle, May 24, 1951, House Committee on Un-American Activities, U.S. 82nd Congress, *Hearings Regarding the Communist Infiltration of the Motion Picture Industry*, p. 632.

23 Testimony of Richard Collins, April 12, 1951, House Committee on Un-American Activities, U.S. 82nd Congress, pp. 220–25.

24 Ring Lardner Jr., *I'd Hate Myself in the Morning: A Memoir* (New York: Thunder's Mouth Press, Nation Books, 2000), p. 100; phone interview of Budd Schulberg by Ronald Radosh, August 13, 2004.

25 Testimony of Richard Collins, April 12, 1951, pp. 220–21.

26 Elia Kazan, *A Life* (New York: Alfred A. Knopf, 1988), p. 459.

27 Testimony of Richard Collins, April 12, 1951, p. 228. Also see: Testimony of Morrie Ryskind, October 22, 1947, House Committee on Un-American Activities, U.S. 80th Congress, pp. 181–187.

28 Rapf, *Back Lot,* pp. 97–98. In retrospect, Rapf, who served on the board four times between 1938 and 1946, and served twice as secretary, realized that his father was correct when he said he was being "used" by the Party.

29 Ibid., pp. 88–89.

30 Testimony of Richard Collins, April 12, 1951, House Committee on Un-American Activities, Executive Session.

31 Jack Newfield with Mark Jacobson, "An Interview with Budd Schulberg," *Tikkun,* May/June 2000.

32 Stephen Koch, *Double Lives: Spies and Writers in the Secret Soviet War of Ideas Against the West* (New York: The Free Press, 1994). The account herein is based partly on Koch's third chapter, devoted to Katz, "The Lieutenant," pp. 75–95.

33 Claud Cockburn, *A Discord of Trumpets: An Autobiography* (New York: Simon & Schuster, 1956), p. 306.

34 Arthur Koestler, *The Invisible Writing: An Autobiography* (Boston: The Beacon Press, 1954), p. 209.

35 Babette Gross, *Willi Münzenberg: A Political Biography* (East Lansing, Michigan: Michigan State University Press, 1974), pp. 310–11.

36 Koestler, *The Invisible Writing,* p. 210.

37 FBI Report on Otto Katz, LA 100-15865, December 10, 1943, p. 14.

38 Ibid., p. 15.

39 Ibid., p. 15; Babette Gross, *Willi Münzenberg,* p. 311; Wendy Smith, *Real Life Drama: The Group Theatre and America, 1931–1940* (New York: Knopf, 1990), p. 249.

40 Theodore Draper, "The Man Who Wanted to Hang," *The Reporter,* January 6, 1953; pp. 26–30.

41 Prince Hubertus zu Lowenstein, *Towards the Further Shore: An Autobiography* (London: Victor Gollancz, 1968), p. 171.

42 Donald Ogden Stewart, *By a Stroke of Luck!: An Autobiography* (New York and London, Paddington Press, 1975), p. 225.

43 Ibid., p. 206.

44 Ibid., p. 213.

45 Ibid., p. 226.

46 Ibid., p. 231.

47 Ibid., p. 232. Also Larry Ceplair and Steven Englund, *The Inquisition in Hollywood: Politics in the Film Community, 1930–1960* (Garden City, N.Y.: Anchor Press/Doubleday, 1980), pp. 106–12

48 Neal Gabler, *An Empire of Their Own: How the Jews Invented Hollywood* (New York: Crown Publishers, 1988), pp. 328–29.

49 Stewart, *By a Stroke of Luck: An Autobiography*, p. 240.

50 Alexander Stephan, *"Communazis": FBI Surveillance of German Émigré Writers* (New Haven, Conn.: Yale University Press, 2000), p. 48.

51 Salka Viertel, *The Kindness of Strangers* (New York: Holt, Rinehart & Winston, 1969), pp. 181–82.

52 Ibid., p. 211.

53 Interview of Elizabeth Frank by Allis Radosh, November 28, 2004.

54 Otto Katz to Fritz Lang, December 10, 1935, in FBI File 65-1763, Report of 6/10/42, p. 15, Otto Katz File, FBI Headquarters, Washington, D.C.

55 Fitz Lang to Otto Katz, n.d., 1936, in FBI Otto Katz File, p. 16.

56 Lilly Latte to Otto Katz, October 8, 1936, in FBI Otto Katz File, pp. 20–21.

57 Fritz Lange to Otto and Ilse Katz, July 2, 1937, in FBI Otto Katz file, pp. 22–23.

58 Ibid., p. 24.

59 Ilse and Otto Katz to Fritz Lang, n.d., 1937, in FBI Otto Katz File, p. 28.

60 E. H. Carr, *The Comintern and the Spanish Civil War* (New York: Pantheon, 1984), pp. 31, 44. Most recently, the esteemed late French historian François Furet offered a sober evaluation of Stalin's real goal: "to put Republican Spain under the Soviet influence and to make it a 'friend of the USSR.'" Stalin's feigned antifascism was meant to kill any actual Republican energy; antifascism "perpetually concealed the pursuit of power [by Stalin] and the confiscation of liberty."

61 COMPIC, Memo of D. M. Ladd, May 27, 1947, to J. Edgar Hoover; in File 100-138754, Serial: 157x1; Part 2, p. 4.

62 Otto Katz to Fritz Lang, July 28, 1936, in FBI File 65-1763,

Report of 6/10/1942, Otto Katz File, pp. 17–18.

[63] Otto Katz to Fritz Lang, July 31, 1936, in FBI Otto Katz File, p. 19.

[64] Otto Katz to Fritz Lang, n.d. 1938, in FBI Otto Katz File, p. 32.

[65] Babette Gross, *Willi Münzenberg: A Political Biography* (East Lansing, Michigan, Michigan State University Press, 1974), p. 312.

[66] FBI Report on Otto Katz, LA 100-15865, p. 12

[67] Ibid., 11/19/41.

[68] Babette Gross, *Willi Münzenberg,* p. 312.

[69] Lillian Hellman, *An Unfinished Woman: A Memoir* (New York: Little, Brown, 1976), p. 82.

[70] Phone interview of Marty Peretz by Ronald Radosh, October 15, 2004. Peretz recalled that when he was visiting her at her Martha's Vineyard home, Hellman told him that Katz had been her lover.

[71] Hellman, *An Unfinished Woman,* p. 104.

[72] Hans Schoots, *Living Dangerously: A Biography of Joris Ivens* (Amsterdam: Amsterdam University Press, 2000), pp. 110, 116.

[73] Quoted in ibid., pp. 124–25.

[74] Fritz Lang to Otto and Ilse Katz, July 2, 1937, FBI File 65-9266-15, Report of 6/10/1942, p. 25; Schoots, *Living Dangerously,* p. 131. There were other showings of the film. The 3,500-seat Philharmonic Auditorium was filled a night later. There were private screenings as well for Joan Crawford and Franchot Tone, and another for John Ford and Darryl Zanuck. See John T. McManus, "Down to Earth in Spain," *New York Times,* July 2, 1937. The paper of record's coverage was written by McManus, who was himself a fellow traveler and a fierce partisan of the Loyalist government.

[75] Schoots, *Living Dangerously,* p. 132.

[76] Viertel, *The Kindness of Strangers,* p. 215.

[77] Budd Schulberg, *Writers in America: The Four Seasons of Success* (New York: Stein & Day, 1983), p. 83.

[78] Ibid., p. 167.

[79] Interview of Paul Jarrico by Patrick McGilligan, in *Tender Comrades,* ed. McGilligan and Buhle, pp. 330–31.

[80] Schwartz, *The Hollywood Writers' Wars,* pp. 82–83.

81 Ibid., p. 84.

82 Fritz Lang to Otto and Ilse Katz, October 11, 1938, FBI Otto Katz file, pp. 33–34.

Chapter 4: The Nazi-Soviet Pact and Its Aftermath

1 Helen Gahagan Douglas, *A Full Life* (New York: Doubleday, 1982), p. 134.

2 Philip Dunne, *Take Two: A Life in Movies and Politics* (New York: McGraw Hill, 1980), pp. 109–10.

3 John Bright, quoted in Ronald Brownstein, *The Power and the Glitter: The Hollywood-Washington Connection* (New York: Pantheon Books, 1990), p. 64.

4 Ibid., p. 64.

5 Ibid., p. 120.

6 Ibid., p. 122.

7 For a discussion of Mooney and the paucity of evidence against him, see: Stephen Schwartz, *From West to East: California and the Making of the American Mind* (New York: The Free Press, 1998), pp. 188–91.

8 Dunne, *Take Two,* p. 123.

9 Ibid., pp. 114, 132.

10 Quoted in Nancy Lynn Schwartz, *The Hollywood Writers' Wars* (New York: Alfred A. Knopf, 1982), p. 146.

11 "Pact Hurts Axis, Browder Asserts," *New York Times,* August 24, 1939, p. 9.

12 W. G. Krivitsky, *In Stalin's Secret Service* (New York: Enigma Books, 2000), p. 53.

13 Melvyn Douglas, quoted in Larry Ceplair and Steven Englund, *The Inquisition in Hollywood: Politics in the Film Community, 1930–1960* (Garden City, N.Y.: Anchor Press/Doubleday, 1980), p. 142.

14 Dunne, *Take Two,* p. 112.

15 Ring Lardner Jr., *I'd Hate Myself in the Morning: A Memoir* (New York: Thunder's Mouth Press, Nation Books, 2000), p. 101.

16 Stalin had been pursuing a two-pronged strategy. While he sought a military alliance with the West through the policy of "collective security," he was at the same time secretly trying to reach an accord with Hitler. His hope was for a protracted war

between Britain and France on one side and Germany and Italy on the other. That conflict, he hoped, would weaken all the powers who were fighting, leaving Moscow with time to increase its power and advance Soviet rule throughout a ruined Europe. See: Robert C. Tucker, *The Revolution from Above: 1928–1941* (New York: W.W. Norton, 1990), p. 345; and Anthony Read and David Fisher, *The Deadly Embrace: Hitler, Stalin and the Nazi-Soviet Pact* (New York: W.W. Norton, 1988), pp. 8–16.

[17] Donald Ogden Stewart, *By a Stroke of Luck: An Autobiography* (New York and London: Paddington Press, 1975), pp. 247–48.

[18] Ibid., p. 249.

[19] Quoted in Nancy Lynn Schwartz, *The Hollywood Writers' Wars*, p. 150.

[20] Ibid., p. 150.

[21] Dunne, *Take Two*, pp. 127–28.

[22] Harold Ickes, *The Secret Diary of Harold L. Ickes*, vol. 3, *The Lowering Clouds: 1939–1941* (New York: Simon & Schuster, 1954), p. 73.

[23] Melvyn Douglas, "Report to the Executive Board of the Motion Picture Democratic Committee," December 18, 1939, Melvyn Douglas Papers, box 15, folder 3, State Historical Society of Wisconsin, Madison.

[24] "Executive Board Meeting of 12/19/39, discussion on resolution presented by Melvyn Douglas," Melvyn Douglas Papers, box 15, folder 3.

[25] Dunne, *Take Two*, pp. 127–28.

[26] Newsletter of the Motion Picture Democratic Committee, "MEMBERS: SPECIAL ATTENTION," February 22, 1940, Melvyn Douglas Papers, box 1.

[27] Dunne, *Take Two*, p. 128.

[28] Newsletter of the Motion Picture Democratic Committee, May 22, 1940, in Melvyn Douglas Papers, box 15, folder 3.

[29] Brownstein, *The Power and the Glitter*, p. 68.

[30] *New York Times*, August 15, 1940, p. 1.

[31] Testimony of John L. Leech, August 16, 1940, House Committee on Un-American Activities, "Printed Testimony from Public and Executive Session Hearings, 1938–1944," pp. 1381–91, Record Group 233, Center for Legislative Archives, National

Archives, Washington, D.C._

32 Testimony of Humphrey DeForest Bogart, August 16, 1940, ibid., pp. 1375–78.

33 Testimony of Franchot Stanilas Pascal Tone, August 27, 1940, ibid., pp. 1753–57.

34 Testimony of Lionel Stander, August 27, 1940, ibid., pp. 1749–53. Years later, Stander was very clear about what he really felt. A supporter of the Nazi-Soviet Pact, Stander explained that he saw it as a "temporary" maneuver, caused not by Stalin but by the "inability of the democracies to line up with the Soviet Union." Moreover, Stander noted that Melvyn Douglas had tried to convince him otherwise, but that he took "the long term view" that it was the destiny of the United States and the Soviet Union to be united against Hitler. He did not, he emphasized, subscribe to "the anti-Soviet Union, anti-Communist hysteria." Indeed, a true believer, Stander told his interviewer that the purge trials in Russia hardly disturbed him, and that he "respected [Stalin] as the leader of the Soviet Union," as well as Earl Browder, the wartime leader of the Communist Party of the United States. But Stander still claimed never to have formally joined the Party, only to have supported "a number of the Party's positions." A quintessential fellow traveler, Stander also worried that if he joined, he could be subject to legal action for denying membership before the Dies Committee. See the interview with Lionel Stander by Patrick McGilligan and Ken Mate, in *Tender Comrades: A History of the Hollywood Blacklist,* ed. Patrick McGilligan and Paul Buhle (New York: St. Martin's Press, 1997), pp. 607–25.

35 Dunne, *Take Two,* p. 131.

36 Thomas Brady, "Hollywood Heckles Its Hecklers," *New York Times,* August 25, 1940, p. 111.

37 *New York Times,* August 20, 1940, p. 21.

38 The discussion on Budd Schulberg is taken from the following sources: Testimony of Budd Schulberg, May 23, 1951, House Committee on Un-American Activities, reprinted in Eric Bentley, *Thirty Years of Treason* (New York: The Viking Press, 1971), pp. 434–58; Budd Schulberg, "Collision with the Party Line," *Saturday Review,* August 30, 1952, pp. 6–8, 31–37; Jack Newfield

with Mark Jacobson, "An Interview with Budd Schulberg," *Tikkun*, May/June 2000; and Dan Georgakas, "Budd Schulberg: The Screen Playwright as Author," in Dan Georgakas and Lenny Rubenstein, *The Cineaste Interviews* (Chicago: Lake View Press, 1983), pp. 360–79.

[39] Budd Schulberg, *Moving Pictures: Memories of a Hollywood Prince* (Chicago: Ivan R. Dee, 2003), p. 203.

[40] Interview of Budd Schulberg by Ronald Radosh and Allis Radosh, March 17, 2004; the rest of this section is taken from this same interview.

[41] Ibid.; and see Nancy Lynn Schwartz, *The Hollywood Writers' Wars*, pp. 154–55.

[42] Nancy Lynn Schwartz, *The Hollywood Writers' Wars*, p. 167.

[43] Interview of Maurice Rapf by Patrick McGilligan, in *Tender Comrades*, ed. McGilligan and Buhle, p. 533.

[44] Testimony of Budd Schulberg, May 23, 1951, in Bentley, *Thirty Years of Treason*, p. 441.

[45] Nancy Lynn Schwartz, *The Hollywood Writers' Wars*, p. 70.

[46] Interview of Budd Schulberg by Ronald Radosh and Allis Radosh, March 17, 2004.

[47] Budd Schulberg, "Afterword," *What Makes Sammy Run?* (New York: Random House, 1990), p. 322.

[48] Lardner, *I'd Hate Myself in the Morning*, p. 104.

[49] Charles Glenn, "Novel: The Story of a Hollywood Heel," *Daily People's World*, April 2, 1941; *Daily Worker*, April 7, 1941.

[50] Glenn, quoted in Nancy Lynn Schwartz, *The Hollywood Writers' Wars*, p. 168.

[51] *Daily Worker*, April 23, 1941.

[52] Interview of Budd Schulberg by Ronald Radosh and Allis Radosh, March 17, 2004.

[53] Quoted in Nancy Lynn Schwartz, *The Hollywood Writers' Wars*, p. 168.

[54] Schulberg, quoted in ibid., p. 167; and Neal Gabler, *An Empire of Their Own: How the Jews Invented Hollywood* (New York: Crown Publishers, 1988), p. 338.

[55] Newsletter of the Motion Picture Democratic Committee, May 25, 1940, Melvyn Douglas Papers, box 1.

[56] Guy Endore, "Let's Skip the Next War and Win a Free House and Lot," Hollywood Peace Forum Publication, in The Edward

Eliscu Papers, Tamiment Institute Library, New York University.

57 Nancy Lynn Schwartz, *The Hollywood Writers' Wars*, p. 157. Guild member William Ludwig recalled a meeting where "we had to censure the top echelon for picketing...the loading of scrap iron bound for Europe or Japan. Now as individuals," Ludwig said, "they had every right to do this, but in statements to the press they all identified themselves as officers and board members of the Guild, which made it look as thought it were an official SWG action. We had to censure them for that because the Guild had to take a nonpolitical stance."

58 Stewart, *By a Stroke of Luck*, p. 252.

59 Ibid., p. 257.

60 Ibid.

61 Quoted in Nancy Lynn Schwartz, *The Hollywood Writers' Wars*, p. 173.

62 Lardner, *I'd Hate Myself in the Morning*, pp. 103–4.

63 Maurice Rapf, *Back Lot: Growing Up with the Movies* (Lanham, Md.: The Scarecrow Press, 1999), pp. 125–26.

64 Lardner, *I'd Hate Myself in the Morning*, p. 101.

65 Interview of Paul Jarrico by Patrick McGilligan, in *Tender Comrades*, ed. McGilligan and Buhle, p. 336.

66 Quoted in Schwartz, *The Hollywood Writers' Wars*, pp. 187–88.

67 Interview of John Bright by Patrick McGilligan and Ken Mate, in *Tender Comrades*, ed. McGilligan and Buhle, p. 151.

68 Edward Dmytryk, *Odd Man Out: A Memoir of the Hollywood Ten* (Carbondale and Edwardsville, Illinois: Southern Illinois University Press, 1986), p. 6.

69 Testimony of Budd Schulberg, March 21, 1951, in Bentley, *Thirty Years of Treason*, pp. 308–48.

70 Interview of Lloyd Bridges on the "50th Anniversary Tribute to High Noon," on 2004 DVD release of the film *High Noon*.

71 Testimony of Lloyd Bridges, October 22, 1951, House Committee on Un-American Activities, Executive Session, Record Group 233, box 51, Records of the Investigative Section, Center for Legislative Archives, National Archives, Washington, D.C.

72 Interview of Robert Lees by Paul Buhle and Dave Wagner, in *Tender Comrades*, ed. McGilligan and Buhle, p. 431.

73 Dmytryk, *Odd Man Out*, p. 8.

74 Bernard F. Dick, *Radical Innocence: A Critical Study of the Hollywood*

Ten (Lexington: University Press of Kentucky, 1989), p. 40.

[75] Ibid., p. 58.

[76] Dick, *Radical Innocence,* p. 58.

[77] Dan Georgakas, "The Hollywood Reds: Fifty Years Later," WBAI Pacifica Radio broadcast, December 5, 2003.

[78] Nicholas Worth, "A State Against Its People," Part 8, in Stephan Courtois et al., *The Black Book of Communism* (Cambridge, Mass.: Harvard University Press, 1999), pp. 159–68; quotation on p. 167.

[79] Taylor told HUAC in 1947 that government officials had prevented him from entering the Navy in 1943 unless he took the starring role in the film. Louis B. Mayer was furious that HUAC released Taylor's closed session testimony, and said that his story was false. As a result of pressure from Mayer, Taylor changed his testimony when he appeared before HUAC in public, saying that he objected to the film's politics, but in deference to the war situation he agreed on his own to take the part. See: Robert Mayhew, *Ayn Rand and Song of Russia: Communism and Anti-Communism in 1940s Hollywood* (Lanham, Md.: The Scarecrow Press, 2005), pp. 44–45.

[80] Ibid., pp. 36–38.

[81] Ibid., p. 112. For years, Rand's reference to the children's smiling faces has been a subject of scorn and ridicule. Most commentators have argued that this was all HUAC could come up with to prove the existence of Soviet propaganda in American films. Even Ring Lardner Jr., as late as 1995, chastised Rand for claiming that the film "distorted" the Soviet Union because it showed children smiling, as if that one sentence were the heart of her testimony. Lardner may no longer have been a Red, but he continued to echo the original smears against Rand made at the time by the Party. See Griffin Fariello, *Red Scare: Memories of the American Inquisition: An Oral History* (New York, W.W. Norton, 1995), p. 261; and interview of Lardner for CNN's Cold War series, 1997, at www.gwu.edu/-nsarchiv/coldwar/interviews/episode-6/lardner1.html. Also see Mayhew, *Ayn Rand and Song of Russia,* pp. 162–64.

[82] Testimony of Ayn Rand, October 24, 1947, House Committee on Un-American Activities, reprinted in Bentley, *Thirty Years of Treason,* pp. 111–19.

Chapter 5: "A Great Historic Mistake"

[1] Joseph E. Davies, *Mission to Moscow* (New York: Simon & Schuster, 1941).

[2] David Culbert, ed., *Mission to Moscow* (Madison: University of Wisconsin Press, 1980), p. 15.

[3] Sidney Hook, *Out of Step: An Unquiet Life in the 20th Century* (New York: Harper & Row, 1987), p. 222.

[4] Davies to Stephen Early, April 4, 1938, Stephen Early Papers, FDR Library, Hyde Park, N.Y., box 3.

[5] Davies, *Mission to Moscow,* pp. 239–46.

[6] Culbert, *Mission to Moscow,* p. 35.

[7] Ibid., p. 11.

[8] Thomas F. Brady, "Joseph E. Davies Explains How Warners Came to Make His 'Mission to Moscow;'" *New York Times,* January 17, 1943, p. X3.

[9] Statement of Jack L. Warner, October 20, 1947, House Committee on Un-American Activities, U.S. 80th Congress, *Hearings Regarding the Communist Infiltration of the Motion Picture Industry,* pp. 9–11.

[10] Jack Warner to Marvin McIntyre, May 17, 1943, FDR Presidential Library, PPF #1050 and President's Official File #73.

[11] Robert Buckner to David Culbert, January 1 and 14, 1978, in Culbert, *Mission to Moscow,* pp. 253, 255.

[12] Robert Buckner to Jack Warner, June 19, 1942, Warner Brothers Archives, box 2085, University of Southern California.

[13] Jack Warner to Joseph E. Davies, June 30, 1942, Warner Brothers Archives, box 2085.

[14] Culbert, *Mission to Moscow,* pp. 18–19.

[15] Victor S. Navasky, *Naming Names* (New York: The Viking Press, 1980), p. 300. Navasky gives a few other examples of attempted propaganda in some films, all minor inserts and all rather comical.

[16] Howard Koch to Jay Leyda, February 20, 1944, Jey Leyda Papers, box 5, folder 10, the Tamiment Institute Library, New York University.

[17] Howard Koch, *As Time Goes By* (New York: Harcourt Brace Jovanovich, 1979), p. 102.

[18] Howard Koch to Thomas Staedeli, August 25, 1992. We would like to thank Mr. Staedeli for giving us a copy of this letter. Portions of it are on line at his website: www.cyranos.ch/

wrik-oc-e.htm.

[19] Howard Koch, *As Time Goes By,* p. 89.

[20] Ibid., pp. 105–7.

[21] Joseph E. Davies to Jack Warner, August 31, 1942, Warner Brothers Archives, box 2085.

[22] Davies to Jack Warner, September 8, 1942, Warner Brothers Archives, box 2085.

[23] See Culbert, *Mission to Moscow,* p. 22. Culbert cites a letter from Davies to Curtiz, September 23, 1942, found in the Joseph Davies Papers at the Library of Congress. We tried to gain access to this collection, but found that it is now closed and that Culbert had previously been given access by Davies' daughters. Without seeing the letter, there is no way to tell what precisely Davies had demanded.

[24] Diary of Joseph Davies, November 23, 1942, Davies Papers, box 12, quoted in Culbert, *Mission to Moscow,* p. 251.

[25] Clare Spark, *Hunting Captain Ahab: Psychological Warfare and the Melville Revival* (Kent, Ohio: Kent State University Press, 2001), p. 334.

[26] Ibid., footnote on p. 657.

[27] Jey Leyda, "Reminiscences," 1981, 2:82, Columbia University Oral History Collection, cited in ibid., p. 651.

[28] Jay Leyda to Joseph Freeman, February 2, 1943, Jay Leyda Papers, box 3, folder 47.

[29] Clayton R. Koppes and Gregory D. Black, *Hollywood Goes to War: How Politics, Profits and Propaganda Shaped World War II* (London: I.B. Tauris, 1988), p. 198.

[30] Al Alleborn to T. C. Wright and Michael Curtiz, "Report for Curtiz, 12th Shooting Day," Warner Brothers Archives, School of Cinema-Television, University of Southern California, Los Angeles, box 2085.

[31] These scripts are to be found in the Jay Leyda Papers, box 19, folder 1. All citations in the text are from these scripts.

[32] Bukharin not only was innocent, but was a major opponent of Stalin's secret dealings with the Nazi leadership. Stalin fabricated criminal connections between his opponents and Nazi Germany, when in reality Bukharin was a man who tried to warn his countrymen in Aesopian language that Stalin was moving

to create a fascist-style regime based on terror, and was seeking an alliance with the Nazi government that would start a war and leave the Soviet Union with Eastern Europe. See: Robert C. Tucker, *Stalin in Power: The Revolution from Above, 1928–1941* (New York: W.W. Norton, 1990), pp. 338–65.

[33] Joseph E. Davies to Jack Warner, April 21, 1943, Warner Brothers Archives, box 2085.

[34] Jack Warner to Joseph E. Davies, April 22, 1943, Warner Brothers Archives, box 2085.

[35] Bosley Crowther, review of *Mission to Moscow* in *New York Times*, April 30, 1943, p. 25.

[36] "Several Faults Are Found in 'Mission to Moscow' Film," by John Dewey and Suzanne LaFollette, May 6, 1943, *New York Times*, May 9, 1943, p. E8.

[37] "Critics Hit 'Submission to Moscow,'" *New Leader*, May 8, 1943, p. 2.

[38] Howard Koch, "A Dramatist's Viewpoint on 'Mission to Moscow,'" May 27, 1943, *New York Times*, June 13, 1943, p. X3.

Chapter 6: The Cold War Begins in Hollywood

[1] The best discussion of the Communists in wartime is Maurice Isserman, *Which Side Were You On? The American Communist Party During the Second World War* (Middletown, Conn.: Wesleyan University Press, 1982).

[2] "Political Notes: Glamour Pusses," *Time*, September 9, 1946, pp. 23–25. All quotations from the *Time* article come from this source. Arthur Schlesinger wrote that the group was wrong for allowing Communists into its membership, claiming that "its celebrities maintained their membership but not their vigilance." The locals may have been sincere liberal groups, but the national organization on foreign policy "backed the Russians or kept quiet." Arthur M. Schlesinger Jr., "The U.S. Communist Party," *Life*, July 29, 1946, p. 93.

[3] In his memoir, the Communist novelist Howard Fast revealed that the 1949 Waldorf Conference, at which he played a major role, was "a conference created by the Communist Party," which he proposed and fought to have accepted by the CP leadership. Dorner was chosen as its executive director. It is unlikely that

the CPUSA would have allowed a conference it set up and controlled to be run by a non-Communist, even a fellow traveler. See: Howard Fast, *Being Red: A Memoir* (Boston: Houghton Mifflin, 1990), pp. 199–203, quotation on p. 202.

4 Hannah Dorner to Jo Davidson, August 2, 1944, HDC Papers, box 2, folder 3, State Historical Society of Wisconsin, Madison.

5 Minutes of ICCASP, October 5, 1945, Report of Hannah Dorner to the Board, HDC Papers, box 2.

6 Speech of John Howard Lawson to HICCASP, November 30, 1945, HDC Papers, box 2, folder 3.

7 Joseph Starobin, *American Communism in Crisis, 1943–1957* (Cambridge, Mass.: Harvard University Press, 1972), pp. 80–81.

8 Harvey Klehr, John Earl Haynes, Kyrill M. Anderson, *The Soviet World of American Communism* (New Haven, Conn. and London: Yale University Press, 1998), pp. 91–106. American Communists had always believed the letter was meant as a message from Moscow, but evidence did not exist to prove its origins. The recent research of historians Harvey Klehr and John Haynes established without a doubt that in fact, the article was written in Moscow, translated into French, and given to Duclos to publish and claim authorship.

9 Earl Browder, "How Stalin Ruined the American Communist Party," *Harper's,* March 1960, p. 45.

10 Report to the Board of Directors of HICCASP, June 22, 1945, HDC Papers, box 6, folder 1, State Historical Society of Wisconsin, Madison.

11 Bruce Cook, *Dalton Trumbo* (New York: Charles Scribner's Sons, 1977), p. 133.

12 Ibid., p. 51.

13 Draft of speech for Olivia de Havilland by Dalton Trumbo, 1946, Dalton Trumbo Papers, box 1, folder 10, State Historical Society of Wisconsin.

14 Dalton Trumbo to Olivia de Havilland, July 27, 1946, Dalton Trumbo Papers, box 7.

15 Dalton Trumbo to Ernest Pascal, n.d., June 1946, Dalton Trumbo Papers, box 1, folder 10.

16 Ronald Reagan, *Where's the Rest of Me?* (New York: Elsevier-Dutton, 1965), p. 141.

17 James Roosevelt to John Cromwell, July 27, 1946, in Dalton

Trumbo Papers, box 7.

[18] Semi-Annual Report of the National Board of Directors, ICCASP, 1946, in HDC Papers, box 6, folder 1.

[19] Dalton Trumbo to Carey McWilliams, September 26, 1946, in Dalton Trumbo Papers., box 1, folder 8. Trumbo's letter bares striking similarity to the letter from Trumbo to Samuel Sillen, editor of the *New Masses*, n.d., 1946, in *Additional Dialogue: Letters of Dalton Trumbo, 1942–1962*, ed. Helen Manfull (New York: M. Evans & Co., 1970), pp. 40–44. This letter contains precisely the same phrases and paragraphs, with substantive omissions from points made in the letter to McWilliams.

[20] The two essential books on the strike, which take diametrically opposed views, are: Kenneth Lloyd Billingsley, *Hollywood Party: How Communism Seduced the American Film Industry in the 1930s and 1940s* (Rocklin, Calif.: Prima Publishing, 1998); and Gerald Horne, *Class Struggle in Hollywood: 1930–1950* (Austin: University of Texas Press, 2001).

[21] "Actors Take Vote on Screen Strike," *New York Times*, March 16, 1945, p. 32.

[22] "Hollywood Riot Flares in Strike," *New York Times*, October 6, 1945, p. 3.

[23] "AFL in California Hits Reds in Films," *New York Times*, June 19, 1946, p. 32.

[24] "AFL Feud Strike Stalls Film Work," *New York Times*, September 27, 1946, p. 3.

[25] Cited in Nancy Lynn Schwartz, *The Hollywood Writers' Wars* (New York: Alfred A. Knopf, 1982), p. 245.

[26] Ibid., pp. 246–47.

[27] Reagan, *Where's the Rest of Me?*, pp. 159, 162.

[28] Testimony of Sterling Hayden, April 10, 1951, House Committee on Un-American Activies, U.S. 82nd Congress, part 1, pp. 142–43.

[29] Reagan, *Where's the Rest of Me?*, p. 172.

[30] Sterling Hayden, unpublished manuscript of *Wanderer*, pp. 802–3.

Chapter 7: Crackdown: The Case of Albert Maltz

[1] Frank Sinatra to Albert Maltz, August 31, 1945; Albert Maltz Papers; box 15, folder 13, State Historical Society of Wisconsin,

Madison.

2 Albert Maltz to Frank Sinatra, September 24, 1945, in Albert Maltz Papers, box 15, folder 13.

3 Albert Maltz, "What Shall We Ask of Writers?" *New Masses,* February 12, 1946. The easiest way to read Maltz's piece is in the appendix in Kenneth Lloyd Billingsley, *Hollywood Party: How Communism Seduced the American Film Industry in the 1930s and 1940s* (Rocklin, Calif.: Prima Publishing, 1998), pp. 290–98.

4 Maltz had thrived in the period of the Popular Front, and was not at home in the new post-Browder epoch. He wrote his article after the Duclos letter had appeared, but before Browder had been removed from the Party leadership and expelled from the Party. Maltz, like the membership at large, had no idea that Browder's days would soon be over. See: Daniel Aaron, *Writers on the Left* (New York: Avon Books, 1961), p. 399. Aaron wrote: "Had [Maltz] written it during the United Front days of 1935–29 or in the war years of Soviet-American cooperation…it might have slipped by without official censure. It appeared, however, well after the famous Jacques Duclos letter of May 1945 presaged the end of peaceful collaboration between the United States and the Soviet Union." By the time the article was in print, Browder had one week earlier been expelled from the Party as a "social imperialist."

5 Testimony of Richard Collins, April 12, 1951, House Committee on Un-American Activities, U.S. 82nd Congress.

6 Interview of Budd Schulberg by Ronald Radosh and Allis Radosh, 2004.

7 Edward Dmytryk, *Odd Man Out: A Memoir of the Hollywood Ten* (Carbondale and Edwardsville, Ill.: Southern Illinois University Press, 1996), pp. 19–21.

8 Mike Gold, "Change the World," *Daily Worker,* February 12, 1946, reprinted in Billingsley, *Hollywood Party,* pp. 299–300.

9 *New Masses,* March 12, 1946, p. 8.

10 Howard Fast, "Art and Politics," *New Masses,* February 26, 1946, p. 6. Ironically, a decade later, Fast would sever his ties with the Party and write a book detailing his growing disillusionment. As for artistic death, he continued for decades to write a steady

stream of popular novels, all of them selling extremely well.

[11] Testimony of Leopold Atlas, March 12, 1953; House Committee on Un-American Activities, *Communist Activities in the Los Angeles Area,* pp. 945–47.

[12] Victor S. Navasky, *Naming Names* (New York: The Viking Press, 1980), pp. 298–99.

[13] Albert E. Kahn to Albert Maltz, February 15, 1946, Albert Maltz Papers, box 15.

[14] Bernhard J. Stern to Albert Maltz, February 18, 1946, Albert Maltz Papers, box 15.

[15] Millard Lampell to Albert Maltz, February 21, 1946, Albert Maltz Papers, box 15.

[16] Maltz to Gurley Flynn, February 18, 1946, Albert Maltz Papers, box. 15. Maltz recalled to Flynn that after Browder's expulsion, she pledged never to refrain from speaking her mind on a subject, even if she differed with the Party leadership. But Flynn had been apologizing for not speaking up against Browder *before* the command from Duclos. Having promptly endorsed the new line, she was not about to come to Maltz's support.

[17] Maltz to Mike Gold, February 18, 1946, Albert Maltz Papers, box 15.

[18] Maltz to Isidore Schneider, February 21, 1946, Albert Maltz Papers, box 15.

[19] Shepard Traube, February 23, 1946, Albert Maltz Papers, box 15.

[20] Quoted in John Pyros, *Michael Gold: Dean of American Proletarian Writers* (New York: Dramatikon, 1979), p. 151.

[21] Sidney Elliott Cohn to Maltz, February 26, 1946, Albert Maltz Papers, box 15.

[22] Joe North to Maltz, March 14, 1946, in Albert Maltz Papers, box 15.

[23] Albert Maltz, "Moving Forward," *New Masses,* April 9, 1946, pp. 8–10, 21–22; first published in the *Daily Worker,* April 7, 1946; reprinted in Billingsley, *Hollywood Party,* pp. 301–7.

[24] Samuel Sillen to Maltz, April 16, 1946, Albert Maltz Papers, box 15.

[25] Dmytryk, *Odd Man Out,* pp. 114–15.

Chapter 8: HUAC Goes to Hollywood

1. Quoted in Larry Ceplair and Steven Englund, *The Inquisition in Hollywood: Politics in the Film Community, 1930–1960* (Garden City, N.Y.: Anchor Press/Doubleday, 1980), p. 248.

2. Robert E. Stripling, *The Red Plot Against America* (Drexel Hill, Pa.: Bell Publishing, 1949), p. 63.

3. Quoted in ibid., p. 64.

4. Ibid., p. 72.

5. Interview of Maurice Rapf by Patrick McGilligan, in *Tender Comrades: A History of the Hollywood Blacklist,* ed. Patrick McGilligan and Paul Buhle (New York: St. Martin's Press, 1997), p. 521.

6. Quoted in Neal Gabler, *An Empire of Their Own: How the Jews Invented Hollywood* (New York: Crown Publishers, 1988), p. 364.

7. Ring Lardner Jr., *I'd Hate Myself in the Morning: A Memoir* (New York: Thunder's Mouth Press, Nation Books, 2000), pp. 12–13.

8. "Red Film Held Forced on Taylor; 'Agent' Halted His Navy Service," *New York Times,* May 15, 1947, p. 1.

9. Ibid.

10. "Hollywood Is a Main Red Center, Adolphe Menjou Tells House Body," *New York Times,* May 16, 1947, p. 1.

11. "Movies Pledge Aid in Inquiry on Reds," *New York Times,* September 30, 1947, p. 21.

12. *Congressional Record,* vol. 93, part 2, p. A2688.

13. Gabler, *An Empire of Their Own,* p. 363.

14. Interview of Maurice Rapf by Patrick McGilligan, in *Tender Comrades,* ed. McGilligan and Buhle, p. 503.

15. Dore Schary, *Heyday: An Autobiography* (New York: Little, Brown, 1979), p. 152.

16. Lester Cole, *Hollywood Red: The Autobiography of Lester Cole* (Palo Alto, Calif.: Ramparts Press, 1981), pp. 271–72.

17. Dorothy Healey and Maurice Isserman, *Dorothy Healey Remembers: A Life in the American Communist Party* (New York: Oxford University Press, 1990), pp. 108–9.

18. Patricia Bosworth, *Anything Your Little Heart Desires: An American Family Story* (New York: Simon & Schuster, 1997), p. 163.

19. Schary, *Heyday: An Autobiography,* p. 159.

20. Edward Dmytryk, *Odd Man Out: A Memoir of the Hollywood Ten* (Carbondale and Edwardsville, Ill.: Southern Illinois University

Press, 1996), p. 38.

[21] Bosworth, *Anything Your Little Heart Desires*, pp. 227–28.

[22] Ibid., p. 227.

[23] Lardner, *I'd Hate Myself in the Morning*, pp. 119–20.

[24] *Anything Your Little Heart Desires*, p. 232.

[25] Albert Maltz, *The Citizen Writer* (New York: International Publishers, 1950), p. 40.

[26] Dmytryk, *Odd Man Out*, pp. 53–54.

[27] Ceplair and Englund, *The Inquisition in Hollywood*, p. 274.

[28] Philip Dunne, *Take Two: A Life in Movies and Politics* (New York McGraw Hill, 1980), pp. 193–94. The account that follows is from this book, pp. 194–208.

[29] Quoted in Lauren Bacall, *By Myself* (New York: Ballantine Books, 1980), p. 212.

[30] Gordon Kahn, *Hollywood on Trial: The Story of the Ten Who Were Indicted* (New York: Boni & Gaer, 1948), pp. 4–7.

[31] Quoted in ibid., p. 19.

[32] Ibid., p. 21.

[33] Testimony of Jack Warner, October 20, 1947, House Committee on Un-American Activities, U.S. 80th Congress, *Hearings Regarding the Communist Infiltration of the Motion Pictures Industry*, pp. 9–15.

[34] Dunne, *Take Two*, p. 206.

[35] "Goldwyn Is Eager for Inquiry Call," *New York Times*, October 30, 1947, p. 4.

[36] "Hollywood Fights Back," *New York Times*, November 2, 1947, p. E1.

[37] Bacall, *By Myself*, p. 213.

[38] "Stars Fly to Fight Inquiry into Films," *New York Times*, October 26, 1947, pp. 1, 26.

[39] "The News of Radio," *New York Times*, October 31, 1947, p. 46.

[40] Ibid., p. 199.

[41] Dmytryk, *Odd Man Out*, pp. 113–14.

[42] Draft of memoir by Sterling Hayden, p. 386, from the private collection of Scott McConnell. The manuscript was edited and published in a different form as *Wanderer*, with much material found in the original deleted by its editor, Angus Cameron.

[43] Kahn, *Hollywood on Trial*, pp. 67–68. Lawson's entire forbidden

statement is printed herein, on pp.72–77; and in Eric Bentley, *Thirty Years of Treason* (New York: The Viking Press, 1971), pp. 161–65.

44 Testimony of John Howard Lawson, October 27, 1947, House Committee on Un-American Activities, reprinted in Bentley, *Thirty Years of Treason*, pp. 153–61.

45 Kahn, *Hollywood on Trial*, p. 78.

46 Quoted in Walter Goodman, *The Committee: The Extraordinary Career of the House Committee on Un-American Activities* (New York: Farrar Straus & Giroux, 1968), p. 212; Kahn, *Hollywood on Trial*, p. 114.

47 FBI Report, Los Angeles, 6/3/43, p. 1; R. B. Hood, Letter to J. Edgar Hoover, 16/4/43; both cited in Alexander Stephan, *"Communazis": FBI Surveillance of German Émigré Writers* (New Haven, Conn.: Yale University Press, 2000), pp. 110–11.

48 R. B. Hood, Letter to J. Edgar Hoover, 14/5/47, cited in Stephan, *"Communazis,"* p. 131. Stephan's discussion of Brecht is on pp. 109–33.

49 Testimony of Bertolt Brecht, October 30, 1947, House Committee on Un-American Activities, reprinted in Bentley, *Thirty Years of Treason*, pp. 207–25.

50 "Asks Rules on Jobs for Communists," *New York Times*, November 20, 1947, p. 18.

51 "Ten Film Men Cited for Contempt in Overwhelming Votes by House," *New York Times*, November 25, 1947, p. 1.

52 Dore Schary, *Heyday: An Autobiography*, p. 164. The narrative is drawn from this book, pp. 165–67.

53 "Movies to Oust Ten Cited for Contempt of Congress," *New York Times*, November 26, 1947, pp. 1, 27. While the producers acknowledged the danger that the policy could lead to an atmosphere of fear and put a damper on creative work, they came up with a mechanism they hoped would prevent such an outcome. They invited the Hollywood "guilds" to work with them to "eliminate any subversives, to protect the innocent, and to safeguard free speech and a free screen wherever threatened."

54 Bacall, *By Myself*, pp. 210–17.

55 Nancy Lynn Schwartz, *The Hollywood Writers' Wars* (New York:

Alfred A. Knopf, 1982), pp. 281–82.

[56] George Sokolsky column, *New York Daily Mirror*, December 6, 1947.

[57] Humphrey Bogart, "I'm No Communist," *Photoplay*, March 1948, pp. 52–53, 86–87.

[58] Jeffrey Meyers, *Bogart: A Life in Hollywood* (New York: Houghton Mifflin, 1997), p. 212.

[59] Cole, *Hollywood Red*, p. 289.

[60] Quoted in Meyers, *Bogart*, p. 213.

Chapter 9: HUAC Returns

[1] Larry Ceplair and Steven Englund, Larry Ceplair and Steven Englund, *The Inquisition in Hollywood: Politics in the Film Community, 1930–1960* (Garden City, N.Y.: Anchor Press/Doubleday, 1980), pp. 338–40.

[2] Edward Dmytryk, *Odd Man Out: A Memoir of the Hollywood Ten* (Carbondale and Edwardsville, Ill.: Southern Illinois University Press, 1996), pp. 94–95.

[3] Interview of Richard Collins by Ronald Radosh and Allis Radosh, May 4, 2004, Brentwood, Los Angeles, California.

[4] Ceplair and Englund, *The Inquisition in Hollywood*, p. 296.

[5] *Hollywood Reporter*, November 26, 1947.

[6] Philip Dunne, *Take Two: A Life in Movies and Politics* (New York McGraw Hill, 1980), p. 213.

[7] Dmytryk, *Odd Man Out*, p. 92.

[8] Melvyn Douglas to Chat Patterson, November 8, 1947, Melvyn Douglas Papers, box 3, State Historical Society of Wisconsin, Madison.

[9] Dmytryk, *Odd Man Out*, p. 92.

[10] Albert Maltz letter, August 5, 1948, box 15, Albert Maltz Papers, State Historical Society of Wisconsin, Madison.

[11] Lester Cole, *Hollywood Red: The Autobiography of Lester Cole* (Palo Alto, Calif.: Ramparts Press, 1981), pp. 319–20.

[12] Dunne, *Take Two*, pp. 213–15.

[13] Norma Barzman, *The Red and the Blacklist: The Intimate Memoir of a Hollywood Expatriate* (New York: Thunder's Mouth Press, Nation Books, 2003).

[14] Betsy Blair, *The Memory of All That: Love and Politics in New York,*

Hollywood and Paris (New York: Alfred A. Knopf, 2003), pp. 204–11.

[15] Testimony of Larry Parks, March 21, 1951, House Committee on Un-American Activities, reprinted in Eric Bentley, *Thirty Years of Treason* (New York: The Viking Press, 1971), pp. 308–48.

[16] Dmytryk, *Odd Man Out*, p. 160.

[17] Patricia Bosworth, *Anything Your Little Heart Desires: An American Family Story* (New York: Simon & Schuster, 1997), p. 252.

[18] Ibid., pp. 305–6.

[19] Dmytryk, *Odd Man Out*, p. 124.

[20] Ibid., p. 144.

[21] Ibid., pp. 150–51.

[22] Testimony of Edward Dmytryk, April 25,1951, House Committee on Un-American Activities, reprinted in Bentley, *Thirty Years of Treason*, p. 379.

[23] Dmytryk, *Odd Man Out*, p. 172.

[24] Maltz to the editors of the *Saturday Evening Post*, May 28, 1951, Albert Maltz Papers.

[25] Dmytryk, *Odd Man Out*, pp. 172–73.

[26] Victor S. Navasky, *Naming Names* (New York: The Viking Press, 1980), p. 401.

[27] Sterling Hayden, *Wanderer* (New York: Bantam Books, 1964), p. 364.

[28] Ibid., p. 347.

[29] Testimony of Sterling Hayden, April 10, 1951, House Committee on Un-American Activities, reprinted in Bentley, *Thirty Years of Treason*, pp. 348–76; quotation on pp. 349–50. The rest of Hayden's account in the text is from this testimony, unless otherwise identified.

[30] Sterling Hayden, unpublished early draft of *Wanderer*, p. 897.

[31] Testimony of Sterling Hayden, April 4, 1951, House Committee on Un-American Activities, Executive Session, Record Group 233, box 51, Center for Legislative Archives, National Archives, Washington, D.C.

[32] Hayden, *Wanderer*, p. 366.

[33] Interview of Richard Collins by Ronald Radosh and Allis Radosh, May 4, 2004.

[34] Ibid.

[35] Interview of Richard Collins by Robert Mayhew, January 10 and 12, 2001; also see: Navasky, *Naming Names,* p. 228.

[36] Testimony of Richard Collins, April 12, 1951, House Committee on Un-American Activities, p. 254.

[37] Ibid., p. 255.

[38] Interview of Richard Collins by Robert Mayhew, January 10 and 12, 2001.

[39] Neil Gabler, *An Empire of Their Own: How the Jews Invented Hollywood* (New York: Crown Publishers, 1988), p. 385.

[40] Navasky, *Naming Names,* p. 229. Collins remembered that Schulberg's being named was front-page news in the *New York Times.* We could find no evidence that this was the case in the paper for that week. Years later, Collins regretted naming Budd. He knew that Schulberg had left the Party years earlier, and thought it would not hurt him. He didn't realize that his testimony occurred just as Schulberg's newest novel was published, and would hurt its reception.

[41] Interview of Budd Schulberg by Jack Newfield, *Tikkun,* May/June 2000.

[42] Interview of Budd Schulberg by Ronald Radosh and Allis Radosh, March 17, 2004.

[43] Testimony of Budd Schulberg, May 23, 1951, House Committee on Un-American Activities, reprinted in Bentley, *Thirty Years of Treason,* pp. 434–57; quotation on p. 454.

[44] Robert Conquest, *The Great Terror: A Reassessment* (New York: Oxford University Press, 1990), pp. 306–7.

[45] Testimony of Budd Schulberg, May 23, 1951, in Bentley, *Thirty Years of Treason,* p. 446.

[46] Interview of Budd Schulberg by Ronald Radosh and Allis Radosh, March 17, 2004.

[47] Quoted in Navasky, *Naming Names,* pp. 239–46.

[48] Walter Bernstein, *Inside Out: A Memoir of the Blacklist* (New York: Da Capo Press, 2000), p. 250.

[49] Elia Kazan, *A Life* (New York: Alfred A. Knopf, 1988), p. 125.

[50] Ibid., pp. 128–29.

[51] Kazan, *A Life,* pp. 130–31.

[52] Ibid., pp. 131–32.

[53] Ibid., p. 231.

[54] Testimony of Elia Kazan, January 14, 1952, House Committee on Un-American Activities, Executive Session, Record Group 233, box 51, National Archives.

[55] Phone interview with Herb London, January 11, 2004. Kazan had told London about the importance of his meeting with Hook before he testified, at a dinner Hook attended at Kazan's home.

[56] Kazan's full testimony is to be found in Bentley, *Thirty Years of Treason,* pp. 484–95.

[57] *New York Times,* April 11, 1952, reprinted in Bentley, *Thirty Years of Treason,* pp. 482–84.

[58] Kazan, *A Life,* p. 466.

[59] Ibid., p. 469.

[60] Larry Swindell, *Body and Soul: The Story of John Garfield* (New York: William Morrow, 1975), p. 238.

[61] Gabler, *An Empire of Their Own,* p. 384.

[62] John Garfield to Dore Schary, October 13, 1950, Dore Schary Papers, box 2, State Historical Society of Wisconsin, Madison.

[63] "House Unit Calls Ferrer, Garfield," *New York Times,* March 7, 1951, p. 15.

[64] Quoted in Robert Nott, *He Ran All the Way: The Life of John Garfield* (San Francisco: Limelight Press, 2004), p. 269.

[65] "Red Links Denied by John Garfield," *New York Times,* April 24, 1951, p. 9.

[66] Quoted in Swindell, *Body and Soul,* p. 241.

[67] Ibid., pp. 241–54; and Nott, *He Ran All the Way,* pp. 272–86. Both of these biographies excerpt the testimony transcript in these pages.

[68] Swindell, *Body and Soul,* pp. 254–55.

[69] Testimony of Hede Massing, May 31, 1951, House Committee on Un-American Activities, Executive Session, Record Group 233, box 50, National Archives.

[70] Testimony of Jean Dillow, June 5, 1951, House Committee on Un-American Activities, Executive Session, Record Group 233, box 50, National Archives.

[71] Quoted in Swindell, *Body and Soul,* p. 299.

[72] Quoted in Nott, *He Ran All the Way,* p. 315.

[73] Joseph Rauh to Lillian Hellman, April 30, 1952, Joseph Rauh Papers, box 51, Library of Congress, Manuscript Division, Wash-

ington, D.C.

74 Lillian Hellman first draft, April 14, 1952, Joseph Rauh Papers, box 51.

75 Lillian Hellman second draft, April 28, 1952, Joseph Rauh Papers, box 51.

76 Carl Rollyson, *Lillian Hellman: Her Legend and Her Legacy* (New York: St. Martin's Press,1988), p. 329.

77 Ibid., pp. 318–19.

78 Quoted in ibid., p. 89.

79 Hilton Kramer, "The Blacklist and the Cold War," *New York Times,* October 3, 1976, Arts and Leisure, p. 1; c.f. Hilton Kramer, "The Blacklist and the Cold War Revisited," *New Criterion,* November 1997, pp. 11–16.

80 Hellman to Schlesinger, n.d. 1976, Joseph Rauh Papers, box 71.

Chapter 10: The Struggle of Dalton Trumbo

1 Bruce Cook, *Dalton Trumbo* (New York: Charles Scribner's Sons, 1977), p. 222.

2 Ibid., pp. 190, 223.

3 Ibid., p. 240.

4 Helen Manfull, ed., *Additional Dialogue: Letters of Dalton Trumbo, 1942–1962* (New York: M. Evans & Co., 1970), p. 301.

5 Quoted in Waldo Salt, "The Legacy of the Hollywood Blacklist: Treatment," p. 4, n.d. after 1985, box 77, folder 19; Waldo Salt Papers; Arts and Library Special Collections, University of California, Los Angeles.

6 Interview of Paul Jarrico by Patrick McGilligan, in *Tender Comrades: A History of the Hollywood Blacklist,* ed. Patrick McGilligan and Paul Buhle (New York: St. Martin's Press, 1997), p. 349.

7 Interview of Norma Barzman (and Ben Barzman) by Larry Ceplair, in *Tender Comrades,* pp. 1–28.

8 Ibid., pp. 15–16. The Barzmans were speaking metaphorically.

9 Norma Barzman, *The Red and the Blacklist: A Memoir of a Hollywood Insider* (New York: Nation Books, 2003), p. 169.

10 Interview of Norma Barzman and Ben Barzman, in *Tender Comrades,* p. 21; also see: Hervé Hamon and Patrick Rotman, *Yves Montand: You See, I Haven't Forgotten* (New York: Alfred A. Knopf, 1992), p. 275.

11 Interview of Norma Barzman and Ben Barzman, in *Tender Com-*

rades, p. 21.

[12] Ibid., p. 28.

[13] Norma Barzman, *The Red and the Blacklist,* p. 434; also see: Larry Ceplair and Steven Englund, *The Inquisition in Hollywood: Politics in the Film Community, 1930–1960* (Garden City, N.Y.: Anchor Press/Doubleday, 1980), p. 402.

[14] Salt, "The Legacy of the Hollywood Blacklist: Treatment," p. 51.

[15] Interview of Paul Jarrico, in *Tender Comrades,* p. 350.

[16] Interview of Allen Boretz by Patrick McGilligan and Ken Mate, in *Tender Comrades,* p. 127.

[17] Lardner focused almost exclusively on writing for television and had tremendous success writing *M*A*S*H.* He was among the minority of writers who successfully made it back to their previous level of income and prestige after the blacklist.

[18] Herbert Biberman to Dalton Trumbo, February 23, 1952, Herbert Biberman Papers, box 1, folder 9, State Historical Society of Wisconsin, Madison.

[19] Quoted in Bruce Cook, *Dalton Trumbo* (New York: Charles Scribner's Sons, 1977), p. 224.

[20] For information about the film, see: Larry Ceplair, "The Many 50th Anniversaries of *Salt of the Earth,*" *Cineaste,* Spring 2004, pp. 8–9; and Herbert Biberman, *Salt of the Earth: The Story of a Film* (New York and Sag Harbor, N.Y.: Harbor Electronic Press, 2003).

[21] Interview of Paul Jarrico, in *Tender Comrades,* ed. McGilligan and Buhle, pp. 342–43.

[22] Joseph Starobin, *American Communism in Crisis, 1943–1957* (Cambridge, Mass.: Harvard University Press, 1972), p. 200. Starobin's discussion of this campaign, on which our account is based, may be found on pp. 199–201.

[23] Harry Haywood, *Negro Liberation* (New York: International Publishers, 1948).

[24] Quoted in Irving Howe and Lewis Coser, *The American Communist Party: A Critical History* (New York: Frederick A. Praeger, 1962), pp. 206–7.

[25] Herbert Biberman to Albert Maltz, March 12, 1952, Herbert Biberman Papers, box 1, folder 9.

[26] Letter reprinted in "Children Always Cry," *The Case of Jean Field*, The Jean Field Committee, Los Angeles, 1950.

[27] Biberman to Trumbo, April 10, 1952, Herbert Biberman Papers, box 1, folder 9.

[28] Trumbo to Biberman, April 26, 1952, Herbert Biberman Papers, box 1, folder 9.

[29] Dalton Trumbo, "Secrecy and the Communist Party," Dalton Trumbo Papers, n.d. circa 1958, box 40, folder 9. See also: Eugene D. Genovese, "The Question," *Dissent*, Summer 1994, pp. 371–76.

[30] Trumbo, "Secrecy and the Communist Party." The discussion of Trumbo's views of this issue in our pages is based entirely on this long memorandum.

[31] Not one Communist, including Trumbo, ever publicly said that they doubted the innocence of Alger Hiss and the Rosenbergs. Had Trumbo done so—putting his own claim to a test—he would have joined the ranks of the anti-Communist liberals like Arthur M. Schlesinger Jr., and would have promptly been condemned as a traitor by his comrades. Thus he qualified his statement by adding that those who informed on "friends who have harmed no one" were nothing but "miserable" scoundrels.

[32] Guy Endore to Trumbo, January 4, 1957, Dalton Trumbo Papers, box 5, folder 5.

[33] Phone interview of Richard Collins by Ronald Radosh, August 11, 2004. Collins acknowledged that Trumbo's wife, Cleo, and his son did not treat him warmly, and made clear their displeasure at Trumbo's continued friendly relationship with him. Interview of Richard Collins, Brentwood Calif., June 4, 2004.

[34] Maltz to Trumbo, March 22, 1973, Dalton Trumbo Papers.

[35] Trumbo to Alvah Bessie, May 21, 1958, Dalton Trumbo Papers, box 6, folder 1.

[36] Victor S. Navasky, *Naming Names* (New York: The Viking Press, 1980), p. 327.

[37] Salt, "The Legacy of the Hollywood Blacklist: Treatment," p. 5.

[38] Waldo Salt to Fred Rinaldo, September 16, 1957, Waldo Salt Papers, box 77, folder 19.

[39] Waldo Salt to Jerome B. Lurie, October 10, 1963, Waldo Salt

Papers, box 77, folder 21.

[40] Waldo Salt, Affidavit to the State of California, November 1963, Waldo Salt Papers, box 77, folder 21.

[41] Jerome B. Lurie to Waldo Salt, November 1, 1963, Waldo Salt Papers, box 77, folder 2.

[42] The entire text of the speech may be found in Helen Manfull, ed., *Additional Dialogue,* pp. 569–70.

[43] Quoted in Navasky, *Naming Names,* pp. 389–90. Navasky deals at length with the exchange between Trumbo and Maltz on pp. 387–401.

[44] Trumbo to Albert Maltz, January 12, 1973, Dalton Trumbo Papers. Trumbo incorrectly dated the letter as 1972.

[45] Lester Cole to Maltz, November 15, 1977, Dalton Trumbo Papers.

[46] Alvah Bessie to Ring Lardner Jr., December 8, 1977, Dalton Trumbo Papers.

Conclusion

[1] TV documentary, *The John Garfield Story,* Turner Classic Movies and Turner Entertainment, a Top Hat Production, written, produced and directed by David Heeley, narrated by Julie Garfield, 2004.

[2] Anne Taibleson, "NYC Honors the Brigade," *Volunteer,* June 2003, pp. 5–6.

[3] "Blacklist Victims' Story Told in Words and Pictures: The Hollywood Film Academy Finally Comes Clean on the Communist Witch-Hunt," *Guardian* (London), August 4, 2001, p. 13.

[4] Lynn Smith, "We Behaved as Badly as Anybody," *Los Angeles Times,* February 2, 2002, p. 1.

[5] Interview of Paul Jarrico by Patrick McGilligan, in *Tender Comrades: A History of the Hollywood Blacklist,* ed. Patrick McGilligan and Paul Buhle (New York: St. Martin's Press, 1997), p. 336.

[6] Eugene Loebl, *My Mind on Trial* (New York: Harcourt Brace Jovanovich, 1976), p. 199; Artur London, *Confession* (New York: Ballantine Books, 1971), pp. 232, 243, 252. Also see: George H. Hodos, *Show Trials: Stalinist Purges in Eastern Europe, 1948–1954* (New York: Praeger, 1987), pp. 78–92; and Karel Kaplan, *Report on the Murder of the General Secretary* (Columbus: Ohio State University Press, 1990), pp. 270–79 for the "confes-

sion" of Katz and letters to his wife written from prison.

7 Tony Judt, *Past Imperfect: French Intellectuals, 1944–1956* (Berkeley: University of California Press, 1992), pp. 148–49. Judt notes that the appeal for clemency for Slansky and his codefendants "was drawn up and then combined with an identical appeal for mercy on behalf of the Rosenbergs," a step made necessary by the reluctance of some French pro-Communist intellectuals to intervene unless a similar protest was made to the United States. Even such a gesture of moral equivalence was not considered by Hellman and her associates.

8 Hervé Hamon and Patrick Rotman, *Yves Montand: You See, I Haven't Forgotten* (New York: Alfred A. Knopf, 1992), p. 361.

9 Andy Seiler and Josh Chetwynd, "An Award, Much Applause for Kazan, Who 'Inspired Us,'" *USA Today*, March 22, 1999, p. 2D. Also see: "Blacklisted Writers Protest Kazan Honor," *Boston Globe*, March 19, 1999, p. D9; and "Oscar for Elia Kazan Is Bringing Few Feelings of Forgive and Forget," *St. Louis Post-Dispatch*, March 19, 1999, p. A2.

10 Editorial, *Philadelphia Inquirer*, September 20, 2003; news story, *Philadelphia Inquirer*, October 4, 2003.

11 James Lardner, "The Gilding of the Blacklist: A Son of the Hollywood Ten Revisits a Heroic Legacy," *Washington Post*, November 2, 1996, p. C1. In a similar fashion, Jeff Lawson wrote that he tried "to get rid of the failed dogmatism of the Communist movement I had been raised in…. [T]he blind adulation of a mass murderer that the American Communists indulged in was bad enough. But I also question what was in the mind of my father…that led [him] to believe so strongly in such false concepts." See Jeff Lawson, "An Ordinary Life," in *Red Diapers: Growing Up in the Communist Left*, ed. Judy Kaplan and Linn Shapiro (Urbana and Chicago: University of Illinois Press, 1998), pp. 54–60.

12 Victor S. Navasky, *Naming Names* (New York: The Viking Press, 1980), pp. 409–10.

13 Ibid., p. 406.

14 Richard Schickel, "The Hollywood Ten: Printing the Legend," in Richard Schickel, *Schickel on Film* (New York: HarperCollins, 1989), p. 96.

15 Bruce Weber, "One-to-One Words of a Blacklistee," *New York*

Times, September 5, 2003; Section E, p. 1.

[16] Terry Teachout, "The Odor of Sanctimony," *Wall Street Journal,* September 5, 2003.

Index